PRAISE FOR PHIL OCHS

"Phil Ochs, Joan Baez, and Bob Dylan were the most important and influential musical voices of the Sixties protest movement that encompassed civil rights, anti-war, feminism, political reform, and a general questioning of blind faith in authority. What made Phil stand out was not just his passion for social justice as expressed in his seminal songs 'I Ain't Marchin' Anymore' and 'There But for Fortune,' or his sardonic wit that shined an unyielding light on society's petty hypocrisies as in 'Love Me, I'm a Liberal' and 'Outside of a Small Circle of Friends,' but the compassion in his more poetic songs like 'Floods of Florence' and 'Pleasures of the Harbor.' To listen for an hour to Phil Ochs's songs is to get an honest yet loving glimpse into the flaws and strengths of humanity." —**Kareem Abdul-Jabbar**, six-time NBA champion and MVP

"Phil Ochs told the truth before it was ready to be accepted, before it was politically expedient. He was the kind of truth teller that made liberal allies nervous because his truth demanded accountability to their own compromise, their own self-serving pragmatism." —**Tim Robbins**, American actor, screenwriter, director, and producer

"Phil Ochs was much more than simply a songwriter. He wrote obsessively, because he had to—from his heart, his soul, his conscience. This collection of Phil's many and varied writings throughout his life sheds new light on his brilliant mind." —**Joan Baez**, American singer, songwriter, musician and activist.

"Phil Ochs was a born writer. He played guitar because that was the language his generation was speaking. Today, his questioning voice chimes as clearly as it ever did." —**Billy Bragg**, British singer, songwriter, and activist

"As much as has been written about the sixties, it's arguable that no one experienced that defining moment in American history more personally than Phil Ochs." —**Steve Earle**, American singer, songwriter, record producer, author, and actor.

"The long lost, largely unpublished, prose of folksinger Phil Ochs does much more than entertain. At the least, it takes us back to a more innocent time. At the best, it awakens the poet in the soul." —**Kinky Friedman**, author, *The Mile High Club*

"Everything Phil Ochs wrote, including this new collection of journalism, poetry, and calls to action, exudes great humanity, heart, and brilliant humor. He was and continues to be a great blessing." —**Anne Lamott**, American novelist and nonfiction writer

PRAISE FOR I'M GONNA SAY IT NOW

"As a teenager my life was changed by Phil Ochs's anti-war songs and his unique ability to combine fierce progressive ideology with a sentimental heart. This remarkable collection of his prose is a reminder that Ochs was simultaneously one of the intellectual leaders of the counter-culture, a writer whose moral clarity was balanced by humor, irreverence, and wisdom. *I'm Gonna Say It Now* is not merely a treasured relic for Ochs completists, it reveals a unique window into a pivotal moment in American history." —**Danny Goldberg**, author of *Serving The Servant: Remembering Kurt Cobain* and *In Search of The Lost Chord: 1967 and the Hippie Idea*

I'M GONNA SAY IT NOW

The Writings of Phil Ochs

Edited by David Cohen

Backbeat Books

Guilford, Connecticut

Published by Backbeat Books
An imprint of The Rowman & Littlefield Publishing Group, Inc.
4501 Forbes Blvd., Ste. 200
Lanham, MD 20706
www.rowman.com

Distributed by NATIONAL BOOK NETWORK

Library of Congress Cataloging-in-Publication Data available

ISBN 978-1-4930-5147-2 (paperback)
ISBN 978-1-4930-5148-9 (e-book)

♾™ The paper used in this publication meets the minimum requirements of American National Standard for Information Sciences—Permanence of Paper for Printed Library Materials, ANSI/NISO Z39.48-1992

Dear Broadside,

I would like to thank you for your extensive and graphic review of my album. However, I must point out one flagrant error; Gregory Peck played Captain Horatio Hornblower, not Robert Taylor.

Sincerely yours,

Phil Ochs

CONTENTS

INTRODUCTION

"Anybody know who Phil Ochs is?" asked Lady Gaga at the Camden Rising concert in the midst of the Democratic National Convention in July 2016, before launching into an impassioned version of Phil's 1967 song "The War is Over." Viewed from one direction it was a surprising choice, a popular singer like Lady Gaga choosing to cover a very political, forty-nine-year-old song written by a not-quite-as-popular left-wing singer-songwriter. On the other hand, Phil Ochs is an artist who keeps being referenced, whether by singers such as Billy Bragg (who reworked the classic "I Dreamed I Saw Joe Hill Last Night" as "I Dreamed I Saw Phil Ochs Last Night") or by writers such as Stephen King (in his novels *The Tommyknockers* and *Hearts in Atlantis*).

A multifaceted creator, a writer of no mean skill all of his life, it is, on that other hand, no real surprise at all that Phil Ochs is continually being rediscovered by artists such as Lady Gaga, with new aspects of his work still being unearthed. In truth, Phil was not only a songwriter, he was a short story writer, a satirist, a critic, a poet ("a poet of the first order" the former U.S. attorney general Ramsey Clark would proclaim at Ochs's Felt Forum memorial in 1976), and yes, a journalist (according to at least one Nobel Prize laureate in literature). In short, a multidimensional wordsmith.

This, then, is a collection of the writings of Phil Ochs, spanning his days as a high school student at the Staunton Military Academy through his college days at Ohio State University to his time on the opposing Gemini coasts of New York City and Los Angeles. It also encompasses his forays into poetry and wends all the way through to his last years and his final elegiac pieces. Reproductions from the rare, and in some cases unique, material held in the Phil Ochs Papers at the Woody Guthrie Center in Tulsa, Oklahoma, augment the text of Phil's works throughout the book under the rubric of Out of the Archives. These looks backstage allow the reader to more closely glimpse the hand of the artist and view the creative process at work, seeing where Phil made corrections, alterations, and emendations. The Out of the Archives section appears at the end of each relevant chapter, with the reproductions in the same order as the texts themselves.

Please note that due to limitations on the use of song lyrics written by other artists, which Phil used to illustrate his critiques, some edits had to be made to Phil's original writings. No artist has been entirely written out, but in a few cases the depth and intent of Phil's narrative is lessened. The chapters affected are "The Guthrie

Legacy," "The Art of Bob Dylan's 'Hattie Carrol,'" "Topical Songs—History on the Spot," and "Man Against Music." Likewise, in the article on "Hattie Carroll," Phil's perceptive summation of the song ("with all this he leaves the listener stunned with a sense of injustice") was excised, as it lacked Phil's intended meaning in the altered context. It is here restored, albeit slightly out of its proper place.

Phil arrived at Staunton Military Academy in 1956, drawn more by his love of music and the marching band than the military discipline of the school. Attracted to writing early on, Phil would contribute to the February 1958 inaugural issue of Staunton's literary magazine, the *Scimitar*, which was edited by Michael Goldwater, son of conservative Senator Barry "In Your Heart You Know He's Right" Goldwater. Phil's story, "White Milk to Red Wine," won the prize for best short story. Less known than his contributions to the *Scimitar* were his days as a features writer for the school newspaper, the *Kablegram*. Phil was noted as being a member of their writing staff from October 25, 1957, through at least February 7, 1958 (unfortunately, the next two issues of the paper could not be sourced and consulted), and the *Kablegram* almost certainly contains his earliest surviving work, most likely a satirical piece. Alas, very few of the features articles contain bylines and none are credited to Ochs, so definitive attribution is not possible, and thus none were able to be included in this collection (however, see the Footnote to History for "The Fight" for one intriguing possibility).

There is no record of any contribution by Phil to the various campus publications during his first two years at Ohio State University. However, after returning from a "sabbatical" in Florida where he wrote his first song, "Three Dreams," co-authored with an African-American songwriter from New Orleans (whose name, unfortunately, appears to be lost to history), Phil seems to have been energized and, starting in his junior year, contributed to no less than three publications.

Ohio State's newspaper, the *Lantern*, would carry not only Phil's early forays into straightforward journalism but also pieces of political content. These included his nuanced and thoughtful letter to the editor "Narrow View"; his first published piece in the *Lantern*, which commented on Castro's Cuba; and his take on the speech by Daniel Rubin of the Progressive Youth Organization Committee in "Red Party Defended by Youth Organizer." When his political views became too controversial for the paper's editorial board, Phil was moved to concert and theatre reviews (Segovia, Roger Williams, Thurber, Ionesco).

At the same time, Phil's love of satire was expressed through numerous pieces in the school's humor magazine, the *Sundial*, where he would be managing editor his senior year. Discovering that satire was one route to express political views deemed unpalatable in more polemical pieces, Phil would share his emerging ideas on such subjects with the broader student body in such pieces as "Only in Cuba; or, listen Ohio Staters" and "Gone with the Wind, Jr."

Phil was never, at any point, a propagandist, but in the conservative atmosphere of Ohio State University in the early 1960s, it became more of a struggle to write what he needed to write from his own evolved political perspective. So he founded his own paper, *The Word*, mimeographed from his dorm, where he could "say what he [had] to say." The vagaries of print run, distribution, and conservation mean that there are no known copies of this fabled paper extant (but see the Footnote to History for "Discussion of Constitution Submitted to Steeb Hall" for a possibility).

A newly discovered chapter in Phil's writing history was his attendance at the Circle Pines Center summer camp in Delton, Michigan, in 1961. While at the camp, Phil was the assistant editor of the *Youth Manual*. There he contributed reviews of the speakers' sessions—as well as a satire and a broadminded overall critique—a myriad of writing styles across a multitude of outlets, something that would characterize Phil's creativity during his lifetime.

Arriving in New York City, the epicenter of the folk music scene, in 1962, Phil would swiftly find his feet on both the music and writing fronts. Even though this was the most explosive period of songwriting for Phil when he would pen dozens of songs, many more than he would be able to professionally record, he still found the time and inspiration to continue publishing his prose. Once again, Phil would not be constrained to a single style or genre. A firm proponent of topical music, Phil would publish many of his articles in *Broadside, Sing Out, Modern Hi-Fi and Stereo Guide* (the issue with Phil's article, "Topical Songs—History on the Spot," is seemingly lacking at all libraries, the sole known source for the article being the pages held in the Woody Guthrie Center), and *Broadside of Boston*.

Often viewed as a rival of Bob Dylan, Phil was consistent in his defense of Dylan's pursuit of his own art. See Phil's "An Open Letter from Phil Ochs to Irwin Silber, Paul Wolfe and Joseph R. Levine" and "Ochs: It Ain't Me Babe" for two full-throated and unambiguous rebuttals of the charge that "true" folksingers should limit themselves to the political or topical.

Phil himself was not content to limit himself to the political or commentaries on the current state of the folk music idiom. He continued to contribute satirical articles to *The Realist* ("Revolt on Campus" and "The Newport Fuzz Festival") and *Cavalier* ("That Was the Year That Weren't"). At a time when lefty singer-songwriters were being accused of being grade-school, quasi-illiterate pamphleteers with no senses of humor, Phil was a strong argument for the contrary position.

In 1967, Phil changed record labels (Elektra to A&M) and moved from the East Coast to the Left Coast (Los Angeles). The same year saw another turning point in Phil's life. Having protested against the Vietnam War for his entire adult life (one of his earliest songs, "Vietnam," dated from 1962), Phil came around to the idea that the only way to deal with an absurd war was with absurdity, by declaring the war over from the bottom up. This absurdist notion was anchored by two public gatherings, in Los Angeles (June 23, 1967) and New York City (November 25, 1967); one song ("The War is Over"); and articles in the *Los Angeles Free Press* and *Village Voice*, all rooted in the idea that "demonstrations should turn people on, not off," and "if there is going to be an America, there is no war." This was a turning point in Ochs's life where he attempted to impose a cinematic, poetic logic on a most uncinematic, unpoetic world. Two other times when Phil would try to bring an artistic sensibility to a decidedly unartistic reality were the Yippie "Festival of Life" at the Democratic National Convention in Chicago (1968) and the "Gold Suit" concerts (1970), where he attempted to meld the politics of Che Guevara with the populism of Elvis Presley. Moments of hope followed by months of despair.

Having been labelled a "singing journalist" and tied to the stake of political topical songs early on, it was a challenge for Phil to explore his more lyrical, abstract, poetic side (although songs such as "Changes" made the point most strongly). At one point in the late 1960s, Phil wrote a fair few poems, although only a handful saw print. Ochs' poems appeared on the backs of albums such as *Pleasures of the Harbor* and *Rehearsals for Retirement*, in *The War is Over* songbook ("Encores," "Cobbwebs," "Coming Attractions"), and in such magazines as *Dare* ("The Torture Garden"). The rest have remained unpublished until now, as have the ringers, the two songs which are included herein: "Love is a Rainbow" and "I Will Not Hurt You." These songs have not been previously published in any magazine nor are any recordings known; this is their first true appearance.

The world may have ended in Los Angeles (as it might have begun in Eden), and Phil hit a severe case of writer's block in 1970. He even updated the "Love Me,

I'm a Liberal" lyric "I go to all the Pete Seeger concerts, he sure gets me singing those songs" to "I go to all the Phil Ochs concerts, I sure wish he'd write some new songs." This always got applause and laughter from the audience, but Phil was not laughing. Returning to his roots, Phil would start writing articles again in 1973. In some ways, these articles represent a recapitulation of his earlier writings. The straight journalism in "Opposes Pot Decriminalization, FREEP Press Passes," the satire in "Brezhnev on TV. Let's Make a Deal," and the political acumen displayed in "Will Elliot Richardson Be Our Next President?" all harkened back to earlier times at Staunton, at Ohio State, and in New York City. The movie review piece "The Last Ten Best List" touches on Phil's lifelong love of the cinema ("I confessed I had been to the movie show/when I was a boy in Ohio"), and one can only wonder what might have been if Phil had been an anonymous movie critic, seeing as many films as he wanted without all the pressure to be "the old Phil Ochs."

"Requiem for a Dragon Departed" is a central piece in Ochs's canon that show-cases his fine journalistic and poetic senses, reporting the story as he might play the piano—one hand on the notes (facts) and the other on the melody (drama) of the realities of Bruce Lee's life and death. Phil realized the strength of the piece at the time, writing to his brother Michael, "Let's spread this around, ok? I like it." It would be Phil's most reprinted piece, appearing in *Take One* (Montreal), *Los Angeles Weekly News*, *Zoo World*, *Time Out* (London), and *Strange Things Are Happening*.

The final pieces date from the last year of Ochs's life, as darkness encroached upon his thoughts. Yet even then, sparks of the old spirit found their way out into the world. "Soho Bar Attacked" is the very model of objective journalism, and Phil is quite honest, even to his own detriment. "The Sale of One City" and "Save New York City" feel like pendent pieces, tied together by Ochs's refusal to see only one side of a situation, answering the cynical with the hopeful.

The question must be asked: Why the writings of Phil Ochs and why now? Phil once noted that life is a series of returnings, and so we return to where we began, with an unexpected person referencing Phil Ochs. In this case it was Kareem Abdul-Jabbar, basketball legend, actor (in another bit of synchronicity, making his debut in Bruce Lee's *Game of Death*), writer, and activist, who referenced Phil in his 2018 "An Open Letter to the NFL Owners," published in the *Guardian*. Righteously taking the NFL owners to task for their hypocrisy in responding to the "controversy" surround-ing players taking a knee in protest (perhaps the first time that respectful kneeling has ever been considered disrespectful), Abdul-Jabbar was reminded of the Phil Ochs song that gives this volume its title, "I'm Gonna Say It Now," which he proceeds to quote in the article. He then goes on to reference a saying attributed to the sage Hillel the Elder: "If not now, when?"

How would Phil, who once wrote "Every newspaper headline is a potential song," have responded to the phenomenon of "fake news"? Perhaps with "Inside a Small Circle of 'Non-existent' Friends"? Would the current refugee crisis—with men, women, families, and unaccompanied children crowded into dirty and dangerous detention centers—have spurred Phil to dust off the unfortunately still-quite-topical lyric "While the people were pressed into camps not called concentration" from his 1965 song "We Seek No Wider War"? Would the president's well-known disagreements with the truth have inspired an update of "Here's to the State of Mississippi/ Richard Nixon," with new lines such as "And here's to the tweets of Donald Trump, for in 140 characters are hid a thousand lies"?

If not now, when?

When?

Now.

Gentlefolk of all persuasions, may I present Phil Ochs.

David Cohen
June 2019

ACKNOWLEDGMENTS

This book could not have come into existence without help from many hands. Profound thanks to all the "links on the chain" that made this book possible.

First and foremost, heartfelt thanks to the Ochs family.

Meegan Ochs: Simply put, this book would not be here without your boundless generosity and longstanding support. Meegan, I hope this book lives up to what you envisioned for your dad's writings.

Michael Ochs: Archivist and gentleman. Thank you for your expertise and munificence regarding your brother in all matters, both photographic and archival.

Phil's sister, Sonny Ochs: Thank you for your passion in keeping Phil's memory and music alive and for your kindness in opening both your "Phil files" and your house by the waterfall to me, in many fondly remembered research trips.

Meegan Ochs, Michael Ochs, and Sonny Ochs have all gifted their individual Phil Ochs materials to the Woody Guthrie Center in Tulsa, Oklahoma, as the Phil Ochs Papers, Michael Ochs Collection, and Sonny Ochs Collection, respectively. The triad of archives are a boundless bonanza of Ochsiana, and they were a fundamental source for much of what appears in this book, including but certainly not limited to the reproductions that appear in the Out of the Archives sections. Among the gems in the Ochs Archives at the Woody Guthrie Center are Phil's notebooks, scrapbooks, correspondence, manuscripts, rare photos, and fascinating realia, such as his gold lamé suit, his mannequin (Miranda), and his backgammon set. The full breadth of the Woody Guthrie Center's Ochs holdings is vast: the primary Phil Ochs collection in the world, a veritable treasure trove waiting for future researchers to delve into its riches. To those authors of future articles, dissertations, and books: a research trip to the Woody Guthrie Center is strongly encouraged: https://woodyguthriecenter.org/

At the Woody Guthrie Center: Sincere thanks to Deana McCloud (Executive Director) for her support of this project from day 1. Special thanks to Kate Blalack, MLIS, CA (Archivist), for providing access to the archives, scanning materials, and performing near-miraculous feats of archivistry in helping us avoid the dreaded deadline doom. A thousand thanks are not enough!

At Backbeat Books/Rowman & Littlefield: John Cerullo (Senior Executive Editor), for initial faith and continuing support; Barbara Claire (Editorial Assistant), for always having the right answer to my 1,001 queries and keeping things on track (all is, finally, "flat"!); Carol Flannery (Senior Acquisitions Editor), for making clear what was once obscure regarding all the pros and cons of book layout (and the images therein).

At Getty Images: Jonathan Hyams (Senior Archive Photo Editor) and Paul Chesne (Senior Photo Editor), thank you for your kind help with the Alice Ochs photographs.

Additional thanks to: Michael Simmons, musician, filmmaker, journalist, and activist, for illuminating Phil conversations, shared finds, and making the connections; Mary Lou Sullivan (author of the fine Kinky Friedman bio *Everything's Bigger in Texas*), for helping us get in touch with the fine folks at Backbeat Books in the first place.

Finally, as ever and always: Thank you, Phil!

STAUNTON MILITARY ACADEMY

THE FIGHT

Scimitar (Staunton Military Academy) 1 no. 1 (28 February 1958)

I had never been so worried in all my life. When I got out of bed that morning a cold sweat came over me. I knew that I had to fight him sooner or later and today was it. He had bullied me once too often, and now I had finally reached my breaking point. If a person is built stronger than others, he does not have the right to pick on people who are smaller and weaker than he is.

When he insulted me in front of my friends, I had to make a stand. In a fit of rage, I challenged him to a fight the next day after lunch. When he heard this, he threw back his head and laughed cruelly.

I went to school the following day feeling like David when he went to meet Goliath. Unfortunately, I had no slingshot to cover me. My morning classes seemed to pass too quickly and the lunch I ate had no taste. When I walked towards the meeting place, I knew how a condemned man feels as he walks the last mile. All of a sudden, a hand gripped my shoulder. I spun around and there he stood. The only difference was that the triumphant look was gone from his face. He stammered nervously and said that he didn't mean to pick on me, and that he didn't want to fight.

With a sigh of relief I agreed, and we walked back to the school to spend another routine kindergarten afternoon.

WHITE MILK TO RED WINE
Scimitar (Staunton Military Academy) 1 no. 1 (28 February 1958)

The silence hung over the deserted highway like a fog. As far as the eye could see there was nothing but emptiness. In the middle of the road sat a milk white rabbit, curled up into a comfortable position, its huge brown eyes staring into the emptiness. Far off in the distance a faint sound which resembled thunder became audible. The sound increased in volume until it was almost deafening. With the sound came a flood of light which illuminated the emptiness.

This sudden explosion of noise and light paralyzed the rabbit with terror; and a circular strip of hard rubber snuffed out the life of this small creature in the same manner as a candle is extinguished. The furry coat was no longer milk white, but wine red, and his two eyes stared blankly into the night.

The four wheeled assassin was loaded with a jubilant crowd of college students. The speedometer had reached the hundred mark and was still climbing. A mile behind this "wonderful" modern convenience was another automobile filled with an equally jubilant crowd belonging to a rival college. They were steadily gaining on the car ahead; their liquor-soaked brains were confident of overtaking and beating the leaders to the finish line which was only seven miles away.

The minutes flew by and soon there was only half a mile to go. The driver in the lead, realizing that victory was in his grasp, was delirious with joy. His mind wandered into the future as he pictured the glory that was to be his.

The picture was destroyed as a road sign appeared straight in front of him and he realized that his car was sliding off the road. In a futile, drunken effort he swung the steering wheel in the opposite direction with all his might.

The wheels screamed in agony and the car was thrown into a rolling motion with terrific force. The twisted heap lay in the middle of the road and the roar of the motor was replaced by the moans of the injured. The last sight that was witnessed by the occupants was the two headlights of their opponents rapidly descending down upon them.

The silence returned to the deserted highway, and the rabbit continued to stare blindly into the emptiness of the night.

OUT OF THE ARCHIVES (STAUNTON MILITARY ACADEMY)

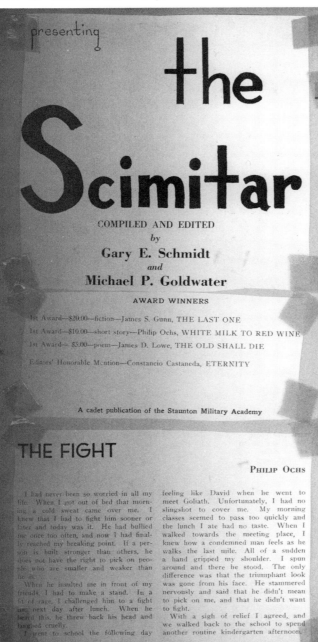

presenting

the Scimitar

COMPILED AND EDITED

by

Gary E. Schmidt

and

Michael P. Goldwater

AWARD WINNERS

1st Award—$20.00—fiction—James S. Gunn, THE LAST ONE

1st Award—$10.00—short story—Philip Ochs, WHITE MILK TO RED WINE

1st Award— $5.00—poem—James D. Lowe, THE OLD SHALL DIE

Editors' Honorable Mention—Constancio Castaneda, ETERNITY

A cadet publication of the Staunton Military Academy

THE FIGHT

PHILIP OCHS

I had never been so worried in all my life. When I got out of bed that morning a cold sweat came over me. I knew that I had to fight him sooner or later and today was it. He had bullied me once too often, and now I had finally reached my breaking point. If a person is built stronger than others, he does not have the right to pick on people who are smaller and weaker than he is.

When he insulted me in front of my friends, I had to make a stand. In a fit of rage, I challenged him to a fight next day after lunch. When he heard this, he threw back his head and laughed cruelly.

I went to school the following day feeling like David when he went to meet Goliath. Unfortunately, I had no slingshot to cover me. My morning classes seemed to pass too quickly and the lunch I ate had no taste. When I walked towards the meeting place, I knew how a condemned man feels as he walks the last mile. All of a sudden a hand gripped my shoulder. I spun around and there he stood. The only difference was that the triumphant look was gone from his face. He stammered nervously and said that he didn't mean to pick on me, and that he didn't want to fight.

With a sigh of relief I agreed, and we walked back to the school to spend another routine kindergarten afternoon.

FEBRUARY 28, 1958　　　　　　　　　　　5

THE OHIO STATE UNIVERSITY

POLITICS

NARROW VIEW
Ohio State Lantern, 27 April 1961

To the Editor:

In Tuesday's *Lantern*, R. Christopher Powell argues that if we had backed the rebels (in Cuba) all the way, we would have sent Communism "reeling back to its own hemisphere."

This view is rather typical of the supporters of such great thinkers as Barry Goldwater. However, it is a very narrow way to look at the situation. The attack, on the contrary, would have solidified Communism's hold on the Western Hemisphere and throughout the world.

Instead of looking at it as an American citizen, look at it as a neutral observer. The picture you will see as a neutral is that of a small country being overrun by a huge imperialistic power who say they are doing it for democracy and the good of the Cuban people even though they have been exploiting these same people for over half a century.

We are told that Cuba is controlled by the Communists even though their party is quite minute when compared to the huge Fidelista party of Castro. We are told that Castro is a demagogic dictator and the fact that he has started to educate his people, bring land reform and begin long overdue building projects is irrelevant.

We are told that Castro is an immense threat to our security, but does this mean security for our lives, or security for our ideas? Our papers are quick to preach how terrible the Castro dictatorship is, but how often do they criticize Salazar, Franco or Chiang Kai-shek?

Had we attacked Cuba we would have alienated every neutral in the world. Even the many people who were sympathetic to the Castro revolution, but who turned away from him because of his dictatorial attitude, would return to his side as the lesser of two evils, and Castro would become a martyr, a Communist saint. Russia's screaming of "Yankee Imperialism" would have a strong ring of truth throughout the world had the attack occurred.

Democracy is an excellent ideal, but in reality do the Cuban people really want it? Did the German people want a democracy, or did they want a Hitler, a leader and a deliverer? Why does the average man in Cuba want to vote if he is eating decently for the first time in his life? They are trying to give democracy to Africa, but chances are they could progress much faster united under the strong leadership of a man like Kenyatta.

Kennedy's mistake was not that he failed to attack Cuba as in all probability Mr. Nixon would have done, but that he didn't have enough foresight to cancel Eisenhower's futile plan when he came into office.

DISALLE, LAW STUDENTS DEBATE CAPITAL PUNISHMENT QUESTION
Ohio State Lantern, 1 May 1961

"The real enemy against society is organized crime, not the isolated murderer, and yet in my adult life in Ohio there has not been one gangster executed," said Gov. Michael V. DiSalle in a panel discussion on Capital Punishment in the Law School Auditorium on Saturday. The discussion was part of the Law Day Program.

Debating for the retention of Capital Punishment were Hubert Dutro, Law-2, and Shelby Hutchins, Law-3. Their opponents were John McDonald, Law-3, and Ronald Endrizal, Law-3.

"Does taking a man's life help insure the health, welfare, and safety of a state?" Gov. DiSalle asked the audience. "With ten million people in Ohio, if we have to rely on nine executions in the past two years to protect us, we are in bad condition."

Serves Two Purposes

He went on to say that punishment serves two purposes: deterrence and rehabilitation.

"There is tremendous publicity given to clemency cases, but the actual executions are played down in the papers," said DiSalle.

He added that we say it is wrong to kill, but we justify it when it is done collectively by the state.

DiSalle concluded his opening statements by saying that he was opposed to capital punishment before he considered his first petition for clemency.

Cites Statistics

"The statistics deal with homicide, but premeditated murder is only 1/5 of the homicide cases," Mr. Hutchins said, starting the opposing argument. The statistics used by the opponents of capital punishment don't prove that it is or isn't a deterrent to murder, he said.

McDonald countered by saying that there is no evidence that capital punishment is a real deterrent. He added that the death sentence is not handed out impartially, and there is no chance to rectify mistakes after an execution.

He also took issue with the argument that killing would save the state the cost of feeding a man with a life sentence.

"If we are interested in saving money, we should execute all criminals, and also the mentally ill," McDonald said.

Stresses Rehabilitation

"We must have an excellent system of rehabilitation before we can consider abolishing the death sentence," Dutro said. He added that the only argument against capital punishment was a constructive one.

VIEWS DISARMAMENT AS BENEFIT TO U.S., RUSSIANS, POOR NATIONS
Ohio State Lantern, 18 May 1961

"Disarmament would provide a little extra luxury for the U.S., convenience for the Soviet Union, and perhaps an economic necessity for the poor peoples of the world," said Dr. Kenneth E. Boulding in a lecture at the Union Conference Theatre yesterday afternoon.

He went on to say that the poor nations are on the threshold of entering the modern world, and if they don't make it over the hump of economic development, they could slip back into a block of misery without hope of recovery.

He classified the history of nations into three phases: pre-civilized, civilized and post-civilized. "The civilized nations of today are the poor countries, while the more advanced nations are in the post-civilized era."

In Unique Position

"We are in the most unique position the world has ever seen," he said. "We have a chance to create a permanent high-level society throughout the world, but if we fail now, the lessening supply of natural resources would prevent us from ever having this opportunity again."

He added that we spend 10 per cent of our income on defense, but the amount of money spent on defense on the world scene is equal to the income of the poorest half of the world.

"The international defenses for peace are very poor, and the vague boundaries that separate violence from peace are often crossed," he said.

Says War Is Obsolete

"War is a dying institution, and we must prepare for the economic and psychological adjustments that we will face with disarmament," he said.

He added that the political leaders of today are thinking in terms of social systems that are disappearing. "It is like piloting a plane, thinking that it is a Model T."

He explained that one of the major sociological problems today is preserving the idea of nationalism. "However, we must prevent nationalism from becoming pathological; any virtue can turn into a vice if it is overdone."

Physical Science Over Emphasized

He said that we are devoting ourselves too much to a scientific system. "50 million for seismology and nothing for sociology seems to be the rule," he said. "When a social system is racing to destruction you must present an appropriate social cure.

"We ought to prepare for a conversion to peace that would let us retain economic stability," he said. "The defense industry has been a boost to our economy because it is the only place that can afford to be extravagant in research and development."

CIVIL LIBERTIES GROUP ORGANIZED ON CAMPUS
Ohio State Lantern, 19 May 1961

The protection of students' civil rights is the main purpose of a recently formed student organization, the Ohio State Civil Liberties Committee.

"We want to avoid becoming a clique or a fanatical group," said its newly elected President, Mrs. Anne Morton, Ed-3. "We have some liberals and some conservatives, and we plan to remain completely independent and nonpartisan."

She explained that the group's purpose was threefold: 1) to educate and inform the students on their civil rights on campus and those guaranteed in the U.S. Constitution, 2) to act as a pressure group for promoting freedom, and 3) to make themselves available to anyone who feels their civil liberties have been violated.

"We plan to provide a well-organized group on campus to protect and project everybody's civil liberties," she said.

Grigsby To Advise
"Some of the issues that we would be interested in are discrimination against Negroes, the restriction placed on girls on campus, and incidents like Mandel and the Von Braun picketers."

The faculty advisor is Dr. Gordon K. Grigsby, an English instructor. He said that their success would depend on how much persuasive power they could achieve, and on what issues arose next year.

He added, "There has been much misunderstanding concerning civil liberties, and we would like to join the individuals in the past who have tried to defend those whose rights have been violated."

Anticipate Much Action
He said that some of the methods they would try to use are petitions, consultation with the administration, acting as a pressure and testimony group in the Student Senate, and acting generally as the representatives of the student body in cases where civil liberties are involved.

Dr. Grigsby was advisor to the Student Peace Committee which he said is an ad hoc group that is undecided as to whether it will petition for official recognition. He was also advisor to the Human Relations Sub-Committee of the Student Senate.

The group hopes to be recognized by the end of May, and has already collected dues and elected their officers for a year. They are Mrs. Morton, president; Bruce Hinely, Grad, vice-pres.; Lynda Friedlander, A-2, sec.; and Carol Grandee, A-3, treas. They are presently meeting in the Law Building, but don't plan on any major action until next year.

SAMUEL FARBER
Circle Pines Center Youth Manual, 1961

"Be careful of what you read, and always check as many sources as you can," is the advice of Samuel Farber, a Cuban studying in the United States. He added that in any given circumstance this is the best way to get an accurate picture; not an absolute, but the best possible approximation.

Mr. Farber feels that from the beginning, the trend of the Castro Revolution has been to consolidate the power of the government in all the fields of life. "There is no effective channel through which the masses can influence the government," he said. "It is wrong for an individual or small group to decide what is wrong or right in any society," he continued.

"You may tell me that Guevara disagrees with Castro on certain things, but the basic evil is that the people are not allowed a vote in the disagreement," he added. He pointed out that the people are allowed to complain to a limited extent, but there is no guarantee that even the minor issues will be given proper attention. Mr. Farber pictures the Cuban government as a blossoming bureaucracy. As an example, he stated that the autonomy of the trade unions is being suppressed, replaced by a dictatorial appointee of the government. He also mentioned the fact that the state farms are increasingly replacing the more democratic cooperatives.

"As far as I know there is no instance in history where a group or individual holding absolute power has given it up of his own free will," he said.

Mr. Farber stated that many liberals in Castro's government have left him either by choice or pressure, even though they agreed with many of his economic reforms. Three outstanding examples are Manuel Fernandez, his first Minister of Labor; Major Eloy Gutiérrez Menoyo, an ardent anti-Franco; and David Salvador, Secretary General of the Cuban Confederation of Labor (CTC), who was arrested while trying to leave the country and is still in jail.

"Castro has said that you are either with me or against me, there is no middle way. Some honest people in America recognize his mistakes but still give 'critical support' to him. This is not fair because this position cannot be taken openly in Cuba. The principle of freedom is a vital point to any government, and without it, there should be no support."

Mr. Farber refuted the argument that revolutions necessarily strangle democracy by pointing out that even Lenin, who is to the left of Castro, always fought for the autonomy and freedom of such institutions as the trade unions.

"If channels of popular decision making are left open to the people, then it is possible to change a society without need of violence. If the situation in Cuba remains static, force may be necessary; however, I would never condone American intervention in Cuba, since history shows that the U.S. would certainly not be doing it for the sake of the Cuban people. He also said that the fact that the recent invasion did not draw any support in Cuba does not necessarily prove the lack of discontent. He added that some of the liberals opposing Castro (e.g., MRP [Movimiento Revolucionario del Pueblo]) were not given any power in the invasion force, and it was mainly a reactionary attempt. "Nothing good could come out of the evil of an American invasion," he said.

Mr. Farber, twenty-two, has just received his B.A. in Sociology from the University of Chicago and plans to attend the London School of Economics.

THURSDAY, AFTERNOON, AUGUST 31, 1961
HAITI
TOM BOURELLY, SPEAKER
Circle Pines Center Youth Manual, 1961

"It is the duty of American youth to be informed about Haiti, and to realize that our problem is theirs, because by helping us they are helping themselves," said Tom Bourelly, a Haitian student studying in America.

After explaining the common Latin American problems such as control by American business interests, dictatorial militarist rule, and widespread poverty and ignorance, Tom gave a historical synopsis of Haiti. "We have been under the domination of Spain and France; and the Negro population was brought there during the period of the slave traffic from Africa." Independence from these countries created a power struggle between the black and mulatto elite which is still present. "The history of our country is one of continual uprisings and revolutions averaging one every four years." He also pointed out that Haiti was the first Negro republic and the first independent country in Latin America.

"The middle class educate their children in Haiti, but the elite are contemptuous of our schools and send their children to study abroad," he stated. He mentioned that French is the official language of Haiti, but only 5% are able to speak it, while the masses speak Creole, a combination of French, Spanish, African, and Indian.

Mr. Bourelly said that the religion of Haiti is a combination of Catholicism and Voodoo, with the latter being the cornerstone of Haitian culture with its African heritage. "Basically, Voodoo is the worship of the spirit of our ancestors to protect the community, roughly comparable to self-hypnosis and telepathy. I have never seen such things as a pinned doll which many people believe is the symbol of Voodoo. An example of the way the two religions are incorporated is that the Virgin Mary is represented by the symbol of a snake, and that natural surroundings are deified, as the goddess of the sun and sea, etc. The villages are controlled first by the military delegate and second by the Voodoo priest, and to win an election you must have the support of both."

He pointed out that the Catholic church is always striving for contributions, for example many priests will not baptize a child or bury somebody properly without a fee ranging from two to five dollars.

"The most popular music and dance in Haiti is the merengue, and some calypso which filters in from Jamaica and Trinidad," he said. "Our popular music is basically African with the drum beat predominant; it is the poetry of our island. American performers such as Harry Belafonte and Nat "King" Cole are also very popular here. We have no real movie industry, and most of our cinema imports are French and American."

Mr. Bourelly described an average peasant weekend as a gathering in huts to perform voodoo ceremonies. This consists of singing ancestral songs with the drum beat prominent, and the serving of food and alcoholic beverages.

"Our island is shared with the Dominican Republic; they have two-thirds of the land and we have two-thirds of the population," he remarked. "Haiti has occupied them twice and this created a vendetta in the mind of Trujillo who enforced strong boundaries. However, there is still a close bond of friendship between our peoples."

He finished by saying that "Revolution (meaning change by violent or non-violent means) is inevitable in Haiti. 95% of the thinking students in Haiti are pro-Castro and the success of our revolution depends partially on his success and support."

Tom, 22, received some of his higher education at a French baccalaureate in Haiti, which is the equivalent of a college in America. He has completed three years of medical school at the University of Illinois and will finish this year in Switzerland. Then he plans to return to the United States to study general surgery. On his mother's side there are plantation owners and his father's side is professional, and he hopes that their differences in ideas will not place them on different sides of the political coin when and if a revolution comes. Tom hopes to serve his country in the field of public health and hygiene after he graduates.

RODRIGO ALAMOS
Circle Pines Center Youth Manual, 1961

"Newspapers in Chile and throughout Latin America are influenced greatly by political parties; sometimes they go to extremes, but they balance each other to prevent widespread distortion," said Rodrigo Alamos, a Chilean student. He added that in Chile the most honest paper was the liberal one because it represented a wide cross section of views.

"Latin America has a very political atmosphere; in the United States people spend their spare time in trivial activities like watching television, but in my country there is a great deal of intellectual discussion," he remarked. "The youth in America care too much about money and other material goods."

He pointed out that in Chilean high schools a group of 25 or 30 students stick together until they graduate. "This allows them to make friends for life and facilitates the communication of ideas and problems; teenagers are not alone as they are many times in the United States," he mentioned. He added that on the college level everyone takes almost the same courses for the first three years of a five-year program. "There is a great emphasis on history and philosophy in our courses, but strangely enough the courses on history since 1900 are minute; the school of thought is that you are not able to acquire enough historical perspective for so recent a period," he said. He also mentioned that the highlights of U.S. history taught on Chile are the role we played in their independence and the American Civil War with emphasis on Lincoln.

On the cultural side, Mr. Alamos said that there are two main types of music in Chile. *Tonadas* is romantic music that is sung and played on the guitar, but not danced to. The *cueca* is a dance derived from the Spanish flamenco and slightly influenced by the natives. It is danced for enjoyment and exhibition and is even used in ballet. "It is interesting to note that Paul Anka is tremendously popular in Chile; the teenagers almost destroyed the airport when he came on a personal tour," he said.

Mr. Alamos considers Jânio Quadros a great leader, but criticizes his tendency to ignore his opposition while putting through his own program. "This is what largely provoked the recent crisis there and his resignation," he said.

Speaking on sports, he said that soccer is the most popular game throughout Latin America, and the players there are the best in the world. "We also play basketball, tennis, and some rugby football," he added.

His favorite politicians in the U.S. are Jack Kennedy and Jacob Javits, Senator from New York. He mentioned that when he reads American papers he only looks at the front page, the movie section, and Ann Landers.

Mr. Alamos, 22, is studying for his master's degree in Business Administration at the University of Chicago. When he completes his courses there, he plans to study Economics at the Sorbonne in Paris.

A CRITIQUE OF THE SESSIONS
Circle Pines Center Youth Manual, 1961

The sessions conducted at Circle Pines were stimulating and worthwhile, but they had several outstanding weaknesses. In the first place, the talks tended to be extremely repetitive because of the similarity of the subjects. The main issue in Latin America today is the need for political and economic reform, but this is not the entire picture. A much better understanding of Latin America could have been achieved if there had been one or two talks on the music, religion, culture, and the daily habits and characteristics of the people. How many people at the institute really know the way of life of the peasants, the middle class, and the aristocracy?

Tim Bourelly provided a beautiful example of the psychology of the revolutionist in Latin America, but what about the psychology of the owners of the latifundias? If somebody representing their interests or those of the corporations like the United Fruit Company had spoken, we could have been exposed to the way their minds work, the way they justify the situation in Latin America today, which would have painted a more detailed portrait of such a complex situation.

The speakers as a whole were excellent, but some had a tendency to be narrow minded. Mr. Rossen is a man of tremendous knowledge and experience, but unfortunately, he seems to have become so addicted to the Castro cause that he can't seem to find any fault with him. I am very sympathetic to Castro's basic economic reforms, as are many liberals, but that does not mean that I have to apologize or try to find an excuse for the authoritarian and bureaucratic trend his government has taken. Many liberals have stated here that the U.S. sees the world as either pro or anti-Communist. But these same people have a tendency to condemn the mistakes of America so much that they fall under the hypnotic spell of a Castro or other Socialist government. The fact that the U.S. is wrong is certainly not proof that another country is right; there are two sides to every picture. I believe that the most effective and realistic speaker here was Mr. Farber. He didn't go out on a limb to revere or curse Castro; he explained that he read as many sources as possible without accepting anything as the ultimate truth. Here is a man who searches for facts, not propaganda to suit his personal biases. If the leaders of today had the same philosophy, this would be a far more peaceful and understanding world.

RED PARTY DEFENDED BY YOUTH ORGANIZER
Ohio State Lantern, 31 October 1961

The Socialist countries of the world and the Communist Party of America were defended last night by Daniel Rubin, 30, a member of the executive board of the Progressive Youth Organization Committee (PYOC).

Rubin's unannounced talk was attended by an ad hoc group of 75 in the third-floor lounge of the Ohio Union.

He stated that the McCarran Act will allow the federal government to arrest any members of the Communist Party and any liberals who fall under the Act's definition of a Communist on Nov. 20, the date the act becomes effective.

He charged that the act "Violates the Constitution and the Bill of Rights and is one of the most extreme examples of far-right legislation ever passed in this country."

"Even President Truman described it as a 'thought control act' and the most potential danger to free speech in America since the Alien and Sedition Laws," he said.

He explained that the PYOC is an attempt to encourage the youth of America to take an intelligent look at world Communism and Marxian principles. "We also want to organize all groups interested in such issues as civil rights and the Negro problem," he said.

In the question and answer period that ensued, Rubin made the following statements:

- I don't believe Russia is Communist, and neither do the Russians; they are Socialist.

- Socialism offers the best solution of the problems mankind faces, and I would like to see it in the U.S.

- Russia is a democracy where the people, in fact, have much to say about government programs.

- There is no capitalistic party in Russia for the same reason there is no feudalistic party in America; each country has decided that the previous system was harmful and should remain extinct.

- The Communist Party in Russia contains all opposing viewpoints of the people except for capitalism.

- Thousands of tourists go to Moscow and those that openly denounce the government are left alone.

- There is a legal right to strike in Russia and strikes do take place. However, they are infrequent since the people realize they are only striking against themselves.

- Marxist thought in America speeds up actions on such issues as integration.

- The majority of people in Hungary today support the Communist government and the Hungarian Revolution had many Nazi and Fascist elements.

- Russia has no intention of advancing by force of arms or subversion. According to Khrushchev, the world will be persuaded to Communism by the example set by Russia and other Socialist countries.

ONE VERSION OF WHY AND HOW NEHRU DID WHAT HE DID TO SEIZE GOA
Ohio State Student Says India Action Is Justified; Hits 'Torrents of Abuse'
Plain Dealer (Cleveland), 31 December 1961

Editor Plain Dealer—

Sir: Your "Look What Nehru Started" editorial fits perfectly into the naïve niche so eloquently and superficially carved by our politicians and mass media. This is yet another consummate example of looking at the world through red sun glasses, and seeking conspiratorial enemies and betrayers surrounding us while our bovine government moos helplessly instead of taking effective actions.

I do not propose to defend Prime Minister Nehru's action since I have not intelligently reviewed the opposing facts and justifications that inevitably come with such an occurrence, as apparently you have, but I would like to present a slightly broader view of the currents and causes of just what exactly Nehru did start.

The fact of the matter is that Nehru started absolutely nothing; on the contrary, in 30 hours he succeeded in finishing an episode that began four centuries ago, and he did it under the shocking principle that India belongs to India, also known as anti-colonialism. There are certain forces in history that, good or bad, can never be prevented. It was a force of history that colonized India, an omnipotent force called imperialism, and now the reverse force of nationalism has liberated Goa from its reactionary chains.

The Communist forces from the beginning have understood and exploited the power of historical movements, while we have either ignored them or paid them hypocritical lip service. Is it any wonder that so many neutrals have fallen under the magnetic spell of the Soviet Union's realistic foreign policy, both in word and deed?

Portugal is a decrepit nation ruled by a conservative dictator who refuses to believe he is living in the 20th century. Nehru's anti-colonialist action produced 50 casualties, but it must be remembered that Portugal's pro-colonialist action in Angola resulted in the brutal slaughter of 50,000 Africans.

You state that President Sukarno now has designs on Dutch New Guinea; poor Dutch New Guinea. In case you don't know it by now, every country that is partially or wholly colonized has designs on their rightful territories, and Russia is backing them all without reservations. It will be incredibly difficult to fight against this invincible movement and maintain the delicate balance we have now in the cold war.

You mention that the Dutch "Cannot in honor yield to his open threats." However, the latest issue of *Newsweek* states, "An ironic touch to Indonesia's threatened invasion of Dutch New Guinea is that the Dutch themselves would like nothing better than to abandon the place." They add that pressure from conservative Australia is keeping them there.

Imperialism is dying! Colonialism is dying! These are the cries of the world today, and we can no longer remain deaf to them. If Nehru has erred in his means, he should be criticized; but since his end was historically and morally justified, there is no excuse for the torrent of abuse heaped upon him by the western powers.

To attack a dying institution is pardonable by historical standards; to attack a growing giant recklessly without realizing its significance could prove to be political suicide.

OVER BILLION WASTED ON CD, YOUNG SAYS
Ohio State Lantern, 23 October 1961

In the past nine years over one billion dollars has been wasted on the boondoggle of civil defense, according to Senator Stephen M. Young, who spoke to the Young Democrats Friday night in the Franklin Room of the Union.

He pointed out the danger of each shelter being a potential fire trap, and the great deal of time and cost ($1,500 average per home) involved in a private shelter.

There would also be many bars, rumpus rooms, and garages built in basements under the guise of a shelter for tax advantages, he said.

He added that the emphasis on shelters should be the large community type built at government expense, and that we shouldn't get into the position of having "fast-buck men" scare people into building shallow basement shelters.

"Our real temporary defense against attack is massive retaliation and the only permanent shelter is peace and disarmament," he asserted.

"It is extremely doubtful whether a shelter program would do any good," he continued, "and the stress on civil defense is a defeatist psychology."

Senator Young has recently returned from Europe, and he made several comments on his trip.

Four major ones were:

- The real purpose of Russian nuclear testing is not to terrorize the West, but to develop an anti-missile missile.

- West Germany is not paying its full share of the arms race.

- There was far less talk of war in Europe than in America.

- Many feel we overrate the Russian threat and that out foreign policy is too aggressive.

Commenting on the loss of the Speaker of the House, Young said: "Sam Rayburn was an excellent Speaker of the House but because of a certain continuity in Congress, I don't feel the President's program will be drastically affected by his loss."

STRADLEY BODY BARS DEFENDER
Ohio State Lantern, 30 January 1962

The Stradley Hall Commission of Justice barred Student Defender Benson Wolman from representing two cases last night.

In a 4-1 decision, the commission cited a statement from the dean of men's office saying that a dormitory student can be defended only by a fellow resident. The commission interpreted this as an absolute rule as opposed to a guideline allowing deviation.

Wolman made the following statement to the *Lantern*, "The decision of the commission to bar the defender is unreasonable at best and appears to be an improper acquiescence to arbitrary guidelines imposed by the office of the dean of men.

"If it is merely a guideline and not a rule, the commission gravely erred in concluding they were bound by them. If it is in fact an absolute rule, then the student courts are not being administered by the students and will become mere rubber stamps of the dean's office."

Both cases were postponed until next week in order to allow the defendants a chance to find adequate dormitory defense. Wolman stated that he would talk to the dean of men in order to get a ruling on the statement.

The Stradley Hall Senate will discuss the validity of the commission's ruling tonight, according to Al Kotsybar, Ed-3, a dorm senator. The two cases which Wolman attempted to defend involved destruction of dorm property and throwing water balloons out of a window.

DISCUSSION OF CONSTITUTION SUBMITTED TO STEEB HALL
Unpublished, circa 1961

The Constitution submitted to the residents of Steeb Hall is an unjust, vague document. The general air of complacency hovering over the students could easily allow it to pass without much discussion or opposition.

This paper covers a few of the main points that are subject to the most dissention and debate. For example, Section 2, Article B states that the chairman shall be elected by a majority vote of the senate. This means that the students at large do not have a voice to express their choice for executive leader of the dormitory. Interest in government on campus is negligible, and is only brought out during elections. If the students aren't even given a chance to elect their chairman, who is essentially the President of the dormitory, interest will wain to an even lower level, and the dormitory government will lose almost all contact with the wishes of the students.

Section 2, Article C states that the qualification for the office of chairman is that he be first elected floor president. This automatically disqualifies 99% of the residents of Steeb Hall from becoming Chairman. Also the Vice-Chairman, the Treasurer, and the Secretary must first be elected floor president; all this makes conditions very suitable for a clique-rule in Steeb Hall because it combines the legislative and executive branches into one group.

The constitution also neglects to define the judicial section of the government. However, this is supposed to be posted before the election.

There is also much controversy on such things as how many counselors should be allowed to vote, and the point-hour qualifications for the dormitory chairman.

The proponents of the constitution say that errors can be revised later, but I think they should have offered the students a chance to revise it before the election, which would take the students' views more into account. Next Monday the students will be voting for more than a constitution; they will also be voting on whether they are really represented or not. Any student who really considers the constitution and its implications will have no recourse but to veto it on Monday.

These are some of the ideas that came up during a discussion of the Constitution on the third floor.

SATIRE

LEFT, RIGHT, LEFT, RIGHT, LEFT, RIGHT
Sundial 49 no. 6 (April 1961)

There were no intelligent political parties running for the Student Senate at Philistine University; each one had its own peculiar level of idiocy. They spent their time calling each other do-nothing parties, and the more severe the name-calling became, the closer they got to truth. Student interest in the campaign seemed to be dropping from the previous year's all-time low, and there were dire predictions that the candidates would outnumber the electorate. Like most of the other students on campus, I tried to avoid the eager candidates, flowing with self-praise and wild promise. Then Philistine U. was introduced to Zelda Flutts.

It seems that the COPS (the conservatives of Philistine) decided that the sleepy campaign was a ripe opportunity to present their version of a typical LOPS (the liberals of Philistine) candidate. The conservative and liberal groups on campus were not affiliated with the office-seeking parties, but the COPS decided to run Zelda, to see how much they could ridicule their worthy opponents. The fictional Zelda was a liberal's liberal, having many qualifications for truly free thinkers. Miss Flutts was described as a 16-year-old Jewish negress with a Catholic mother and a father with a long criminal record. She advocated such leftist policies as changing Philistine into a welfare campus with a progressive tax program, a minimum allowance for students, and student ownership of the book stores. According to the COPS, she believed in changing everything without thinking, and then changing the changes.

Overnight Zelda became the toast of the campus. The LOPS could not be found for comment, for they had all disappeared into their locked, secluded office. I figured that Zelda would be forgotten in a couple of days until I was introduced to Nanu Funk the next day.

LOPS did not intend to remain the fool for long, so they employed the principle of massive retaliation. Nanu was an 87-year-old white Protestant, whose ancestors had come over on the Mayflower. There was even a school of thought that Nanu, himself, had come over screaming that sailboats were too radical. He believed in the complete freedom of the individual from the campus government service, and felt that all the students were rugged enough to take care of themselves. He advocated such policies as abolishing the curve used in grading by the teachers, abolishing the much too socialized student health center, and applying the isolationist doctrines to Philistine with respect to other colleges.

Philistine seemed to come out of its hibernation, and debates and parades were omnipresent. Not wishing to be attacked by either side as I walked to the library that night, I carried both Nanu and Zelda buttons with me in case I ran into an overzealous crowd of partisans on the oval. I also stayed away from the extreme right and left sides of the oval, in case somebody got the wrong idea.

When I got back to the dormitory a stalwart COP was trying to raise votes for Zelda and was promising a more radical Zelda to be unveiled the following day. I escaped up the stairs, but when I reached my floor I was confronted with an overheated LOP who was handing out more literature promising a more reactionary Nanu to combat the ultra-ultra Zelda.

Classes were forgotten the next day as the candidates' policies became more and more extreme. Zelda decided to recognize Red China, condemn the House Un-American Activities Committee, and extend student ownership to the dormitories and the classrooms. She wanted the teachers of each subject to form labor unions, and she screamed against the imperialistic policies of the administration.

Not to be outdone, Nanu decided that to be conservative was actually a cover-up for being extremely radical. The good old days became the great good old days, and Nanu decided that the industrial revolution was leftist in origin and advocated a mercantilistic policy. As his rightist mind raced on, he decided that the whole concept of democracy was actually Communist inspired, and the only way to protect the university was to bring in a monarchy. The professors would become Lords and the students, serfs. As beginning instructors became knighted, Philistine could replace the team-conscious football games on Saturday with jousting tournaments which really placed the value on the individual man.

"Dictatorship of the Proletariat students" screamed Zelda in reply. "The time has come to end the exploitation of the masses." She proposed that the university be divided into communes with students and professors receiving the same pay. Free love would be introduced as the men's, women's, and married students' residence halls were made one and the same. She also stated that private property must be abolished in order to have really free students, and she offered her back issues of the *Daily Worker* to the student community as a token of good faith. She ended up by saying, "A spectre is haunting Philistine! Students of all universities, unite! You have nothing to lose but your chains!"

For some reason the whole campaign seemed to have become slightly exaggerated. The student body swayed from one side to the other, depending on who appeared to be the most ridiculous at the time. Rumors sprang up that there actually was a living Nanu and Zelda on campus, and an entire day and night was spent in an intensive search for the symbolic idols of the campus.

Meanwhile, back at the Student Senate, the forgotten regular parties made their first and last bid for attention by proposing a massive tug-of-war on the oval between the rival factions as the only real means to settle the campaign. But when they heard the rumors that both Nanu and Zelda had suggested using the rope for lynching the Student Senate, they quietly disappeared from the campus scene.

The day before the elections promised to be unusual, to say the least. Zelda started the day off by deciding that television sets had to be placed everywhere to facilitate the watching of "Big Brother." In the afternoon, she promised that Big Brother and the State would wither away in a couple of days and the University would reach complete Utopia. Carrying it just one step further she concluded by saying that there was actually no need for her being elected because there was no need for the Student Senate, or any government, even the University.

Philistine did not have to wait long for Nanu's reply. Declaring himself a Caesar, he denounced the leftist religion, Christianity, and promised to bring gladiator battles to the Stadium. His final step forward (or rather backward) strangely resembled Zelda's. I had an idea of what he had in mind when I saw an engraving of a cave man's club on his final pamphlet. Denouncing the invention of the ultra-radical wheel, he also decided that the Student Senate was not needed and therefore neither was he. After he declared a state of anarchy on campus, he stated the only way to become completely rightist and free from society is for everybody to become a hermit.

The election day was phenomenal; nobody showed up at the polls. Everybody on campus had taken either Nanu's or Zelda's side, and taken their undisputed word, nobody voted. I don't know whether the COPS or the LOPS were more surprised when they read the campus newspaper the next day. The headline said, "Connie Francis Unanimously Elected to Student Senate on Write-in Vote from Florida." The sub-heading read, "Student Senate Abolished by Dazed Trustees."

I'm not sure what the effect of the whole campaign was, but the other day I overheard two professors talking after classes. One asked, "Who was that liberal I saw you with last night?" The second professor replied, "That was no liberal; that was Barry Goldwater."

HOW GREEN WAS MY GAMBOLING
Sundial 49 no. 7 (May 1961)

Most of the students at Gamboling Green were blue except for those who were purple with rage. The university president, Barry Beria, commonly referred to as Der Führer, had laid another 300 yards of barbed wire around the university, and was doubling the guards at the machine gun towers. The rustling of chains could be heard as the students shuffled their feet in the cafeteria and drank their milk. Many were still grumbling over the new law restricting the sale of "tooth rotting" soft drinks on campus.

Jock Heiferbull, the star football player, was displaying the thirty vicious welts he had received for straying off the cement paths on the oval. "I'll never forget Barry's hyena-like laughter as he was washing the whip afterwards," Jock mumbled. There were also rueful predictions that Dash would be served for Sunday dinner. The only person in the cafeteria who didn't seem run down was a Chinese waiter who walked around with a secret smile on his face. Suddenly both cafeteria doors opened wide, and a hushed silence fell over the room. A tall, dark, mustached man dressed in black appeared in the doorway and slowly gazed around the room.

The Chinese waiter's face broke into a grin as he bounded across the room.

"I knew your new MG would make it from San Francisco, you old son of a gunfighter," the waiter said.

"Mao, I haven't seen you since UCLA . . . I got the clippings you sent me about the trouble down here, and also that snapshot of the cheerleaders."

"What are you here for?" asked Jock, rising from the table.

The stranger's craggy features took on a serious look as he rambled into the room and threw a card down on the table. It read, "Have lost my Trendex. Will do anything for money."

"Now what seems to be the trouble?" muttered the stranger as he leafed through a copy of *Bartlett's Quotations*.

Just then a horrible gasp was heard from the doorway, and the broken body of a student stumbled into the room. He looked as if he had wrestled an alligator and lost.

"It's Patrice," screamed a coed as she ran to him and took him in her arms. "What have they done to you? Are you hurt?"

"No," said Patrice, bitterly. "I'm bleeding for credit hours."

"What did you do to deserve this?" asked the stranger.

"I couldn't help it . . . I couldn't control myself . . . I was walking across the oval with my girl and I had to do it."

"Do what?" the students asked.

"I had to . . . I just had to grab her hand!"

"Well, why didn't you just pay your $5.00 fine to avoid punishment?"

"I tried, but they wouldn't accept $4.95."

Upon hearing this, the stranger's face grew dark and angry. Gruffly he said, "Take me to your leader."

A crowd started to follow the stranger on the oval as Jock pointed out the watch towers. When they reached the third one, the stranger was informed that one of the cheerleaders was locked in the tower. He paused and slowly said, "Take me to you ladder, I'll see your leader later."

Suddenly, shrill laughter burst the calm. The students started to shudder as they recognized the eerie cackle of Barry Beria.

"So . . . daddy's little children insist on rioting and storming the towers," he chortled. "And who might this be?" he asked, glancing at the stranger.

"My name's Palomine. I've come here to stand up for the rights of these poor suffering students."

"You sound like an un-American riot inciter," sneered Beria as he gleefully twisted a shiny thumb-screw and stepped on a passing ant.

Before Palomine could answer, a look of sheer horror crossed Beria's face. Scrambling past the crowd, he let out a shriek as he reached down to pick up something. "Who . . . who . . . what miserable peon dared to drop this Kingston Trio album here"—with a pleading voice he whimpered, "You know I can't stand them!" After drawing mustaches on the cover, he carefully ground up the record.

Nobody moved a muscle as Beria stalked in front of the crowd. Realizing the potential homicidal maniac had escaped, Beria snarled, "From now on, we are going to hold two fingernail inspections instead of one." Seeing the downhearted faces of the students, his laughter returned.

Facing Palomine again, he smiled, "I'll give you till high noon tomorrow to clear off this campus. Otherwise, I'll be waiting for you on the oval." After giving the petrified students a final glare, he climbed back into his tank and drove off in a fit of chuckles.

The students waited expectantly for a reply from their hero. Palomine's lips quivered as he faced them and said, "I need a cigarette . . . where can we go?"

Jock led the way to the Men's Room and they all lit up. Nobody felt much like talking as the room gradually filled with smoke. Suddenly, Beria's shrill voice poured into the room. "Throw out your cigarettes and come out with your arms raised!"

Palomine looked out the window and with clenched teeth said, "If you want us, you'll have to flush us out."

It was dark outside, but Beria could be seen picking up the phone in his tank, as a crowd of students started to gather around. Nobody knew who he was calling until they heard the familiar: Hup, Two, Three, Four.

"It's the ROTC division," said Jock. "And that's all she wrote."

Strangely, without even being given "At Ease," the troops wandered into the building, despite the loud protests of Beria. It was evident that the students had decided to take a stand. Palomine, seeing his chance, decided to use his new forces, and laid out plans to take over the administration-controlled territory.

They started pushing back Beria and the school police until they were stopped at the library by the newly assembled National Guard. Trapped in the library, they decided to wait it out by turning on the television. As the station came into focus, President Kennedy appeared on the screen in a news conference. He said, "Fellow Americans, I regret to say that Gamboling Green has surpassed Laos as the world's number one trouble spot according to the latest Gallup Poll." Turning to the large map in back of him, he picked up a pointer and said, "The students have taken over the northern segment of the university and are threatening to advance."

There was wild rejoicing in the library as the students realized they had gained national recognition. As the noise died down, feverish knocking was heard. "Let me in . . . let me in . . . . it's Patrice."

As he came in he stammered, "We've won . . . we've won. Beria has disappeared and they're calling off the troops."

Anarchy reigned supreme all through the night as the students celebrated their hard-won victory. The newly uncensored newspaper came out with the headline, "BERIA FIRED." The article stated, "At last we are free from tyranny and subjugation. Our new President is a man known far and wide, a just and honorable man whom we can put our faith in, a man named Eichmann."

LETTER TO BE READ BY JACK PARR ON HIS
"LETTER FROM CAMP" DEPARTMENT
Circle Pines Center Youth Manual, 1961

Dear Mommy,

The revolution is coming! Gee, I'm so excited now that I've seen a true picture of the world. Remember how Daddy used to make fun of me because I was only thirteen and thought I knew more than he did? Well, what do you expect from a businessman?

Well, I gotta go listen to this guy talk about developed girls in under-developed countries, but before I go I must ask you to put family sentiments aside. It's very important for me to know; which side are you on?

Historically, absolvingly yours,

Raoul

ONLY IN CUBA; OR, LISTEN OHIO STATERS
At last, the first true and uncensored story of
the beginning of the Castro Revolution
Sundial 50 no. 1 (October 1961)

"But dad, I told you a million times already, I don't want to be a lawyer!"

"Look, Infidel, you gotta understand . . . you can't become another bum like your old man. Hey! Quit hitting me in the face with your elbow."

"I'm sorry, dad, but you ought to be getting used to the crowded conditions by now. Y'know I can still hear that guy digging outside. What's he trying to do, anyway?"

"You know these nutty Americans, Infidel. They're not even satisfied with taking the money out of Cuba. Their rugged individualist nature makes them want to take everything else. When that guy gets tired of sending trees back to America, there's no telling what else he'll want. Even his little boy is learning fast; I heard he mailed a couple of pails of dirt to his friends in Chicago. Tell your mother to move a little. Her knee is pushing against the small of my back."

"She told you already she can't move. She's crowded up against the wall because Royal is pointing his toy gun at the American digging out there."

"How can he see through so many people; the guy couldn't be any closer than three miles?"

"Well, you know Royal, he's got a great imagination; remember that great bit he did about dropping an A-bomb on New York?"

"Yeah, that was pretty good, but don't you think he overdoes it when he froths at the mouth every time he sees an American newspaper?"

"It's hard to blame him, though. Remember he used to take his aggression out by climbing trees? They really meant a lot to him. Then those American tourists argued for three hours over which forest they were going to ship back to Long Island, and when they picked this one, it was just too much for him. Besides his claustrophobia keeps acting up all the time, and that's not a good disease to have when ninety percent of the people live on 1/85 of the land."

"Maybe it wasn't such a good idea for the American ambassador to ask for land reform. We backed him because we thought by 'land reform' he meant dividing it up more equally. And here we are; families having to take shifts swimming in the water because we can't all fit on the land."

"Well, I'm going to the city to watch the executions. I hear they're starting on Oriental Province this afternoon. Sometimes it's hard to believe there's so many Communists in this country, especially 12-year-old ones."

"You know how Badbeasto is: he just doesn't seem to trust anybody after he lost the last election when he was counting the ballots himself."

Infidel crawled over the masses of squirming bodies for a few miles until he reached the sugar plantation. Over the gate hung the body of a peasant with a note tied to his leg. "This man was caught growing a tomato: for the last time, this is a one-crop economy." Infidel was horrified at the sight. Crying out "what a waste," he took off the olive-drab army jacket and tried it on. *Perfect fit*, he thought as he entered the city and met his friend José Miro Gardenia. They sat down in a café and began their usual discussion on politics. José said as usual, "You must realize that evolution is better than revolution," brushing a dead child off the table.

"Yes, that may be so academically, but this is an emergency."

"What do you mean, an emergency?"

Before Infidel could answer, a group of militia marched in, carried away their table and picked up José and his chair. They took them out to the street, and a man in a Hawaiian shirt and Bermuda shorts said in a booming voice, "I'll take them, sonny, but I don't want the guy in the chair. Wait'll the boys back in Texas see this furniture match the interior of the peasant hut we got yesterday."

"That's what I meant," said Infidel when José came back, "Well, I guess I better be leaving you; we're going to storm the barracks again."

"Don't you ever get tired of that bit. I mean it must be pretty embarrassing having the guards laughing at you while you and your friends try to climb the wall."

"What can I say. History will ab—"

"Please . . . please . . . not that line again. You've been saying that ever since you got that ticket for jaywalking. What are you, some kind of repetitive nut?"

"Every leader must have a motto."

With that statement, Infidel rose abruptly and left the café. When he arrived at the fortress, his excited friends rushed to greet him. "Infidel, Infidel, they left the door open, now's our chance!"

Infidel took immediate advantage of the situation, and after an impromptu three-hour speech on foreign imperialists, they rushed through the gate.

The captain of the guards saw them coming and yawned peacefully. "Here come those damn students again. I guess we'll have to teach them a lesson by sending them to Badbeasto." Walking outside he nonchalantly raised his hands over his head and said, "I surrender . . . come . . . I'll show you where Badbeasto is."

Most of the men were taken aback by this statement, but Infidel's natural qualities of leadership shone through as he asked, "Gee, do you really mean it?"

"Sure, just climb the turret and make a left past the torture chamber; you can't miss him."

In his most virile posture, Infidel led the way and knocked on the door. A gruff voice from inside yelled, "Who is it?"

"Nobody but us Communist dupes."

"Okay, all you peasants keep outside and intellectuals come in; we try to maintain a policy of keeping our rugs clean."

Infidel screened his men carefully, and said sadly, "All you guys wait out here." When he walked in, he got the shock of his life. There was Badbeasto sitting on the lap of a well-dressed American. For the first time at a loss for words, he said, "Oh, excuse me, I didn't mean to interrupt anything."

The American smiled cruelly and said, "Wait a second; sometimes looks are deceiving. United Fruit gives me state-side union wages plus a bonus every few months for sitting with this dummy. Sure beats vaudeville."

"You mean . . ."

"That's right kid. The Commies don't know how right they are when they say Badbeasto's an American puppet. But anyway, what the hell do you want?"

"Oh, I forgot. This is a revolution. History will . . ."

"Hey, hold it kid. You're supposed to take control of the army or something first, aren't you?"

"You're right. I knew I forgot something."

"Look, kid. Why don't you go home and read Lenin or something; we're pretty busy around here."

"I'm sorry, but I can't stop now."

"What's with you guys, anyway? You had a revolution a few years ago. Where do you think you are? Algeria? What's so important about doing it now?"

"It wouldn't be so bad, but I got this beautiful speech prepared."

"Prepared for what?"

"For my trial. Every revolutionary leader must have a trial."

"I don't know, kid. That means we'd have to find a judge someplace and clean out one of the courtrooms . . . uh, what the hell, we haven't had anything to censor for a long time. Tell me, what are you calling this movement?"

"What do you mean? Do we have to call it something?"

"Look, kid, I don't have any time to waste. What's today's date?"

"Uh, July 26."

"Okay, we'll name it by the date. Let's see now . . . you'll be under J, so be there late tomorrow morning."

Infidel rose and walked to the door, saying, "History . . ."

"Kid, what d'ya say, huh? Save it for the trial."

And thus began the long revolutionary road of Infidel Custard who was to go down in American history with such names as Yogi Bear, King Kong, and Robin the Hood.

The End.

GONE WITH THE WIND, JR.
Sundial 50 no. 3 (January 1962)

"Flight 509 loading on runway seven . . . all aboard." The two bearded youths looked at each other and smiled though their cigars.

"And it was written, let there be birdmen, and it came to pass that we are like here," said Wolfgang, the elder and more prolific of the two. "C'mon Leonardo, leave us make this scene on cue."

Leonardo lifted his huge 235-pound frame to his natural 6'3" height, his eyes darting around the room. "Like now, daddy?" he asked as he picked up a huge stalk of bananas.

"Leonardo, am I reaching you when I tell you I will tune you in on the main action when it jives? Just cool it till you are notified." The passengers boarded the plane without incident except for Leonardo being gently warned by the stewardess not to leave banana peels on the loading stairs.

As the engines began to rev, Wolfgang's musical senses were stirred. Snapping his fingers in time with the pistons, his whole body began to vibrate. Between his cigar and banana, Leonardo began to feel the electricity of the uninhibited beat, and feverishly joined in by tapping his feet. An occasional sputtering of one of the engines provided an ecstatic offbeat, heightening the acute rhythmic sense. Their reverie was interrupted by a cool, well-manicured hand on Wolfgang's shoulder. "Really, gentlemen, it's nothing to be afraid of. As a matter of fact, it's safer than being in your car. Now just fasten your seat belts and relax while I get you an aspirin."

They looked at each other in amazement as she walked away.

"It speaks . . . it must be alive," said Wolfgang, astounded. When she returned with some pills and two glasses of water, he looked into her innocent eyes and muttered with a grin, "no thank you; we brought our needles with us." Since this occasion was not covered in the rule book, she excused herself in a polite but bewildered manner.

The plane taxied down the runway and soared gracefully into the air. "Like now, daddy?"

"Cool."

Meanwhile, in the cockpit, the pilot, Lance Steelgirder was very satisfied with himself. He was approaching the twilight of his career, and he was yet to have a mishap during a flight. His confidence was in direct contrast to his nervous copilot,

Chick Greenyellow. This was his first commercial flight, and he was so unsure of himself that every time they hit an air pocket, he reached for his parachute.

"Take it easy, Chicky. There's one thing you'll have to learn if you want to be a pilot, and that is you don't have to cover your face with your arms every time you see another plane. You'll get used to them. Well, I guess we can put the auto pilot on, and see how friendly that new stewardess is."

All of a sudden, the cockpit door opened, and Wolfgang and Leonardo entered. "What's happening, baby?"

Lance glared at them, trying not to notice the guns pointed at him. "Who are you? What do you want?"

"Like money, success, women; what does anybody want? What's that guy doing under the seat?"

"Oh, that's Chicky. Don't mind him; it's his first flight."

"Crazy. Now let's ooze her into passing gear and drop into Havana like a falling red star."

"So, you're one of them?"

"What can I say, baby? We beards gotta stick together. Well, I guess you better make a hero-type speech to the passengers so that they can have something to talk about while you make with the new flight plan over the radio."

"*You'll be sorry, you dirty rats,*" Lance thought to himself as he left the cockpit. When he faced the passengers he said, "I'll come straight to the point . . . we're going to Cuba." The crowd broke into a buzz of shock and disbelief, but the pilot tactfully said, "There's really nothing to get excited about."

But few heard him as their minds raced just ahead of their tongues on the possibility of what could happen.

A teenage girl in the front seat perked up and squealed, "Oh, this is so thrilling, my first hijack," whereupon she immediately pulled out her diary and began writing feverishly. A plump, middle-aged woman pointed her shaky finger at Wolfgang, and shouted something into her husband's ear, her lips moving almost as fast as the propellers outside.

Wolfgang tapped the enraged pilot on the shoulder and asked, "Man, where is that draft coming from?"

Lance looked over his shoulder and mumbled, "From that broken window in the cockpit." As their minds digested this strange fact, it suddenly dawned on them that planes shouldn't have broken windows, so they both bolted for the cockpit at the same time.

"What happened?" they asked Leonardo who was tossing a banana peel through the opening.

"I just asked the guy why he was like putting on his parachute, and then he knocked a hole in yonder window and left the scene."

"Didn't he say anything?"

"He said goodbye."

Wolfgang tried to comfort the shocked pilot. "Dad, think like in terms of not losing a copilot, but of gaining an air conditioning unit."

Lance mechanically turned on the radio and said, "I am changing my course to Havana under extreme left-wing type pressure."

A bored voice on the other end of the line answered, "Again?"

However, the reaction throughout the rest of the country was not as calm. The Senate was half empty when the news arrived in Washington, but it miraculously filled up as one senator after another gave as patriotic and indignant a speech as was possible. Their attitude was best summed up by Senator Saltwater. "Piracy!" he screamed. "This is exactly the same as piracy on the high seas, and there is only one penalty appropriate for such a heinous crime." The crowd waited breathlessly as he paused for a glass of water. "They must walk the plank!"

After the deafening applause had died down he continued, "Fellow American flag-loving patriots? As you know, I have warned you of this menace 90 miles off our shore many times, and this is just another example of the un-Americanism I have known to exist before. I have here in my hand a secret report just given to me by my special assistants. It identifies the hijackers as five known Communist atheists. They were trained in China by Russians using Cuban textbooks and Yugoslavian planes. When I think that these dastardly villains have threatened the lives of 68 fine, upstanding, decent, loveable Americans and four Algerians, I . . . I . . . get darn mad. Now this is no time for fuzzy thinking and appeasement; if Cuba gets this plane they'll think they can get away with anything, and they'll hijack everything we have in the air. But they won't stop there; they'll end up with everything that moves on land or sea too. Our merchant marine, our children's bicycles . . . when is the last time you people have seen your cars?"

Meanwhile, back on Flight 509, the plane landed in Havana, and a Cuban official met the hijackers as they walked onto the runway.

"Yanquis?"

"Si, Mantle and Maris."

"Ah, I have heard much of you. But why do you stop here? Fidel is getting tired of all these planes."

"Fidel Castro?"

"No, Fidel Schwartz, the busboy. He says he carries all the luggage to the hotel, but nobody gives him a tip. Look, here comes Dr. Castro."

The bearded leader approached and sized up the unexpected visitors. "I'm afraid I'll have to place you under arrest," he said.

Leonardo was so frightened by this statement that he dropped his bananas, but Wolfgang remained calm and said, "Cool, cool, but first, how about an autograph?"

Obviously pleased, Fidel asked his aide for a pencil, but Wolfgang slipped a card into his hand first. The flourishing handwriting read, "Like sincerely yours, Wolfgang Mantle and Leonardo Maris."

Enraged, Fidel screamed, "Seize them!" but the wily hijackers had already drawn their guns, and were backing up toward a Cuban plane saying, "Like the first cat that cools it is going to be creamed."

After entering the plane, the pilot needed little persuasion when he saw the nervous artillery of the beatniks. The return trip was uneventful, and as the plane was taxiing in at the Miami airport, a crowd of people descended on them. They decided to surrender peacefully, and they walked out with their hands raised. To their surprise the crowd was cheering them, and a smiling man with a microphone walked up and extended his hand, saying, "Gentlemen, it is an honor and a privilege to meet two men with the courage to defect from such a regime. How did you do it?"

Wolfgang was stunned for a second, and then a broad grin broke out on his face. "Like uh, how you say . . . really nothing to it."

The smiling man stretched his smile even more, but his next comment was interrupted by a hustling man with dark glasses. "Pardon me, I represent a Miami advertising firm, and we have just claimed this plane in lieu of certain debts." Grabbing the microphone, he faced the crowd and yelled, "For God, country, and your babies, who will make a bid for this fine plane?"

A temporary silence was broken by a powerful voice yelling, "$10,000."

The auctioneer heaved a sigh of relief, saying, "Sold to the man with the Tshombe button."

As the crowd turned their attention to this new diversion, Wolfgang and Leonardo slipped away quietly and boarded a Greyhound. They found a vacant seat with a newspaper, the headline reading, "More Freedom Riders Enter Mississippi." They looked at each other and smiled, and as Leonardo reached for another banana he said, "Like now, daddy?"

SCIENCE FOR IDIOTS
Sundial 50 no. 5 (March 1962)

A study in nonscience. An article which brings the complexities of modern science down to the level of the feeble-minded (the *Sundial* reader).

CHAPTER I
See the ball. The ball is round and it bounces. All round things bounce. A brick does not bounce. It can't because it is not round, it's rectangular.

Pull a brick off one of the school buildings and throw it at someone's head. Even though the brick is rectangular, it will still bounce because the person's head is bound to be round if my theory is sound.

As the campus police chase you up the stairs, climb to the roof and jump off. Having jumped off of several buildings myself, I know from past experiences that you don't bounce like a ball, you crumble like a brick. Since you are not round and since you don't bounce, therefore the earth cannot be round.

CHAPTER II
When John Glenn tries to orbit the earth, we will never see him again since the earth is flat. However, I won't miss him much because through my secret formulas I have concluded that he isn't really an astronaut, he is a wombat. A wombat is an Australian nocturnal marsupial resembling a small bear. It is easy to see that Glenn is a wombat by the way he hugs his children on television.

Most people think the Cold War is the real menace to the world today, but I know different. The wombat is the real menace. The real reason you have never seen a wombat is that they are so fantastically shy they can't stand to be near other animals because they are afraid they won't know what to say. This is why they inhabit places like opera houses in America and churches in Russia. The thing a wombat hates more than anything else is other wombats. This is because they live alone so long they consider themselves a society unto themselves, and unfortunately they are very ethnocentric.

Therefore, they never get near enough to each other to reproduce their species. However, they have managed to survive by their WITS (wombat intestinal tract system) which winds through their entire body. Having grown up without parental guidance, they developed nasty habits like sucking their paws. They became so addicted to this habit that the paw grew into a regular appendage of the mouth, thus creating an endless intestinal tract, a vicious but delicious circle.

The wombat has the extraordinary ability to change his form because of its years of practice in hiding from other animals. Noted wombats who have been mistaken for humans are Frank Buck and Walt Disney.

No wombat can ever be sure he won't be discovered and through the centuries he has searched the daily papers for a perfect way out, continuously being frightened by reports that the world is getting smaller.

Finally, with the advent of the missile age, the wombats realized at last they could be truly alone. You see the wombat is the only animal, besides myself, who realizes the world is flat. That is why they disguise themselves as astronauts so they can drift happily in space, sucking their paws without fear of interruption.

Since wombats are the only animals who don't lower their standards by the crushing weight of mass mediocrity, they are able to surpass normal human beings in the physical and mental tests required for taking the flight.

Now, all science students know that air is composed of several chemicals including nitrogen, oxygen, hydrogen, and a minute mixture of gasses comprising less than one percent. Some fractions of this one percent are not known by anybody; anybody but me, that is. I have secretly observed wombats all my life, and one night I was fortunate enough to grab a little cloud of gas hovering above a sleeping wombat with my magnetic ice cream scoop.

Carefully cupping my hand over it, I braced myself and dashed through my wind tunnel. Holding a Pepsi bottle over it upside down, I feverishly watched the slowly rising vapor struggle past the temporary carbonated water downflow and settle comfortably at the bottom.

I spent the remainder of the day analyzing my wombatgas, and after discovering all its unique properties, I constructed the world's first wombat strainer, and carefully wrapped it around the end of my favorite plastic straw. Sucking strenuously in all corners of the room, I proceeded to dewombatize the area. Suddenly, I was shocked to realize that my mind was weakening and I was flapping in the air with both hands.

As the room was being dewombatized, I was slipping to the mentality of the goony bird. The goony bird has the lowest mentality of the all the animals on earth because it is so frustrated that it can't think. It is frustrated because it is classified as a bird, and so it is always trying to fly even though it has no wings.

Fortunately, the wombatgas escaped from my straw and I was restored to my normal brilliant self. I had discovered the effects of dewombatization, a situation the world would have to reckon with when the last wombat departs into space.

Now the old unscientific arguments against going into space began to appear logical to me. For instance, dad used to say, "If God wanted us in space, we'd have been born with space goggles on." And before she died, my wife would moan, "Why worry about going into space while people are starving to death in this world." She just couldn't understand that my research was more important than her stomach.

However, for every scientific problem there is a solution, if you employ the scientific method. In order to survive, mankind must

A.   Be on the lookout for anyone over three who still sucks his thumb

B.   Make every astronaut swear that he is not now nor ever has been a wombat

C.   Award me the Nobel Prize

D.   Acknowledge the world is flat and begin a massive campaign of de-Columbusization

Unless these and other steps are taken immediately, mankind will deteriorate into a flock of flapping goony birds. This would leave intriguing scientific possibilities, but I had better cease before this magazine does. So, until the next issue, happy zorchathrons.

Source Material—
ROTC textbooks and *Big Deal, Who Needs the Wheel, I've Got Rockets* by Wernher von Braun.

JOURNALISM

11 AFROTC INSTRUCTORS MAINTAIN FLIGHT STATUS
Ohio State Lantern, 29 May 1961

"I feel safer flying an airplane near the speed of sound than driving a car 60 miles per hour on a highway with cars passing less than six feet away," said Captain Owen Davies, USAF, relaxing in his office after classes.

He was one of three AFROTC instructors interviewed by the *Lantern* concerning requirements for remaining on flight status.

Eleven of the 22 officers in the Air Force detachment at Ohio State are on flying status, and must log at least 100 hours of flying time a year.

Use Jet Trainers

They use T-33 jet trainers and C-47 transports which are based at Lockbourne Air Force Base. Of these 100 required flying hours, at least 15 must be at night, and 20 must be on instruments in bad weather.

The primary purpose of this program is to maintain the flying proficiency of those officers who are on flying status. "It's the same idea as a mathematician," said Captain Bernard Lorenz. "If he didn't work out problems for two or three years, he would get rusty and it would be hard for him to go back to his work."

The flights usually average about two hours at an altitude of 20,000 to 30,000 feet. These pilots go all over the country, but never leave the continental United States unless they get special permission, the captain said.

Pass Rigid Tests

Also, every year before his birthday, an officer must pass an instrument test and a rigid physical examination. If an officer's eyesight starts to go bad, he will immediately be grounded.

Every officer who remains on flight status receives at least $100 extra pay per month, and this increases with rank and length of service.

"We don't spend all our time in the air as pilots," said Captain William Hansen. "Sometimes we do navigation or radio work, or once in a while we just go up as co-pilots."

None Have Crashed

"There's never been a crash in our group that I've seen or heard about," said Captain Davies. "However, one of our T33's was destroyed under another pilot a while ago."

Captain Davies, who also checks out other officers in flight, said that he ran into trouble recently while landing at Maxwell Air Force Base, the home of AFROTC in Alabama.

"The plane started to shudder for no apparent reason, and the temperature of the engine began to climb.

"After circling the field a couple of times, I brought her in safely, and found out that one of the turbine blades had broken off and the engine was virtually falling apart in the air."

Chances Very Slight

"However, chances are something like this would only happen once every two or three thousand flying hours," he added with a grin.

A chart of every officer's flying time is kept on the third floor of the Military Science Building. A flyer's hours are marked in black if he is caught up on his time, and in red if he is falling behind.

The chart room also contains up to date flying literature and the ever-changing maps and charts which the flyers must continually read. There is even a monthly booklet that gives changed landing instructions for every airstrip in the country.

Keep Close Watch

Close watch is kept on all planes in the air, and a pilot is notified any time he comes within 20 miles of another plane. "When I'm up in the air I've got a pretty good idea that anybody else up there is sober and knows what he's doing," said Captain Davies.

Whenever a long trip is required, the pilots usually fly at high altitudes which sometimes burns as little as 1/4 as much fuel as at lower altitudes. "The Air Force also uses these training missions to carry information and cargo from one place to another," he said.

SEE AIRPLANE LAND ON OVAL; ONE OF 20,000 PHOTOS HERE
Ohio State Lantern, 25 September 1961

Need a photo of a plane landing on the Oval or of some Ohio State buildings draped in black crepe mourning the death of a U.S. President?

You can find these among the more than 20,000 historical photographs in the Department of Photography's collection in the basement of Brown Hall.

To get into the collection, a photograph must be at least 15 years old and related to the University.

Kept in Vault

The photos are kept in a fire-proof vault at constant temperature and humidity. A card file is kept on about half the pictures.

The file for this pictorial history of Ohio State can be found in the office of Miss Martha Ruth Jones, photo historian, or more correctly, librarian. Director of the photo history division of the department is Assistant Professor of Photography, Harry Binau.

Those who look at the photographs are interested in historical research for the most part. The pictures are also used for class reunions and whenever they are taken from the vault, they are put in celluloid sleeves for protection.

Started In 1931

The Photo-History Division was started in 1931 by Prof. Joseph M. Bradford, the first instructor of photography at Ohio State.

There are many sources for acquiring photographs, but the two main ones are from professors and alumni.

Miss Jones' job is a continual process of checking for deteriorating photographs and negatives. If one starts to become bad, it can ruin others near it.

Identification Is a Problem

She also has the problem of identifying thousands of unknown people and objects in the photographs. The vault has many old *Makio*s and University bulletins to aid her in this tremendous task.

The oldest known photograph in the collection was taken in May 1884, when High St. was a toll road, and many of the sidewalks on campus were grass.

HERE COMES THE SMUT, MARTHA
An interview with the slightly fabulous Limeliters
Sundial 50 no.1 (October 1961)

"You killed 130 men, old buddy, and now you want to settle down," comes from a satirical song that gives more insight into the absurdities of modern television than a handful of FCC reports. The song is "Gunslinger" and it comes from the balanced repertoire of the Limeliters, the most successful folk singing group since the Kingston Trio.

Lou Gottlieb, 37, does most of the composing and arranging for the group, and is a distinguished musicologist in his own right, having received a PhD at UCLA. He acquired his interest in folk music from a ballad scholar named Sigurd Hustvedt and decided to attempt a career upon the successful advent of the Weavers. He joined the Gateway Singers who met with moderate success; they were known in folk circles as the Re-Weavers because of their resemblance to the most respected group in the business.

Meanwhile, back at the Limelite, a café in Aspen, Colorado, owned jointly by two other minstrels, Glenn Yarbrough and Alex Hassilev, Lou heard them sing together and persuaded them to form a trio, and since that fateful day in May 1959, they have met with one success after another. Lou describes his singing as "something to do until I grow up," and when he "grows up," he plans to return to his study of music.

Alex, the youngest of the group at 28, was born in Paris, the son of a Russian engineer. His first interest in show business was in professional acting, where he worked in off-Broadway shows and finally appeared in one of the phenomena of American culture, a horror movie. He supported himself in Hollywood by singing folk, and made the acquaintance of Glenn Yarbrough who was making Elektra albums with limited success.

Lou plays the bass fiddle and introduces most of the songs with an occasional threatening wave of his bow at the audience. Typical of his remarks is, "RCA has asked us to knock some of the polish off our performance. Tonight, I believe we have succeeded beyond their wildest expectations." He said that his humor is not designed for the big laugh, but rather to evoke emotion from the audience for the tense experience of the songs. "We have seen groups crack irrelevant one-line jokes between numbers, but it's not germane without a basic comic view throughout their program," he remarked.

Lou doesn't understand people who say new groups are not truly original. He feels that every group tries to sing the best way they know, and even Pete Seeger is a trained musician who doesn't consider himself authentic.

Alex sings baritone and doubles on the guitar and banjo. He speaks a dozen languages and ensures the proper pronunciation in foreign songs. "Even though its heresy, I kinda dig Rock 'n' Roll, not specifically the form, but the performers like Presley, whom I consider a great talent," he said. "It has certain folk antecedents in rhythm and blues and country music, and introduced a real emotional quality which was badly needed in the pop music field."

Alex sees the current rise in popularity of folk music as part of the revolution in the recording industry since World War II with the introduction of the LP. "It also came with the desire of people for songs with more to say than 'I'll See You in My Dreams.'

"Every act has an inadequate repertoire in their own opinion; when you get more popular you have less time for creative work. Overexposure outruns our ability to create, and that is the bane of any successful group," he explained.

Glenn, 31, carries most of the solos with a hauntingly beautiful tenor voice. Oddly enough, he doesn't enjoy singing that high, but does it to improve the sound of the group. All three have mature voices, but Glenn's lilting tones produce their distinctive sound. His singularly poignant version of "Lass from the Low Country" completely captivates audiences wherever they go.

So, in case of massive trauma, follow Lou's advice and "Race home, jump into bed, assume the pre-natal position, and turn the electric blanket up to nine," but don't forget to add the extra ingredient of a Limeliters album.

THE NEW KINGSTON TRIO
Sundial 50 no.2 (November 1961)

The three young men in ivy-league shirts picked up their instruments and ran back to the center of the stage for their sixth encore of the show. Had you seen them walking down the street, they would have impressed you as typical college students, but the thunderous applause that greeted them when they faced the audience indicated immediately that they were the Kingston Trio, the most popular folk group this country has ever seen.

From their natural and unassuming manner, it would be hard to know that their first five albums have already sold over a million copies apiece, and their first single record, "Tom Dooley," has sold over five million, including overseas sales. Their success in personal appearances has been phenomenal, and they have recently completed a tour of New Zealand, Hawaii, and Japan.

The man behind the Kingston Trio is their bearded manager, Frank Werber, who first heard them sing at the Cracked Pot in California. Since then he has skillfully guided them from obscurity to the top of the music industry. They chose the name Kingston Trio because of the immense popularity of calypso in 1957, the year of their formation.

When the Trio goes on tour, their road manager, Don MacArthur, goes along and remains backstage during the show, giving lighting and other technical directions. During their recent engagement at Vet's Memorial, Don discussed the Trio's amazing success. "What they do looks very simple, and consequently any college kid can grab an album and a guitar and copy them to a certain degree. Besides, they put on a damn good entertaining show; so many groups, especially in rock 'n' roll, get a hit, and then disappoint people on their tours since they know so few songs and have so little showmanship in person."

The three members of the group are Nick Reynolds, 28, Bob Shane, 27, and John Stewart, 22. They try to form themselves into personality types that the audience can easily identify; Nick is the short, cute comedian, Bob's rugged good looks provide the sex symbol, and John has a withdrawn, shy quality.

Energy is a key word in describing Nick Reynolds. The animation and spirit he puts in a song, and his obvious enjoyment on stage, stimulates his audience and adds a contagious vigor to the group. He sings tenor and plays several instruments including various drums. He has a degree in Business Administration, and his interests range from sports cars and skeet shooting to photography.

Bob Shane was born and raised in Hawaii where his father was a distributor of toys and sporting goods. He met Nick at business school, and after a brief fling at retailing in Hawaii, he came to California to join his former schoolmate in show business. He has a whiskey baritone voice, and Nick describes him as the most natural talent of the three.

John Stewart is a former rock 'n' roll singer who spent his childhood traveling around the race track circuit since his father was a horse trainer. He is an excellent composer of folk music, having written such well-known songs as "Molly Dee" and "Johnny Reb." John was originally with a mildly successful group, the Cumberland Three, who have now disbanded. He has been in contact with the Trio since 1958, and because he wrote and arranged several songs for them, he was a natural to take Dave Guard's place when he quit recently.

According to Nick, the trouble with Dave was that he wanted everything exactly his way. "He was a self-appointed leader who wouldn't listen to our side of the argument, and it finally got to be too much. We're really happy to have John with us now, because we only argue about normal things. At least we don't have to listen to 'it's my way or I'll quit' anymore."

He added that being in a group is like being married with none of the advantages and all of the disadvantages. "Actually, most groups will be all right if they make it through the first year."

"We always try for that extra surge on stage, and we give it everything we have," said Bob. "It's a great feeling to know you've done a good job at something you've worked hard for."

John is delighted to be working with the Trio now. Comparing them with the Cumberland Three he said, "It's like going from managing a general store to managing Sears; there is five times more pressure. It's very hard to fill someone's shoes, especially a friend like Dave. You don't know whether the audience expects you to be the same or completely opposite. I couldn't keep my self-respect if I walked in and became just a copy of Dave Guard."

They feel that part of the present success of folk music is due to the fact that colleges were trying for material that was easy to sing. "Folk music tells a story, has a meaning, and can be sung by almost anybody; it may be hard to accept, but we believe that in a hundred years or so, many rock 'n' roll songs of today will become folk songs."

Their favorite folk group is the Weavers, and discussing their differences, they said, "We don't want to get mixed up in politics, because once you're in the business, there's no sense in cutting your own throat. Besides, we're out to have fun by entertaining people, and we don't think audiences pay money to listen to lectures."

When you see the Trio in person, it's hard to tell who enjoys themselves more, the entertainers or the audience. Their show is a combination of ad libs, comedy stunts like doing the twist and jabbing at each other with guitars and banjos, and great music. They have that rare ability to dissolve the longest distance in show business, the distance between the stage and the seats.

The Kingston Trio on tour is joined by a young comedian named Ronnie Schell who describes his routine as "subtle slapstick and satirical clowning." He has the difficult task of warming up the audience with humor, and judging from his reception in Columbus, he has a very bright future ahead, even though he describes himself as "America's slowest rising young comedian." One of his best lines is "I've never met a man I didn't like . . . with the possible exception of Will Rogers."

PLAY REFLECTS THURBER WIT
Ohio State Lantern, 15 January 1962

The spirit of James Thurber returned to Ohio State Friday night in the form of "A Thurber Carnival" at Mershon Auditorium.

The entire production was professional at every level, but unfortunately, the humor lost some of the brilliance of Thurber's original medium, the written word.

However, any change of presentation is bound to lose in translation, and the *Carnival* script was witty enough to provide a nostalgic and penetrating view into the personality of a great talent.

For example, *The Secret Life of Walter Mitty* failed to achieve the intimacy necessary for entering a man's thoughts.

The cast played every line for all it was worth, exploiting every facet of the comical situations. Arthur Treacher surpassed anything he has ever done, as he titillated the audience out of any impression they might have had about his ability to play other roles than his stereotyped butler.

Imogene Coca maintained her usual standard of excellence, while King Donovan's sense of comedy enhanced the show, especially when he portrayed Thurber.

During *The Last Flower,* an interpretation of history, a series of drawings were shown while Miss Coca narrated a clever view of life in perspective, which pointed out the inherent wisdom in his humor.

Thurber's effect stems from his association with common sentiments and everyday experiences with which his audience can identify.

The material teases the audience without preaching; it is sophisticated enough to chide without provoking. Thurber's genius was a product of his deep insight into mankind, and his humor was a product of his deeper love.

MOOTS TELLS REPORTER OF YEAR IN OFFICE
Ohio State Lantern, 23 January 1962

The major weaknesses of Student Senate this year have been its inability to establish reciprocal communication with the student body, and its failure to involve a large number of students in campus government, according to Senate President Philip Moots, A-4.

The 21-year-old student added that while the role of the administration is to enforce the rules, the Senate's function is to examine them and make suggestions where changes are needed. "Our power of suggestion is largely dependent upon our ability to mobilize student opinion," he said.

Reflecting on his almost completed term of office, he listed the major accomplishments of Senate as (1) the application of pressure which forced the decision on compulsory ROTC, (2) the initiation of "due process" changes in the Student Court system and the creation of the Student Defender, and (3) the institution of the district system of representation which will make Senate more geographically responsive.

During his interview with the *Lantern,* Moots gave his opinion on several controversial topics:

"At the time of the Rose Bowl decision I wanted the team to attend, but since then I have changed my mind because of the disgusting pressures and reactions of the Columbus community who attempted to distort the role of education at Ohio State.

"It is ridiculous to believe a wave of conservatism is sweeping Ohio State; there is a general increase in all student movements brought on by such actions as the sit-ins, and the Conservative flurry is simply a reaction to the challenge of the Liberals.

"Dean Bonner is sincerely interested in working for the students, but we have radically different ideas on what is good for the students and the methods of improving the campus. The office of the Dean of Student Relations is inherently a difficult one since his task is to block policies the administration doesn't want to be carried out.

"I am not convinced that Bob Sherman and the school of anti-Communism fulfill a valid role in the legitimate fight against Communism. The process of mass condemnation on hearsay evidence and the use of wild emotionalism can be destructive to our nation."

Moots explained that Senate receives pressure from many sources, but some-times he feels they are unethical. For example, during the ROTC controversy, an administration official subtly hinted that if a demonstration took place, the pictures taken might be used against Moots if a prospective employer asked for his record.

"Faculty members have to worry about advancement, but students are indepen-dent enough from University authority to take a few risks," he said. "However, the administration is not as bad as some people say; they are not opposed to all change, and sometimes they initiate reforms themselves."

He feels that in the future the Senate should concentrate on a revision of the speaker's rule in regard to "subversives," greater financial autonomy from the admin-istration, and a model course dropping procedure.

Moots was born and raised in Bellefontaine, Ohio, and was first elected to the Senate in 1960. After being appointed Educational Affairs Commissioner, he was elected president as an Inde-greek.

Upon completing his major in social science, he plans to enter law school this fall. In the coming elections, Moots, a member of the Student Congress Party, will support "Those candidates who are devoted to the concept that students should have a vocal and responsible role in determining the policies of Ohio State."

SEGOVIA PLAYS TO ENTHRALLED, PLEASED FANS
Ohio State Lantern, 25 January 1962

The poetry of the world's greatest classical guitarist, Andrés Segovia, enthralled a capacity audience in Mershon Auditorium last night.

The music ranged from a Bach lute transcription to selections by Mario Castelnuovo-Tedesco, who has written a new work for Segovia almost every year since 1932.

The simple dignity of Maestro Segovia complements the high quality of his playing. He has the quiet sensitivity of a truly great virtuoso, the bearing of a singularly talented artist.

In "Allegro" by H. Vieuxtemps he displayed his remarkable technique, a technique distinguished by the artist's awareness of the music in each individual note in spite of the marvelous speed.

With every note of the transcriptions from piano works by Granados and Albéniz, he made it impossible to believe that these pieces could have been written for anything but guitar.

Segovia seems to ignore his surroundings as he caresses each note with a knowledge that only years of practice can bring.

The lilting melodies of great composition are at his command, while the unique sound of the guitar chords provide a splendid background.

Under the skilled hands of Segovia, the guitar loses its identity and becomes a piano, a string ensemble, an entire orchestra. It is a part of him, and through him it is a living part of the audience.

DERBY PRESENTS ABSTRACT PLAYS
Ohio State Lantern, 2 February 1962

Two avant garde plays, *The Chairs* by Eugene Ionesco and *The American Dream* by Edward Albee, opened last night in Derby Theatre for the first of eight performances.

The Chairs at times is so abstract it almost defies description. The plot revolves around an old man and woman who carry on an esoteric conversation about their 100-year existence in limbo.

There are points of recognizable satire as invisible guests arrive to hear the old man's message to mankind. The empty chairs seem to symbolize the empty people who supposedly occupy them.

Man's ignorant respect for status and his inability to communicate are brought out in this play which has as its strongest point a stimulus to thought.

John Fields was superb as he portrayed the mature insanity of the old man. He made excellent use of his body motions and his marvelously expressive face registered every slight change of emotions. Sharon Kent complemented him well as the woman, but at times she appeared too theatrical.

The American Dream symbolically portrays the sterility of America, the absence of her goals, with the shell of outwardly magnificent features covering a vacuum of ideals.

Nancy Penry is appropriately venomous as the neurotic, materialistic wife, and William Bushnell is effective as the meek, effeminate husband.

The latter play is great theatre and is close enough to reality to be a truly educational and fascinating experience.

PIANIST GETS TOP APPLAUSE
Ohio State Lantern, 26 February 1962

The applause at the Roger Williams concert at Mershon Auditorium Friday night was so extensive that it almost hindered the progress of the show.

The pianist captivated his audience from beginning to end as he established a perfect rapport with them through his marvelous playing and his charming stage presence.

He explored the entire range of piano from the classical "Prelude in A-Minor" by Bach-Liszt to a rousing rock 'n' roll number called "I Wanna Ask You a Question, Baby!" à la Jerry Lee Lewis. In conjunction with the latter he said, "Rock 'n' roll is bad grammar set to music."

The best part of the program was a playing commentary on the history of popular piano styles in which he reminisced musically about such greats as Frankie Carr, Carmen Cavallaro, and Eddy Duchin.

He becomes emotionally involved with each number, and his rendition of "Exodus" provided one of the most moving few minutes on the Mershon stage this year.

He was aided and abetted in his triumph over the audience by a fascinating rhythm section known as "The Quiet Men." Consisting of two guitars, a harp, a bass, and various percussion instruments, they added an unusual and highly dramatic complement to an artistic performance.

He delighted the audience with his finale in which he played two pianos simultaneously; using a spinning stool he alternated between classical on a Steinway grand piano and light popular on a spinet.

In a word, his technique is comparable to that of the finest classical artists, and his polish as a performing concert pianist is second to none.

MASTERS OF DECEIT
Sundial 50 no. 4 (February 1962)

The tall Negro stepped up to the plate and with a practiced eye he watched the pitcher take his wind-up. Ordinarily, this scene would not be considered unusual, except in this case it was occurring during a basketball game.

After sliding safely into home plate, the ball was awarded to the opposing team, and as one of the players approached the basket, the former batter screamed in an hysterical high-pitched voice, "Stop it . . . stop it!" Naturally, this threw the shooter off balance, and the unannounced announcer comforted him by yelling, "Nice shot, but you missed!" The loquacious athlete was Meadowlark Lemon, star of the Harlem Globetrotters, and basketball's "court jester" for seven years.

The Globetrotters were formed 35 years ago by owner and coach Abe Saperstein, who has probably done more for basketball than any other living man. They have played in eighty countries, and last summer they served as good will ambassadors at the request of the U.S. State Department when they traveled to Poland, Hungary, and Romania.

They have been defeated 309 times during the last 34 years, but between these defeats they have managed to chalk up 7,125 victories. This record has been compiled against some of the best teams and players in the country, including the annual world series of basketball between the Globetrotters and the College All-stars.

Saperstein's superb showmanship is displayed by the way he presents a basketball game. When the Globetrotters played at the Ohio State Fairgrounds last November against the Washington Generals, they were joined by a ping pong match between world champions, a Japanese trick bicyclist, a baton twirler, a juggling act, and the rousing songs of Cab Calloway.

The Globetrotters' season usually lasts nine or ten months, and they have a two-week training period to break in rookies. Their main supply of talent, like all professional teams, comes from colleges and high schools.

Charles (Tex) Harrison, one of their most outstanding players since he joined them in 1953, discussed their trip behind the Iron Curtain after their game in Columbus. "We brought along out own opposition since the players there aren't of the same caliber as this country. We had a tremendous reception wherever we went, but we were restricted in dealing with the local people, few of whom spoke

English, and all of whom seemed reluctant to talk to foreigners. We were really given the red-carpet treatment in Russia in 1959, but even though we were impressed by Moscow, the showplace of communism, we were more than happy to leave after our tour."

He said it was a difficult task to present good basketball and good comedy at the same time. "It requires complete concentration, because on a split second's notice the team might have to go into a comedy routine en masse. Some of our comedy is traditional, like the baseball caper, while others are added as we go along. Mr. Saperstein originates some of the routines, and all suggestions from the players are given careful consideration."

He added that the team was originally all Negro, and it was built on this basis; this is one tradition they will maintain since it is their trademark. Tex explained that because of this fact, they don't play in southern states where there are extreme segregation laws or heavy opposition to their race.

He complimented Ohio State on having one of the best teams in the country today, and said, "I was surprised when they lost in the finals last year, but it's one of those upsets that eventually happen to every good team."

The captain of the Globetrotters is Clarence Wilson who is enjoying his 13th year with the team as player and assistant coach. Some of the high spots in every game are the dribbling of Murphy Summons, and the fantastic accuracy of Willis Thomas and newcomer Tony Wilcox.

They practice their trickery with such skill that sometimes even the audience is left behind by their dazzling speed. Some of Lemon's favorite tricks include leaving the ball on the floor as he feints a break from his position, and returning in a split second with a wide grin and two points. After making a difficult shot he will ignore the rest of the players to carefully repeat his exact movements with mock bravado. He also makes life hilariously uncomfortable on the court by demanding four shots after he has been fouled, untying the shoelaces of various opponents, and occasionally interrupting the game in order to pass a ball back and forth with one of the spectators.

If 35 years at the top of their profession is any indication, the Harlem Globetrotters will be around as long as basketball is. Abe Saperstein's idea of merging comedy and basketball on a professional level has brought success to hundreds of ballplayers, and laughter to millions of people. They are without a doubt a boon to their sport, an asset to their country, and a credit to their race.

WILLIAMS RISKED HIS HANDS AS PARTNER FOR JOHANSSON
Ohio State Lantern, 7 March 1962

One of Ingemar Johansson's sparring partners during the Patterson fight series was an amateur pugilist named Roger Williams whose hands have made him the best-selling instrumentalist of all time.

Williams, who appeared at Mershon Auditorium last week, acquired his interest in boxing from his father, a fighter who became a minister after witnessing the death of a friend in the ring.

When asked about the danger to his uninsured hands, Williams shrugs, and with his ever-present grin says, "Hands were made to use in many ways, so why limit them?"

He is completely engrossed in his music, spending most of the year in personal appearances and recording sessions while practicing eight to ten hours a day, when he can find the time.

The personable artist was born and raised in Des Moines, Iowa, where he began playing at the age of three under his mother's guidance.

He was able to play 13 instruments upon his graduation from high school, and he decided to move to New York to continue his studies and eventually turn professional.

His early years were a commercial failure and looking back on them he reminisced, "Some of the world's great musicians died in poverty, but what I objected to was living in it."

The turning point in his career was the recording of "Autumn Leaves" which established him as a major piano stylist. "I think my success was largely due to the fact that I treat the piano as though it were my voice, and memorize the words to phrase the melody line as a singer would," he said.

He met his wife, Joy, after a concert when she approached him for an autograph. He was so impressed with the striking brunette that he invited her out for dinner and proposed to her the same evening.

Williams describes himself as an ear pianist. "An eye pianist sees the music as he plays and turns pages in his mind," he said. "I learn songs by listening to melodies and working out my own arrangements; I never use sheet music when learning a song.

"I like all types of music, and the only attitude I don't like to see in a musician is a preference for one kind of music that is so extreme it excludes all others," he remarked.

Williams' most impressive feature offstage is his sincere friendliness and lack of affectation. His ability to project this affable nature and his perfect musicianship will undoubtedly insure him of a long and deservedly successful career.

OUT OF THE ARCHIVES (OHIO STATE UNIVERSITY)

The Constitution submitted to the residents of Steeb hall is an unjust, vague document. The general air of complacency hovering over the students could easily allow it to pass without much discussion or opposition.

This paper covers a few of the main points that are subject to the mo st dissention and debate. For example, Section 2, Article B states that the chairman shall be elected by a majority vote of the senate. This means that the students at large do not have a voice to express their choice for the executive leader of the dormitory. Interest in government on campus is n egligible, and is only brought ou t during elections. If the students aren't even given a chance to elect their chairman, who is essentially the President of the dormitory, interest will wain to an even lower level, and the dormitory government will lose almost all contact with the wishes of the students.

Section 2, Article C states that the qualification for the office of the office of chairman is that he be first elected floor president. This automatically disqualifies 99% of the residents of Steeb Hall from becoming Chairman. Also the Vice-Chairman, the Treasurer, and the Secretary must first be elected floor president; all this makes conditions very suitable for a clique-rule in Steeb hall because it combines the legislative and executive branches into one group.

The constitution also neglects to define the judicial section of the government. However, this is supposed to be posted before the election.

There is also much controversy on such things as how many counselors should be allowed to vote, and the point-hour qualifications for the dormitory chairman.

The proponents of the constitution say that errors can be revised later, but I think they should have offered the students a chance to revise it before the election, which would take the student's views more into accoun t. Next Monday the students will be voting for more than a constitution; they will also be voting on whether they are really represented or not. Any student who really considers the constitution and its implications will have no recourse but to veto it on Monday.

These are some of the ideas that came up during a discussion of the constitution on the third floor.

Philip Ochs

THE OHIO STATE LANTERN

Just before quitting
Journalism School
winter "62"

NEW YORK CITY

TOPICAL SONGS AND MUSIC CRITICISM

THE NEED FOR TOPICAL MUSIC
Broadside 22 (March 1963)

Before the days of television and mass media, the folksinger was often a traveling newspaper spreading tales through music.

It is somewhat ironic that in this age of forced conformity and fear of controversy the folksinger may be assuming the same role. The newspapers have unfortunately told the truth, the whole truth, and nothing but the cold war truth so help them, advertisers. If a reporter breaks the "code of the West" that used to be confined to Hoot Gibson movies, he'll find himself out on the street with a story to tell and all the rivers of mass communication damned up.

The folksingers of today must face up to a great challenge in their music. Folk music is an idiom that deals with realities and not just realities of the past as some would assert. More than ever there is an urgent need for Americans to look deeply into themselves and their actions and musical poetry is perhaps the most effective mirror available.

I have run into some singers who say, "Sure, I agree with most topical songs, but they're just too strong to do in public. Besides, I don't want to label myself or alienate some of my audience into thinking I'm unpatriotic."

Yet this same person will get on the stage and dedicate a song to Woody Guthrie or Pete Seeger as if in tribute to an ideal they are afraid to reach for. Those who would compromise or avoid the truth inherent in folk music are misleading themselves and their audiences. In a world so full of lies and corruption, can we allow our own national music to go the way of Madison Avenue?

There are definite grounds for criticism of topical music, however. Much of the music has been too bitter and too negative for many audiences to appreciate, but lately there has been a strong improvement in both quantity and quality, and the commercial success of songs like "If I Had a Hammer" have made many of the profit seekers forget their prejudices.

One good song with a message can bring a point more deeply to more people than a thousand rallies. A case in point is Pete Seeger's classic "Where Have All the Flowers Gone" which brought a message of peace to millions, including many of the younger generation who do not consider themselves involved in politics.

Folk music often arises out of vital movements and struggles. When the union movement was a growing, stirring, and honest force in America, it produced a wealth of material to add to the nation's musical heritage. Today, there regrettably seem to be only two causes that will arouse an appreciable amount of people from their apathetic acceptance of the world; the Negro struggle for civil rights and the peace movement. To hear a thousand people singing "We Shall Overcome" without the benefit of Hollywood's bouncing ball is to hear a power and beauty in music that has no limits in its effect.

It never ceases to amaze me how the American people allow the hit parade to hit them over the head with a parade of song after meaningless song about love. If the powers that be absolutely insist that love should control the market, at least they should be more realistic and give divorce songs an equal chance.

Topical music is often a method of keeping alive a name or event that is worth remembering. For example, many people have been vividly reminded of the depression days through Woody Guthrie's dust bowl ballads. Sometimes the songs will differ in interpretation from the textbooks as with "Pretty Boy Floyd."

Every newspaper headline is a potential song, and it is the role of an effective songwriter to pick out the material that has the interest, significance, and sometimes humor adaptable to music.

A good writer must be able to picture the structure of a song and as hundreds of minute ideas race through his head, he must reject the superfluous and trite phrases for the cogent powerful terms. Then after the first draft is completed, the writer must be his severest critic, constantly searching for a better way to express every line in his song.

I think there is a coming revolution (pardon my French) in folk music as it becomes more and more popular in the U.S., and as the search for new songs becomes more intense. The news today is the natural resource that folk music must exploit in order to have the most vigorous folk process possible.

THE GUTHRIE LEGACY
Mainstream 16 no. 7 (August 1963)

The legacy of Woody Guthrie encompasses much more than the thousand songs he put together and the years he spent singing around the country. His legacy is the same as all the great poets of history; that of truth or the search for truth.

The seed he planted in his contributions to folk music is now blossoming forth into a wave of writing that has reached amazing proportions at the beginning. There is no way of foretelling how widespread it will get but it has all the indications of a major revolution in the folk music of today.

Guthrie's work now stands as a model of technique for the new writers that have taken over his task. He showed that a folk writer does not necessarily have to create an entirely original work to add to the folk process. Rather it can be desirable to adapt themes from the vast reservoir of folklore keeping a continuity between generations.

The power of simplicity was demonstrated time and time again in "So Long," "This Land is Your Land," and "Clean-O;" his sympathy for human suffering was displayed in "Deportees" and "Tom Joad;" and his narrative skill in "Pretty Boy Floyd" and "Ludlow Massacre." He also had the uncanny ability to portray the viewpoint of the working class, as in "Talking Miner."

One of the sad aspects of the growing fame of Guthrie and his songs is the lack of understanding by some and the prostitution by others. I have run across some people who seem to consider him solely as a writer of great camp songs. They cannot fathom or don't want to fathom the political significance of a great part of his work.

Even worse are some fine musicians, who should know better, talking about "Hard Travelling" or "Pastures of Plenty" strictly as good commercial songs. How many intelligent men have leafed through Guthrie's work struggling to find some way to adapt the work of an artist for the consumption of a 13-year-old mind that seems to control the market. It is a tribute to the greatness of "Pastures of Plenty" that it has been able to survive so many abominable arrangements.

The legend of Guthrie continues to grow in the new generation of writers and singers. The best interpretation of his material is done by Jack Elliott, one of the finest folk musicians in the country. He has developed a stage personality that can move from light hilarity to tragic depth with surprising ease. He presents himself almost as a reincarnation of Guthrie, complete with cowboy hat, drawling tones, and western mannerisms. His growing stage maturity and his sense of theater has made him less of an imitator and more of an interpreter.

Of the new crop of writers, the most powerful and most poetic is Bob Dylan who came to New York to meet Guthrie and is one of his greatest admirers. As a philosopher in dungarees, a preacher with a guitar, a politician with the truth, he has hit the folk scene like a tornado. Originally, he was noted as a fine country and blues singer adapting the styles of the best blues men, but it wasn't long before his writing came to the spotlight and now he performs almost entirely his own material.

His ability with words approaches genius; his lyric poetry is a pleasure to hear in this age of the stilted verse, but even more striking is the way he can condense complex thoughts in a few words without sacrificing clarity. With a voice as tough as leather and soft as fog he punches out verse after stunning verse on a myriad of subjects.

Dylan's ability with deep tragedy is shown in "Hollis Brown," the story of the frustration of poverty causing a man to destroy himself and his family.

The description of his poverty—

> You looked for work and money and you walked a ragged mile
> Your children are so hungry they don't know how to smile.

Guthrie's influence is apparent in Tom Paxton who also hails from Oklahoma. The most striking feature in his work is the beautiful simplicity he is able to achieve, musically and lyrically. Of all the new writers I have seen perform, Paxton has been the most effective in getting audiences to learn his tunes and join along. The idiocy of war is examined in "The Willing Conscript," a study of a naïve draftee.

> To do my job obediently is my only desire
> To learn my weapon thoroughly and how to aim and fire.

Dramatic presentation is the forte of Peter La Farge, who has helped fill the void in the woefully ignored area of Indian protest songs. With brutal irony and bitter sadness, he sings of the exploitation of the Indian while expressing the nobility of that forgotten American. One of the finest choruses ever written in a protest song comes from his "Ballad of Ira Hayes."

> Call him drunken Ira Hayes, he won't answer anymore
> Not the whisky drinking Indian, or the marine who went to war.

I think the most charming writer-performer around today is Mark Spoelstra, who is also one of the most original guitarists to be found. With a twelve-string guitar and a mustache that won't stop, he beguiles audiences using a beautifully underplayed style. Subtle humor abounds in his "Shelter Sign"—

> I've got more Band-Aids, more ice-cubes and more iodine
> Just in case it hurts some friends of mine.

The absurdities of modern life are dissected marvelously by Malvina Reynolds whose volume of songs seems to increase by the hour. One of her most moving songs is "What Have They Done to the Rain," popularized by Joan Baez. The power of her pen appears in "Non-Ads."

> Put a tattoo on your hand and whiskers on your chin
> It fills your lungs with cancer and that's how old men die.

One of the best educated of the new writers is Len Chandler who holds a master's degree in music. Many of his songs have philosophical overtones and several tunes show an intricate knowledge of musical composition. One of his topical songs is "Turn Around Miss Liberty."

> Every eye in the whole wide world is lookin' toward the U.S.A.
> Miss Liberty stands with her torch held high, but she's lookin' the other way.

Most of my songs have been satires of ballads. From "Talking Cuban Crisis"—

> He said here comes the President but first this word from Pepsodent
> Have whiter teeth cleaner breath when you're facin' nuclear death.

From the "Ballad of Medgar Evers"—

> Too many martyrs and too many dead
> Too many lies too many empty words were said
> Too many times for too many angry men
> Oh let it never be again.

If there's one man who deserves the credit for inspiring the outburst of writing it would be Pete Seeger. Throughout the fifties he kept the ball rolling with his recordings, his writing, but most of all, his enthusiasm. Thousands of young people, including myself, were introduced to topical music through his singing, and his encouragement and advice have helped many a beginner. Everyone identified with the topical song movement has learned and will continue to learn from his humility and his humanity.

Topical music is growing as more and more people realize that if they can talk they can sing, and if they can memorize a song they can almost as easily write one. The best way you can help the song revival is by writing one yourself. We are all potential song-writers; the last letter you wrote probably contained some great song material that only needs a few rhymes and an old melody you can dig up someplace.

As the revival is spreading many are asking where is it all going? Guthrie's close association with the unions exemplified the traditional connection between folk music and social movements. With the explosion of the peace and integration movements of the sixties, it was inevitable that folk music would follow its natural tendency of commentary and identify itself with the times. In a word, the one compelling reason that has caused so many people to write so many songs is this; they are all writing for the day when there will hopefully never be a need to write another protest song.

REQUIEM FOR A HOOTENANNY
Broadside of Boston (4 March 1964)

Hey you blacklist you blacklist I've seen what you have done
I've seen the men you've ruined and the lives you've tried to run
but the one thing that I've found is the only ones you spare
are those that do not have a brain or those that do not care

and you men who point your fingers and spread your lies around
you men who left your souls behind to drag us on the ground
you can put my name right down there I will not try to hide
for if there's one man on the blacklist I'll be right there by his side

for I'd rather go hungry and beg upon the street
than earn my bread on dead men's souls and crawl beneath your feet
and I will not play your hater's game and hate you in return
for it's only through the love of man the blacklist can be burned

From a song on John Henry Faulk

If you swallowed something poisonous and had to throw up immediately you might use your thumb, eggs and mustard, or perhaps tune in the ABC-TV *Hootenanny* Show. This documentary series on the degeneration and corruption of American folk music has no equal in the annals of cultural castration.

However, like the McCarthy hearings, I invariably end up watching it whenever I have the masochistic opportunity. When the show started, it wasn't half as bad as it is now, mainly because it was only half as long. Throughout the series, they have had a steady group of good commercial singers like Bob Gibson, Ian and Sylvia, and Judy Collins, who have all been an important factor in helping Jack Linkletter to keep a straight face on the air. Smilin' Jack, folk sideburns and all, comes ambling up to the camera and usually says something like, "Hi, there. Welcome to the scenic Birmingham Military Academy, deep in the beautiful Caucasian Valley. We have a special treat for you tonight. The local citizens' council is sponsoring a new group, the Marauders, singing a song they wrote themselves, 'Freedom Later.'"

After about one minute of singing, they cut to Jack again, who says, "Hi, there. Just a reminder that our sponsors tonight are *Hootenanny* Enterprises, dealers in

Hootenanny shoes, socks, pants, shirts, perfumes, and your friendly Loyalty Oath Insurance Company," ad nauseam.

This travesty is supposedly watched by several million families each week. Fortunately, many of the country's finest folk musicians have refused to appear on the show, ranging from relative unknowns to folk music's major selling artists— Joan Baez, Bob Dylan, Kingston Trio, PP + M, Jack Elliott, Tom Paxton, Jackie Washington, Barbara Dane, John Herald, and Jim Kweskin.

A fairly recent development has been that several performers who appeared on the show at first now refuse to go on any longer. This list includes Judy Collins and Leon Bibb. Aside from the poor quality of the show, the inane censorship and re-shaping of material to fit their Bugs Bunny concept are among the main reasons for these late drop-outs.

A little while ago *Hootenanny* reached a new low even at their level. They had a show with only one known folk group, the New Christy Minstrels. The rest of the program was Nina Simone, the Four Preps, and a couple of comedy acts. Usually a big-name group is allowed to do four numbers in the hour-long show. This time the Christies did close to ten songs. From all appearances, it seemed that for the first time a network television show actually was hard up for acts.

Many of the arguments about the show seem to me to be irrelevant. For example, some people carry the notion that any kind of show on folk music is better than none. This is simply avoiding the basic issue of the blacklist. We're not just talking about Pete Seeger who is among the lucky few who can command a huge audience without the aid of a 21-inch tube. We're talking about countless numbers of unknown writers and actors and others working in the arts who are virtually destroyed by the poison pen.

Every time a singer agrees to go on that show, he's driving the blacklist dagger deeper and deeper into the backs of the very people who would be most likely to improve the show's quality and the quality of television in general. Is the phony applause worth the lives and careers of so many people?

It's really unbelievable. These people go on the show playing a banjo that was popularized by Pete, using arrangements originating with Pete, even doing songs actually written by Pete. They sing about freedom, they sing about John Birch, they sing about Pastures of Plenty (leaving out the verse that ends, "we'll work in this fight and we'll fight till we win"). They think they're working within the system while the system ends up working within them. I wonder if Robert Welch and H. L. Hunt feel the enemy coming closer when they watch *Hootenanny*.

It is somewhat surprising that neither of the other two networks has tried to compete with *Hootenanny* without a blacklist. Supposedly the networks want the highest ratings and the best reviews. I think a show starring Pete Seeger, Joan Baez, Bob Dylan, and the Kingston Trio might make a small dent in the ranks of the New Christy Minstrel following.

Ironically, the formation of this show on folk music may turn out to be one of the most powerful blows ever struck against the blacklist by giving it so much unwanted publicity and making so many people aware of a well-disguised problem. It has also forced many singers to analyze their principles and their roles as folk performers. If the show is renewed for another thirteen weeks, there is a good chance that the original dissenters and those who were later disillusioned will combine in signed statements and other levels of action against the blacklist.

One of the worst aspects of blacklisting is the runaround you get from various producers and executives. First, you hear the story that they don't want Pete or the Weavers because they want to fill their show with quality acts like the Smothers Brothers. Last week one of their quality folk acts was the Geezinslaw Brothers. The next logical step would appear to be Jack walking out and saying, "Hi, there. And now we take great pride in presenting a *Hootenanny* discovery, Jack Ruby and the Avengers, singing, 'Don't Think Twice, It's All Right.'"

Now they come to the old weapon of political controversy, the loyalty oath. "Sure, we all love Pete, but you understand, ha ha, it's not up to us. We're only the producers." I guess the only answer is a *Hootenanny* coloring book with the first page reading, "I am a list, color me black."

I think *Hootenanny* and all the other shows of our vast wasteland have been best summed up by one man, Bob Gibson. At the end of one of the shows he was on, they were scheduled to sing "Kumbaya" as the closing sing-along. All of a sudden, an executive runs up and says, "Hey, we're running out of time; you'll have to do Kumbaya twice as fast."

"You can't do that, it's a lullaby," said Gibson. "Let's do another song."

"Sorry, Bob, it's listed in the program. Ha ha. You understand."

Comes the end of the show and the first singer sings, "Someone's prayin', Lord."

The second sings, "Someone's sleepin', Lord."

Gibson walks up to the microphone, smiling ever so slightly, "Someone's kidding, Lord."

THE ART OF BOB DYLAN'S "HATTIE CARROLL"
Broadside 48 (20 July 1964)

After Judy Collins' N.Y. Town Hall concert in which she performed Bob Dylan's "Hattie Carroll" (*Broadside* 43), I overheard a well-known commercial folk singer criticizing it as "another one of those black and white songs." Another act I know said the song was no good because it was too preachy.

It's a sad comment on the folk community when normally intelligent people can totally misunderstand such an important work. I believe this song could add a new dimension to topical songs that has been missing too often in the past. I'd like to use the song as an example to some of the writers who contribute to *Broadside*.

There are many pitfalls that Dylan might have fallen into while treating such a delicate and difficult subject. It would have been easy to describe the event and ask, "Wasn't that a terrible shame, don't her die in vain," and put the usual sarcastic "land of the free" line at the end. I think this all too simple artless approach is what the *Little Sandy Review* critics are rightfully opposed to.

In line after poetic line Dylan brings out all the pathos and irony of a tragic crime. He never gets trapped trying to fit a thought into a prescribed rhyme form. What more effective beginning could he have chosen than to use the sound of the name William Zantzinger and the description of the weapon, "with a cane that he twirled round his diamond ring finger," to carry over to the man?

He gives the setting in the first verse and asks those who would shed a tear over the murder to wait and listen to more. In the second verse he describes Zantzinger's connections with "high office relations in the politics of Maryland who reacted to his deed with a shrug of the shoulder." Once again, he deftly understates the evil, never making the mistake of calling him a brute or coward and ruining the narration.

Dylan describes Hattie Carroll as a "maid of the kitchen," not a downtrodden maid or a poor Negro woman. He brings out the pathos of her life perfectly with, "she never sat once at the head of the table."

The description of the murder has to be one of the classics of American folk music: "the cane sailed through the air and came down through the room, doomed and determined to destroy all the gentle." I listened to Bob's third record with him before it was released, and the song that moved him most was "Hattie Carroll."

The use of poetry is paramount to his effective narration, and one of his most important techniques is that he always avoids the obvious. Probably the main thing wrong with so many of the songs sent to *Broadside* is that they overstate the obvious when it doesn't need to be stated at all.

The understatement, the subtle lyric, the ironic twist, are demonstrated time and again throughout the song. There is no empty cry of shame, or bland pleas for decency. There is no justification for a bad song no matter how important the cause, and I sincerely hope some of the *Broadside* songwriters will learn some of the lessons taught so well in "The Lonesome Death of Hattie Carroll."

THE YEAR OF THE TOPICAL SONG
Newport Folk Festival Program (23–26 July 1964)

In spite of the Fire and Police Research Association of Los Angeles and the *Little Sandy Review*, the topical-song movement has continued to expand beyond its phenomenal growth of last year.

Even the commercial groups are reflecting that it is time to think about the songs of our times. I wouldn't be surprised to see an album called *Elvis Presley Sings Songs of the Spanish Civil War* or the Beatles with *The Best of the Chinese-Indian Border Dispute Songs*.

Broadside magazine (Box 193, Cathedral Station, N.Y. 25, N.Y.) has provided the main outlet for the new songs. It averages about four new subscriptions a day, and even though it comes out every two weeks, it's only able to print a small portion of the great volume of songs being sent in.

In the year since the last Newport Folk Festival the main development in topical music, aside from its commercial success, has been the involvement on a personal level by many of the songwriters. This has been mainly with the integration and unemployment issues. Some of us have visited various areas of the South and have come in contact with a real movement for the first time. The understanding and emotional involvement you get from real contact can't be achieved by reading about it though newspapers and magazines. It is also a challenge to sing your own songs to the people directly involved, and to see if they understand and appreciate what you've done. This is probably the greatest test of a protest song.

Another group went down to Hazard, KY., and witnessed what may be the roots of an organized unemployment movement that could be carried to other areas of Appalachia and the country. The excitement of being exposed to vital issues on a first-hand basis is sure to have an effect on the quality and importance of the great bulk of writing that is yet to come.

There has also been a marked increase in the number and variety of rallies the songwriters are appearing at. An organization has been formed called the Committee for Performing Artists to coordinate the schedules of artists for rallies and to promote more benefits.

Some of the most important work in protest music is being done by Guy Carawan. He has spent the last couple of years in the South collecting and compiling songs to be used in the Freedom Movement. He was also responsible for the recent

Freedom Song Conference in Atlanta, which brought together singers from all areas of the South and some topical writers from New York.

Many people are skeptical about the effect of topical songs, but I think I have found a definite purpose for the songs aside from what musical value they may have. For example, I wrote a song called "William Worthy" about a reporter who went to Cuba and was arrested because of the State Department travel ban. Through the use of satire many people have laughed at the illogical overtones of a travel ban and have heard of Worthy for the first time through the song. Some of these are people that could easily skip over a small item on Worthy in their local paper and might normally not even question the validity of a travel ban. Now other performers are picking up the song and it appears possible that literally millions of people may become aware of the case, and the lessons to be drawn from the Worthy example will have definite farther-reaching implications.

Another example is Bob Dylan's "God on Our Side," which doesn't publicize a specific case, but is powerful enough to affect people's reasoning on a general level. I personally know of people who have had some of the thoughts of the song in the back of their minds, but the song dramatically opened their eyes to a greater extent and made them more intelligent observers. Of course, the song couldn't switch someone's thoughts completely around, but I think it does prove that a topical song can be a catalyst to the minds of the listeners and can serve a practical function.

I don't know what there is left to say about Bob Dylan. His success is unparalleled and about the only thing that keeps pace with his writing are the rumors about him.

I think he's slowly drifting away from song-writing because he feels limited by the form. More and more of his work will probably come out in poetry and free verse, and I wouldn't be surprised if he stopped singing altogether, considering the over-adulation of his fans and the lack of understanding of audiences that identify with him.

Tom Paxton is probably the best songwriter of the group as far as the craft of writing songs. He really knows how to fit words into simple melodies and make them singable.

Len Chandler has been singing around the country. He has been building a bigger and bigger following. He went to Atlanta with Tom and me and was almost stunned by the power and beauty of the Southern freedom songs. He was so impressed that he decided to stay down South and travel to different areas instead of coming back to New York.

Buffy Sainte-Marie has emerged this year as the finest female writing talent on the scene. One of the most dynamic performers in folk music, she has covered a wide variety of subjects with uncommon intensity.

The major addition to the folk writers this year is 21-year-old Eric Andersen. Tom Paxton heard him in California and wisely persuaded him to come to New York. Within a couple of weeks, Eric had a Vanguard recording contract, a *New York Times* write-up, and jobs in some of New York's best folk clubs. He is at his best with tender love songs, and he could have the most musical voice of all the writers.

Malvina Reynolds became a year younger and a good number of songs richer. "Little Boxes" rose to national prominence through the singing of Pete Seeger and Leon Bibb and she made quite an impression during a recent trip to New York, visiting, making friends, and appearing at more rallies than I could keep track of.

There are many other writers contributing important songs to the folk revival who deserve mention here. They include Billy Edd Wheeler, Dick Weissman, Fred Hellerman, Mike Settle, Jim Friedman, Shel Silverstein, Bob Gibson, and Ernie Marrs. There are also a couple more newcomers that I believe are soon going to surprise a lot of people: Dave Cohen from New York and Patrick Sky from Georgia.

All these songwriters are creating a musical documentary of our times, and more significantly, they are putting into words the feelings of discontent of an aroused generation.

BUFFY SAINTE-MARIE—IT'S MY WAY (VANGUARD RECORDS VRS 9142)
Broadside of Boston (15 April 1964)

When Buffy Sainte-Marie was in Florida last year she had bronchitis, but she still did some of the best singing I've ever heard on a folk stage. Although this debut album doesn't capture all the excitement of Buffy in performance, it is still one of the most striking and original albums to be released in a long time.

Buffy can sing with the beauty and clarity that equals most of the modern female balladeers, but she can also belt out a gutsy blues as well as most of her contemporaries who specialize in that area. Additionally, she has the all-too-rare ability to experiment with folk music tastefully and end up with a totally unique concept of styling and arrangement.

On top of all that, she is also one of the finest songwriters dealing in the folk idiom, and of her songs, I believe "Cod'ine" will clearly emerge as one of the classic musical statements on drugs.

The weaknesses of the album are all of a minor nature, such as the occasional straining of her voice, the sometimes repetitious driving flatpick, or a few trite lines which can be found in some songs.

The only thing that bothers me about Buffy is that sometimes you get the feeling that someone is trying to make a star out of her. For example, there is an insane button being passed around asking "Are You the Universal Soldier?" The profits go to UNICEF, of course, with no thought in mind of promoting Buffy. Oh well! Maybe we can start a trend with other buttons, like "Are You the Master of War?" or "Are You the Boston Strangler," or, "Are You Serious?"

PATHS OF VICTORY, HAMILTON CAMP (ELEKTRA EKL 278)
Broadside of Boston (28 October 1964)

My favorite folk group is the combination of Bob Gibson and Bob Camp which, unfortunately, didn't last long enough to make its deserved mark on the national scene. Camp dropped out of sight for a while and turned up in San Francisco where he established himself as a master actor and comedian in the satirical revue "The Committee" which recently opened in New York to critical raves.

Now under his real name of Hamilton Camp, Elektra has issued a stunning debut album in a period when the folk market has been saturated with many a bland and repetitive release.

Camp has the vital ability to communicate the modern folk idiom to the urban ear without having to affect phrasings or styles that are alien to his own background. For example, he is the only singer I have ever heard to effectively perform the country and western classic "Satisfied Mind" without the twang that has always been associated with the song.

Like Joan Baez, Camp has a voice that demands to be listened to because of a unique vocal timbre, in Camp's case a piercing, almost whining quality in his tone which creates a sense of urgency and excitement.

He is also the first performer to do a number of Dylan songs as well as Dylan and interpret them intelligently into some new areas. The album is of tremendous value if only because of the quality of material which includes several early Dylan numbers unknown to most people and a brilliant song by California-based Dino Valenti called "Get Together."

With his first album, Camp has established himself as one of the very finest vocalists in the commercial folk field, a field that unfortunately has been too barren of creativity. As folk music adapts itself to the realities of an urban world, Camp will be one of the most important talents of the transition.

BROADSIDE SINGERS (LINER NOTES)
Folkways (1964)

This is the third record of a series inspired by the New York topical song magazine *Broadside*, and, of the three, I believe it will turn out to the most significant. The songs are performed by the Broadside Singers, a group made up of nine of the major contributors to the magazine, a sort of left-wing New Christy Minstrels. In a sense, it is a continuation of the spirit of the Almanac Singers of the forties, since both are strictly topical groups commenting on the political and social issues of their times with original compositions.

It is the most representative record of its kind, since it covers the 14 most prolific topical writers in the country. The major limit on the choice of material was the elimination of important songs which didn't lend themselves to group singing because of their structure, length, etc. Whenever possible the individual authors made the decision on which songs were to be used.

Since it is incredibly difficult to get nine performing artists in town at the same time, the choosing of songs, rehearsals, and recordings were made in a few days. Schedules were too busy to allow even one rehearsal to be fully attended, and, by necessity, the record was made in one three and a half hour session with no editing.

The rehearsals were marked by a combination of confusion and excitement, as brand-new songs were being memorized and arranged simultaneously. The discussion of different points inevitably led to other songs and other writers and ten minutes would elapse before returning to the arrangement, but a musical militancy prevailed and finally the coffee cups were empty, the ash trays were filled, and the songs were familiar.

Into the valley of the recording studio rode the nine nameless writers, and while the mikes were being arranged a large glass of rum and coke was passed around. After greeting each other, tuning up, clearing up throats, and taking recording levels for about an hour, the session began and rolled with surprising ease.

This record is coming out at a time when the folk market is saturated with overdone and hackneyed material. Although it is basically a spontaneous production, the intensity of the singing and the honesty of the writing gives it a validity lacking in many releases of professional groups who seem to have lost touch with the roots of folk music, if indeed they ever had any.

People forget that many of the early folk singers who achieved prominence came out of left-wing trade union singing. This left-wing tradition formed an important part of the foundation of the modern folk revival as we know it.

Around 1915, the radical union Industrial Workers of the World, known as the Wobblies, produced several functional topical song writers who usually set their words to popular tunes of the day. The best known of these was the Swedish immigrant Joe Hill who wrote the sarcastic "Pie in the Sky" song popular during the depression.

Aside from his writing, Hill was actively involved with the rough-and-tumble union activities of the time, and after a controversial trial where he was apparently framed on a murder charge, he fell before a firing squad in Utah at the age of 36.

During the twenties, the bloody mining strikes of Kentucky and West Virginia produced several important topical writers, including Aunt Molly Jackson, whose earthy singing helped out many a difficult strike. Her song on the death of Harry Simms, a young organizer, is a graphic documentation of the period.

The next major figure in topical music was Woody Guthrie, the Oklahoma dust bowl balladeer who remained almost a one-man movement through the thirties and forties. He wrote and adapted approximately a thousand songs, some of which have already been accepted as authentic folk music since they have worked their way into oral tradition.

After Woody was incapacitated with a nervous disease, Pete Seeger spread the topical political gospel through the fifties, popularizing the songs of Woody and other writers and producing such works as "Where Have All the Flowers Gone."

During 1962 several young writers were making their mark on the New York folk scene. I don't think it's possible to ascertain why these writers from different areas appeared and started producing so close together. Perhaps it was inevitable, with so many people learning to play the guitar during the folk boom, that a certain percentage would come to discover they could express themselves by writing in the folk idiom.

Also, the civil rights movement, the Kennedy image of action, the peace marches, and the general increase in political interest among the generation of the sixties were all somewhat conducive to this flurry of writing.

In this period *Broadside* magazine has served as the main focal point in the writing revival; it has been a stimulus and a catalyst to most of the writers and has given many of them their first recognition, while serving as the only forum for the discussion of topical songs.

Like the record, the magazine is essentially non-professional in approach. It is edited by an elderly couple from Oklahoma, Sis Cunningham and Gordon Friesen, and is turned out by hand on a mimeograph machine by Gordon's brother Ollie.

They are great people to talk to in a cold, disinterested city like New York. Sis will reminisce about the days she played accordion with the Almanac Singers and how they were blown out of Oklahoma in the dust bowl days, and Gordon, who once had a novel published, will talk about his days as a journalist when he once authored a rumor about a gold strike out west and started a mild rush with the unknowing assistance of the Associated Press.

The *Broadside* office is their small apartment in a low-rent district in uptown New York. Their living room is distinguished by piles of back issues, unanswered mail, literally hundreds of unpublished songs, and a few cats, rabbits, and other pets belonging to their daughter Jane.

The magazine is scaled in such a way as to make profit almost impossible, and the workload has grown so heavy with their increasing success that they were forced to change from a bi-weekly to a monthly.

Fortunately, they received some money from the Newport Folk Festival Foundation and will be getting some extra money from the sales of Broadside Records and a new series of songwriters' concerts at the Village Gate in Greenwich Village.

I think these notes might be a good place to straighten out some possible misconceptions about the young writers themselves. I've noticed several attempts to idealize them as sort of twentieth century knights. None of the writers I know considers himself exceptionally noble, and most of them have a good healthy streak of ambition. This point is especially directed to the starry-eyed 13-year-old radical fans who comprise a good portion of the topical audience.

The body of work achieved by these writers I believe will clearly emerge as the single most important contribution of the folk revival. With so many hundreds of good songs being written, there is bound to be quite a respectable number of great ones. On this record you have a priceless composite selection of some of the finest efforts.

SONGS OF PHIL OCHS—INTRODUCTION
Songs of Phil Ochs (1964)

I got interested in politics after wasting a couple of years drifting through college. Around the same time, I became interested in learning the guitar, and luckily won an old Kay in a bet on the election of John Kennedy for President. As a journalism major, I was writing for several campus papers, so it was pretty natural to slip some of my ideas between the chords I was learning.

This book contains about a fifth of the songs I've written since then. Many people have asked me how I write a song, and after thinking about it for a while, I decided that all my good songs were written subconsciously. That is to say, I'm never able to sit down and decide that I'm going to write a song. Rather, a song idea will come out of the blue and I'll get the proverbial light-bulb sensation. But I always try to keep my mind conditioned to thinking of new ideas. When I get one, my brain almost acts like a reflex muscle in following up a new thought. Sometimes I have stayed up past daylight pursuing a song idea until it was trapped in rhyme. But once you get the original idea, the rest is relatively easy—and rewarding. Some of the most exciting and satisfying moments of my life have been in the writing of a song.

I hope this book will inspire some readers to try their hand at songwriting. You'll never know how good you might be without a few honest attempts. I think many potentially good songwriters have been still-born by their own inhibitions.

Most of my early songs were straight journalistic narratives of specific events, and the later ones have veered more in the direction of themes behind the events. All of them, though, are trying to make a positive point, even the ones that deal with tragic events. However, I do have to concur with some of the right-wing groups that consider topical songs subversive. These songs are definitely subversive in the best sense of the word. They are intended to overthrow as much idiocy as possible, and hopefully, to effect some amount of change for the better.

I'd like to dedicate this book to the memory of Joe Hill, the Wobbly songwriter, who received his royalties in the form of bullets from a firing squad.

TOPICAL SONGS — HISTORY ON THE SPOT
Modern Hi-Fi & Stereo Guide (1964)

The commercial folk boom has reached its peak and is now on the decline, but I believe that several related trends will continue to grow in both quality and appeal. The most important of these is the rebirth of the topical-song movement.

Topical songs are those which sing about the times, whether they treat a specific event like the sinking of the Thresher submarine or a theme behind the news like nuclear disarmament. Historically, these songs occur predominately in times of crisis or exciting events such as elections. The major catalyst for topical songs in the early part of this century was the union movement, first the ripple of the Wobblies around the time of the Russian Revolution and then the larger wave of the AFL-CIO organization drives of the '30s.

The Wobblies were members of the left-militant union, Industrial Workers of the World. One of the most famous was a songwriter of Swedish descent named Joe Hill who became the major topical writer of his day. He was actively involved in strikes and meetings in the western part of the country and he became a legend in his own lifetime. In order to spread his ideas as rapidly as possible, he wrote his own words to the popular songs and hymns of the day.

Unfortunately, he was shot by a firing squad at the age of 36 after being accused of robbery and murder. He is generally considered to have been framed, but the point will probably never be proven since the court records have disappeared. Joe Hill's sentence aroused widespread interest at the time, and he was executed over the protests of thousands of citizens, the Swedish Consul, and even President Woodrow Wilson. One of his better-known satires is "The Preacher and the Slave" about the Salvation Army:

> You will eat by and by,
> In that glorious land above the sky.
> Work and pray, live on hay,
> You'll get pie in the sky when you die.

During the same period came the muckraking novels such as *The Jungle* by Upton Sinclair. One purpose of topical songs, then and now, was to provide a simpler vehicle for spreading a message. For example, Woody Guthrie in the '30s condensed

The Grapes of Wrath into a long ballad called "Tom Joad," and introduced many non-readers to the story.

Woody was the major topical song writer of the depression and World War II. He came out of the Dust Bowl during New Deal days and blew all over the country recording hundreds of scenes and stories in traditional tunes.

He sang with Pete Seeger and other young musicians in the Almanac Singers, a group that specialized in topical songs. At the height of his creativity he was struck with a rare nervous disease that has kept him incapacitated since 1952. No one will ever know how many brilliant songs have been lost to the whim of fate.

Here's an example of his simple, evocative writing style. The song, called "Pastures of Plenty," is about the plight of migrant workers.

> Out of your dust bowl and westward we rolled
> Through your deserts so hot and your mountains so cold.

During the '50s there was a vacuum in topical song-writing filled only occasionally by such people as Malvina Reynolds, Les Rice, and Pete Seeger. Interest in topical songs reached a low level that mirrored the complacent attitude of the general public during the years of the Eisenhower administration.

Then in 1958, with the advent of the Kingston Trio and other singing groups, there came a fantastic explosion of general interest in folk music. Unlike the Weavers, who made their commercial mark in the early '50s, the new groups lacked any real depth in their material; it was a very sugary and superficial kind of folk music that reached the mass audience.

I believe that 1961 marked the rebirth of topical songs. Around that time several young writers appeared and started to turn out songs in volume. It is impossible to say exactly why this happened, but some probable reasons are these:

First, thousands of students were playing guitars in '61 and '62, and many were doggedly searching for new material. Perhaps it was natural that a certain number of these discovered they had the ability to write songs that satisfied them as much or more than the old ones.

Another possible reason was the general mood of change that arrived with the Kennedy administration. Kennedy's image of youth and action inspired many people to come out of their non-political shell and identify more with what was going on in the world.

A third reason was the civil rights explosion that produced the first semi-revolutionary mentality since the '30s and generated the kind of excitement and tension that produces creativity in all fields of the arts.

All of the outstanding new topical songwriters are from urban middle-class backgrounds, as are many of the new young blues singers. I believe their music evidences a rejection of their own backgrounds and provides an avenue to a more involved life and a deeper morality. Topical lyricists now become involved with their subjects by going to places where there is a real struggle going on, rather than just writing songs out of the newspapers.

There are many reasons for writing topical songs. The first is to express immediate feeling on a given subject or issue. Topical songs can also be written to publicize a significant event so that it won't go unheeded in its own time or to provide an historical document in music so that one day people can better understand the attitudes and happenings of previous generations.

The major writer today is 22-year-old Bob Dylan, who brought topical songs to a new height with the quality of his poetry. His "Blowin' in the Wind" has already become a folk standard though the singing of Peter, Paul and Mary, and Dylan himself has emerged as one of the top selling artists in the business.

In a gravelly voice heavily influenced by country blues, he communicates his long ballads with beautiful stage presence. The contrast between Dylan and James Dean illustrates the difference between decades. Dean was the rebel without a cause in the '50s; Dylan maintains the rebel image while speaking out on the basic moral issues of our day. His lyrics, including those of "Blowin' in the Wind," could be considered the clarion call of the '60s:

> How many times must the cannon balls fly
> Before they're forever banned?

Since I've had training in journalism, my songs are usually more specific. I've tried to make much use of humor to get my points across. For example, in "Draft Dodger Rag":

> Sarge, I'm only 18, I've got a ruptured spleen
> And I always carry a purse.
> I got eyes like a bat and my feet are flat
> And my asthma's getting worse.

Oh, think of my career, my sweetheart dear,
My poor old invalid aunt.
Besides I ain't no fool, I'm going to school
And I'm working in a defense plant.

Also hailing from Guthrie's Oklahoma is Tom Paxton who is a master at the craft of writing songs. He sometimes achieves an almost perfect union of words and music as in "Daily News":

Daily news, daily blues
Pick up a copy any time you choose.

Len Chandler, the only negro in the new crop of writers, is spending much of his time in the South and has been arrested several times for participating in demonstrations. His best civil rights song is called "Turn Around Miss Liberty":

Every eye in the whole wide world is looking toward the U.S.A.
Miss Liberty stands with her torch held high, but she's looking the other way.

Other songwriters who are making major contributions include Buffy Sainte-Marie, Mark Spoelstra, Eric Andersen, and Peter La Farge, and new talents will certainly appear.

Practically all the above-mentioned writers had their songs first printed in a mimeographed publication called *Broadside*. Edited by Sis Cunningham, formerly of the Almanac Singers, it comes out every two weeks or so and contains six or seven songs about recent events. It has sparked interest in the topical song revival and has become the focal point for discussion of the trends of protest songs.

Folk music in general should end on a higher plane than ever after the boom is over, and topical songs will certainly be a vital part of the folk movement. Whether topical songs can be considered folk music right after they are written is a controversial point, but one thing is sure: many of the topical songs written now will work their way into oral tradition and become a permanent mirror of the folkways and social issues of our time.

AN OPEN LETTER FROM PHIL OCHS TO
IRWIN SILBER, PAUL WOLFE, AND JOSEPH E. LEVINE
Broadside 54 (20 January 1965)

Just between you and me, I would like to ask you to sheath your critical swords so I can get a word in edgewise. I couldn't help but notice the frontal attack on brother Bob Dylan lately, who is being criticized a lot more than most of us thought possible.

It is as if the entire folk community was a huge biology class and Bob was a rare prize frog. Professor Silber and student Wolfe appear to be quite annoyed that the frog keeps hopping in all different directions while they're trying to dissect him.

It seems the outrage occurred at Newport, and there are many different, confusing versions of what went on. Was Dylan raped by success? Did Dylan rape his fans? Did Dylan's fans rape Elizabeth Cotton? Nobody seems to know for sure.

And so, Irwin Silber wrote an open letter to Bob telling him he couldn't really write about the world honestly without writing protest songs and accused him of relating only to himself and his cronies.

I agree, and I would like to add my name to the list of accusers. I hereby publicly smack Bob's hand and demand that he be made to stand in a dark corner, preferably at Newport, and be forced to write "Forgive me, Joe Hill" at least a thousand times.

Who does Dylan think he is, anyway? When I grow used to an artist's style, I damn well expect him not to disappoint me by switching it radically. My time is too precious to waste trying to change a pattern of my thought.

If you're reading this, Bob, you might as well consider this an open letter to you too. Where do you get off writing about your own experiences? Don't you realize there's a real world out there, a world of bombs and elections, folk music critics and unemployed folksingers? Instead of writing about your changes like "My Back Pages," for example, you could write a song about Joanie called "My Back Taxes." Oh well, you'll get yours. See if they try to give you any more medals.

In order to prevent this from happening to another angry young man of song, I hereby suggest the formation of an annual prize for the most militant protester in the form of a Silber bullet, on which is inscribed "Go get 'em, kid!"

In the last issue of *Broadside*, Paul Wolfe handed me the topical crown saying I had won it from Bob at Newport and stated that the future of topical music rested on me. Then he went on to attack the former champion for the low level of his new writing and his lack of consideration for the audience at Newport.

Well, I'm flattered by the compliments, but I'd like to point out several misconceptions in the article. In the first place, it's not really important who is the better writer and it's pointless to spend your time arguing the issue. The important thing is that there are a lot of people writing a lot of fine songs about many subjects and what concerns me is getting out the best number of good songs from the most people.

In point of fact, when Bob came to Newport he had completely changed the basic subject matter of his songs, and his only real choice as an artist was to be honest to himself and the work he was doing at the time, not how his fans would react to the change. To cater to an audience's taste is not to respect them, and if the audience doesn't understand that they don't deserve respect.

It didn't take any more nerve for me to go on the Newport stage and sing strong protest material since protest songs are so accepted. In reality, I didn't show any more respect for the audience than Bob did, because we were really doing exactly the same thing, that is writing naturally about what was on our minds.

With so many good writers around, the future of topical music clearly rests in many hands. And if you want to give credit where credit is due, I pay the greatest homage to Guy Carawan, who not only writes songs, but devotes his full time to the Civil Rights Movement in the South, actively working in a real struggle, promoting workshops on how to use music in the movement, and getting his banjo broken over his head on a picket line.

As for Bob's writing, I believe it is as brilliant as ever and is clearly improving all the time. On his last record, "Ballad in Plain D" and "It Ain't Me Babe" are masterpieces of personal statement that have as great a significance as any of his protest material. How can anyone be so pretentious as to set guidelines for an artist to follow?

As a matter of fact, in order to save you folks out there from needless aggravation, you may now consider me sold out, completely depraved, and happily not giving a damn about where your tastes happen to be at the moment. I am not writing out of nobility; I am only writing out of an urge to write, period.

My major concern is how honest and well-written I can make a song, not how well it can be used by the movement or how well it fits into the accepted pattern.

These rigorous requirements for songwriters could really get out of hand. Before long you may hear some enraged voice screaming backstage at a *Broadside* Hootenanny, "You're sorry? . . . You're sorry? . . . You wrote a non-topical song and you're sorry?"

It seems you just can't win: no matter what you do these days you're criticized. I really don't see what's so wrong with Bob and I putting all our royalty money into chemical warfare stock.

And so, the question still remains. Can I withstand the pressures of fame? Will I be chewed up by the American success machine? Perhaps I might mold topical music into a significant voice in a new and revolutionary America. Or on the other hand you might pick up the *Times* one day and read the startling headlines:

"Ochs Turns Tables on Topical Traitors . . . Underground FBI Informer Astounds Folk World by Arresting Dylan and Paxton at Hoot . . . Cites Tape Recordings of Secret Conversations as Damaging Evidence."

As for you, Mr. Levine, some of your movies are really quite bad.

I AIN'T MARCHING ANYMORE (LINER NOTES)
Elektra (1965)

And so, people walk up to me and ask, "Do you really believe in what your songs are saying?"

And I have to smile and think back to the songs and the hours stolen by flickering thoughts dancing just out of my reach occasionally being drawn in by the magnet of an aroused mind.

And I think of the absurd fears that gripped me as I drove down to Mississippi last summer listening to the accounts of the freshly discovered bodies. Or I think of my car spinning wildly out of control on a Kentucky mountainside just before spending Christmas in Hazard, Kentucky.

I remember climbing up rickety ladders to the tops of speaker-trucks to sing in the cold weather at countless rallies, watching the familiar faces of frustrated radicals.

And my vanity flutters as I hear again the cheers of audiences of thousands applauding an entertainer, or perhaps applauding the slim hope that all is not phony.

And I force myself to wonder that perhaps I am as phony as the world I criticize and that I am the greatest fool of all. I realize that I can't feel any nobility for what I write because I know my life could never be as moral as my songs.

I know I'm sticking my neck out and I know I'll be attacked. I remember the attacks of the reactionaries and I have to laugh; I remember the attacks of those I came to respect and the hurt is still there.

I wonder if I'll be investigated and what I could say to a Congress consisting of too many spineless men for whom I could hold nothing but contempt.

And I wait for the faceless American Legionnaire from Ohio to grab me by the collar and yell, "What about Korea, kid?"

And I am warned again—"Write only of your own experiences, only the naïve would be so pretentious as to write 'finger-pointing' songs." And the longer I write, the longer the list of complaints.

There's nothing as dull as yesterday's headlines.

Don't be so ambitious.

Sure it's good, but who's gonna care next year?

I bet you don't go to church.

Don't be so negative.

I came to be entertained, not preached to.

That's nice, but it really doesn't go far enough.

That's not folk music.

Why don't you move to Russia?

And yet every once in a while, an idea grabs me and the familiar excitement returns as I turn myself on with the birth of a song. And I know again that I'll never kick the habit of writing.

And so, people walk up to me and ask, "Do you really believe in what your songs are saying?"

And I have to smile and reply, "Hell, no, but the money's good."

For what else could I say to such a question.

I AIN'T MARCHING ANYMORE (SONG NOTES)
Elektra (1965)

Side One

I AIN'T MARCHING ANYMORE

This borders between pacifism and treason, combining the best qualities of both. The fact that you won't be hearing this song over the radio is more than enough justification for the writing of it.

IN THE HEAT OF THE SUMMER

Scenes and images of the riots last summer in Harlem. As is usually the case, the loudest bursts of outrage came from those most responsible for the debacle.

DRAFT DODGER RAG

In Vietnam, a 19-year-old Viet Cong soldier screams that Americans should leave his country as he is shot by a government firing squad. His American counterpart meanwhile is staying up nights thinking of ways to deceptively destroy his health, mind, or virility to escape two years in a relatively comfortable army. Free enterprise strikes again.

THAT'S WHAT I WANT TO HEAR

There are many fine sentimental out-of-work songs floating around, but as unemployment figures grow larger, so grows the need for more realistic songs and, consequently, actions. I can spare a dime, brother, but in these morally inflationary times, a dime goes a lot farther if it's demanding work rather than adding to the indignity of relief.

THAT WAS THE PRESIDENT

My Marxist friends can't understand why I wrote this song and that's probably one of the reasons why I'm not a Marxist. After the assassination, Fidel Castro aptly pointed out that only fools could rejoice at such a tragedy, for systems, not men, are the enemy.

IRON LADY

A century from now, intelligent men will read in amazement about the murder of Caryl Chessman and wonder what excuse for a society flourished in these times.

The idea for the song was given to me by a social worker in Ohio who had taken the phrase from a poem written by a man on death row.

THE HIGHWAYMAN

I never could follow poetry in school, but this work by Alfred Noyes has completely captivated me since my childhood. It is a classic study of romantic narrative that seemed to have been made for music.

Side Two

LINKS ON THE CHAIN

Historically, labor unions have been a catalyst to social change, and in my opinion have a definite responsibility to be in the vanguard of important battles. When the civil rights struggle came to a head, they had become such a part of the establishment that the old lions of the left were the new pillars of the segregated structure. But I'm sure they'll be able to straighten out this embarrassment at one of their many White House meetings.

HILLS OF WEST VIRGINIA

On one of my trips to Hazard, Kentucky, I drove through West Virginia with Eric Andersen and found myself renewing an old habit of pretending I was taking pictures with my mind. When the trip was over, I set down these images which really don't have any special message.

THE MEN BEHIND THE GUNS

I saw this in a collection of bland patriotic poems, but there were so many ringing phrases in this one, I found myself re-reading it several times and reaching for my guitar. My apologies to the author, John Rooney, for changing a few lines, but the discipline of music had to win out in the end.

TALKING BIRMINGHAM JAM

In Birmingham, tourist city of the South, you can bomb the church of your own choice with the apparent blessing of Governor George Wallace. Birmingham is one of the cities that made the FBI what it is today.

BALLAD OF THE CARPENTER

The State Department has a nasty habit of blocking the entrance of Ewan MacColl into this country, and undoubtedly one of the reasons is songs like this. All political considerations aside, if you take a serious look at the quality of culture in America, you can see that the State Department can ill afford such a tactic.

DAYS OF DECISION

The American politician has developed into a gutless master of procrastination with a maximum of non-committal statements and the barest minimum of action. This moral vacuum is exceeded only by the apathetic public who allows him to stay in power. How feeble is the effect of a song against such a morass, but here it is.

HERE'S TO THE STATE OF MISSISSIPPI

This song might be subtitled "Farewell to Mississippi," for in order to write a few more songs like this, it might be wiser for me to stay away for a while. I was down there last summer and must admit that I met some nice people and that the state isn't as bad as my song implies, unless you are a Negro who has forgotten his place, or unless your last name was Chaney, Goodman, or Schwerner.

SON OF "MY BACK PAGES"
Broadside 57 (10 April 1965)

At the *Broadside* hoot on the first Sunday of February, the Village Gate was packed solid with an enthusiastic crowd while scores of others were being turned away at the door. Every song that was introduced was greeted with fervent applause and the spirit of the songwriting revolution seemed to reign supreme.

However, there was only one aspect that bothered me and a few other observers. That is, that with the exception of four songs (two of them by Eric Andersen), none of the other works could justify themselves as artistic creations. I've been writing topical songs too long to let a few clever lines, or an unusual twist, apologize and fall short of a completely successful and satisfying song.

The protest song movement has now achieved an all-time high in popularity, and I don't think it will reach its peak until a year or two from now. You might say that with experimental songs you can expect too much and be too critical, but I feel that in a period when the songwriting scene is coming to national attention and soon will be recognized by the mass media, the highest standards must immediately be imposed from within the movement rather than waiting for a justified critical axe in the hands of some all-too-sophisticated reporter from *Time* magazine.

With all the honest excitement and zeal that is generated at the *Broadside* hoots, unfortunately, I have to look at the enthused response as an exercise in artistic self-delusion. If a mature, aware, and honest person had heard about the protest revival and decided to see what the excitement was all about, and had shown up at the *Broadside* hoot to check it out, he would have had to have made tracks for the exit or the bar by intermission time. If the spirit and enthusiasm permeated his soul, it would not be unlike the hopeful feeling you might get watching enthusiastic but shaky folk dancing from all kinds of liberal countries at a progressive left-wing summer camp.

Am I saying stop writing and forget it? No, I'm saying don't be so ready to go wild over any song that puts down Barry Goldwater and the landlords. Non-violence must be applied to art also.

The folk music revival is still hanging on to the market, although much of it has become bland and stale. Now the topical area is increasingly winning over the old folk crowd because of its vitality and the freshness of new ideas being infused into the folk idiom. Is there any songwriter who wants to allow such a large part of the foundation of this growing expression to be bland and stale at the beginning stages? Insignificant attempts merit kindness; true creativity merits challenging criticism.

It is an easy error to get the parochial view that protest is the most exciting movement going on in American music. I believe there is an equally important revolution being generated by the Beatles and several other groups in the popular area. For example, I would highly recommend for all people interested in songwriting and real communication through music tune in to a record produced by Phil Spector called "You've Lost That Loving Feeling," sung by the Righteous Brothers.

There are so many beautiful things going on in that record that it leaves the listener almost stunned; it has passed the test of great popular communication, an artistic endeavor that can turn you on and leave you turned on. There is no reason why the social realism of topical songs can't emulate that beauty and even surpass it in its impact. But the only way the protest movement can hope to do it is by a sincere and agonizing reappraisal of the level of its work.

Oftimes in the past, topical songs were functional; they were written on order for a meeting or a strike and consequently the quality suffered. Today, there is a much broader view of this kind of writing and consequently it must undertake new responsibilities to itself. It's just not enough to state the obvious anymore.

What I am saying is this: how many of you think that if Sheriff Jim Clark had wandered into the Village Gate that Sunday, would he have felt threatened?

BUFFY SAINTE-MARIE AND ERIC ANDERSEN
Broadside 39 (7 February 1964)

There are two fine songwriters that *Broadside* has inadvertently missed in the past because of lack of contact. We plan to print some of their songs in the future. The first is Buffy Sainte-Marie, who is my favorite female writer and singer. She could be the most exciting new talent since Bob Dylan. Watch for her first Vanguard recording, which is due any day now. The second is a young man from Berkeley, CA, and Buffalo, NY, named Eric Andersen. He is especially adept at poetic love songs, and his singing can best be described as the logical musical extension of Elvis Presley. Just a few days after arriving in New York he was also signed by Vanguard. I predict that by the end of the year they will both be among the most important names in folk music.

THE BALLAD OF GORDON LIGHTFOOT
Broadside 60 (15 July 1965)

There I was in Canada, stoned out of my mind at 5:00 in the morning, swapping songs, jokes, and bottles with Ronnie Hawkins, the Arkansas rock 'n' roll singer who runs an out of sight bar in Toronto, and Gordon Lightfoot, who is the Canadian Hank Williams.

The best music is usually done in situations like that, where there's no stage, no mic or lights, and no unnatural need to please a strange audience. You're just singing to have a good time, communicate with people who understand you, and create those mad moments that become cherished memories when you're too old to do it anymore.

Also, when you get rolling like that you can find out who has it and who doesn't because you've drunk away all your hang-ups. And as I listened to Lightfoot sing away that intoxicated morning, I knew he had it.

Every time I see Lightfoot he ends up apologizing to me because he's not writing "important" protest songs. "I'm just starting to get beneath the surface, and I know my stuff is just too trite," he told me on Wednesday night in a coffeehouse packed with people there to hear him and a long line waiting outside for the next show.

He says, "Damn, your Mississippi song sure knocks me out," the week that Marty Robbins has made his "Ribbons of Darkness" (see this issue of *B'side*) number one on the country and western charts. Then this paradoxical man picks up his two guitars and walks guiltily to the stage and wipes out another audience which could never fully realize that his stage humility was not put on at all.

Lightfoot, aside from having the greatest real last name of anybody in folk music, is destined to become a pivotal figure in bridging the gap between folk music and country and western. He can sing, play, entertain, write, put himself down with a flair that marks an original. He's the kind of guy who can work a bar and cut through the booze with honesty; there's a strange poetry that lives within the country bar crowd that demands to hear the simple truth served on a platter of realism. Ingrained in the natural Lightfoot is the same spark of human insight that carried Hank Williams, Jimmy Rodgers, and Johnny Cash out of show business and into immortality.

Now everybody has his faults, and Lightfoot is no exception. He plays golf. But that can be rationalized if you consider that he really is an outdoor type, hunting and fishing, skiing, and who knows but somewhere in his past innocent years he might even have swum naked in some chilly Canadian lake. Think about that the first time you see him.

Those of us who know Lightfoot now are, of course, concerned that he won't fall into the well-travelled pitfall known in some circles as the success syndrome, of ignoring his responsibility to us, and writing just for himself and a few cronies, you might say.

Lightfoot (notice how many times I take advantage of that groovy sounding name) was born and copywritten on Nov. 17, 1938, in Orillia, Ontario, and the rumor has it he killed himself a b'ar when he was only three (see how easy it is to start a legend, folks).

He got a professional music degree from Westlake College in Los Angeles, and sold out for the first time when he became a studio singer for the Canadian Broadcasting Corporation doing over 250 shows, mostly in choral work. Not content with selling out in one country, he went to England and did his own hour-long country show in a summer replacement and reached over four million people. At the end of the summer, not having been knighted, he left in a huff to ramble in Sweden where he married his Swedish wife, Britta (all young record buying type girls please forget you read that). Living overseas put him through several changes and cleared up his mind to the point of definitely deciding to be a writer and so he returned to his native Canada.

His friend Ian Tyson, of Ian & Sylvia, became more and more impressed with his songs and finally asked one of his managers, John Court, to fly up to Toronto and watch him perform. Court sat in the shadows, puffing on his Tiparillos, and as he became convinced, the chemistry of a large management office took effect: Peter, Paul & Mary's next release was Gordon Lightfoot's "For Loving Me."

The first time you see Lightfoot, if he's not singing you might walk right by him, mistaking him for a statue. He's got classic Greek features with an *Argosy* magazine jawline, and long flowing blond locks of hair always neatly combed. So you see, he doesn't have to write songs, he could become a sculptor's model.

Lightfoot has established himself as a recording artist in his own right, having had a couple of records at the top of the charts in Canada. He's also one of the major drawing cards there, and now he has to happen in the States. He'll be at the Newport Folk Festival in July, and will make his club debut at Mother Blue's in Chicago. I forgot to mention before, he records for Warner Bros., publishes with Witmark, and frankly his 16-month-old son doesn't really dig his songs.

Gordon Lightfoot may become the greatest country and western writer of all time. But, on the other hand, he may become a forest ranger.

OCHS: IT AIN'T ME, BABE
Village Voice (12 August 1965)

Dear Sir:

After reading Arthur Kretchmer's article on Newport (*Voice*, August 5) I feel I must protest. Because of the nature of Bobby Dylan's songs and mine, I am periodically being used as ammunition against him. He is erratic while I am normal, he has forsaken his principles while I'm dedicated to the cause, etc.

But it ain't me, babe. I'm not the white hope against neurosis; I'm only a writer who, as a matter of fact, goes out of his way to defend Dylan and his changes, and I have never been so badly misquoted as in last week's article where I am represented as saying that Dylan has gone astray, that he's not blunt enough, and that he's forsaken his ideology.

On the contrary, I have written thousands of words in several articles in various publications taking the exact opposite view on this very point. For example, in the September '65 issue of *Sing Out!* I wrote, "The only thing that counts about Dylan's writing in the end is how good it is, not what it's about."

And in the New York *Broadside* on Dylan at Newport: "As for Bob's writing, it is as brilliant as ever and is clearly improving all the time. Some of his works are masterpieces of personal statement that have as great a significance as any of his protest material."

Bogged Down

Mr. Kretchmer has covered Newport from an outsider's point of view—and some of his observations are the sharpest and most honest I've seen on the festival, but, unfortunately, under the handicap of unfamiliar terrain he has overreached himself by trying to analyze Dylan too deeply from too far away. The folk scene has continually suffered from a vacuum of perceptive, intelligent comment, and it's a shame to see welcome new penetrating critics getting bogged down in petty observations about Dylan's "flunkies" and his behavior patterns.

I'd like to straighten out a couple of other common misconceptions that have been floating around. Dylan and I are not in competition with each other; we're in competition with our individual creative processes, trying to stimulate our minds to produce the greatest amount of quality we can. Of course, I hope someday to write ten times better than Dylan, but I also sincerely hope that Dylan will someday write ten times better than Dylan. We're trying to grow if you'll only give us room.

And I can't emphasize strongly enough that there must be no shackles put on any writer to force him to cover certain subject material or use certain styles. Dylan is being violently criticized for using amplified rock 'n' roll as his medium on the Newport folk stage. Just wait and see if we invite you again next year Bobby Teenybopper. I can just imagine some of the cops at Newport who happened to be folk purists reaching for their holsters muttering, "That's not folk music."

Musical Point

I understand that even most of the festival directors were quite upset at his performance there, and I think the best way to judge for yourself who was making the most valid musical point is to listen to a couple of Newport records of previous years and then listen to Dylan's new single which he sang at Newport called "Like a Rolling Stone."

Some people saw fit to boo Dylan after each song, and I think they were getting a needed dose of musical shock treatment. Dylan, as usual, was doing the unexpected, but was quite responsibly doing what any real artist should, that is performing the music he personally felt closest to and putting his own judgement before that of his audience. To cater to an audience's taste is not to respect them, and if an audience doesn't understand that, they don't deserve respect. The people that thought they were booing Dylan were in reality only booing themselves in a most vulgar display of unthinking mob censorship. Meanwhile, life went on all around them.

As for the reasons for my not being invited to Newport I wouldn't presume to guess their motivations, but I couldn't help but wonder, perhaps it's my breath?

TOPICAL SONGS AND FOLKSINGING, 1965
Sing Out 15 no. 4 (September 1965)

There are two major revolutions going on in music today: one is the revolution in songwriting, adding perceptive protest and valid poetry; the other is the solidifying of the pop revolution of the fifties started by Hank Williams, Elvis Presley, Buddy Holly, and Chuck Berry and now being carried on by the Beatles, the Rolling Stones, the Righteous Brothers, and the Loving Spoonful; that is, the firm entrenchment of rhythm and blues slightly flavored by country and western that led to the sudden and final destruction of the big band sound.

Both of them are extremely important because they manage to communicate reality with such an abundance of beauty, soul, and entertainment that they plant themselves in your mind, never to leave.

The topical song movement has now reached a crucial stage of development and has a responsibility to take itself more seriously and look at itself more discriminately than ever before. The fact of its popularity has been accepted in many areas, but it has carried with it an underlying weakness that may lead to its own destruction. Too many bad songs are being accepted and applauded simply because they have the right message. If protest songs are to make a serious dent in American culture, the writers can't be lulled into a false sense of security because of the temporary cheers of an immature audience. Critical standards have to be raised to much higher levels than they are now.

I'm at the point in my songwriting where I give much more consideration to the art involved in my songs rather than the politics. I'm trying to weld sharper, more cogent, and more original use of language and music. The messages in my songs are now secondary to that part of my mind that creates. For example, as bad as it may sound, I'd rather listen to a good song on the side of segregation than a bad song on the side of integration. In order to grow to my greatest capacities, I feel I must understand myself to the fullest and express my deepest emotions regardless of where they stand in the political and social spectrum.

This brings me to one of my most criticized songs, "Here's to the State of Mississippi." This also happens to be my favorite, although on the surface, it goes against the basic policies of all the civil rights groups and the established rational voices of the Left. Before I go any further, here's a verse and chorus of it:

> Here's to the cops of Mississippi,
> They're chewin' their tobacco as they lock the prison door,
> and their bellies bounce inside them as they knock you to the floor,
> no, they don't like taking prisoners in their private little wars,
> and behind their broken badges there are murderers and more.
> Oh, here's to the land you've torn out the heart of,
> Mississippi, find yourself another country to be part of.

Now, normally, you might say the important thing is to encourage moderate business elements of the power structure of the state, bring about the vote, and get Mississippi back into the Union. I agree with that on a rational political level; but, artistically and emotionally, I wrote that song the day the nineteen suspects were allowed to go free. It's a song of passion, a song of raw emotional honesty, a song that records a sense of outrage, and even though reason later softens that rage, it is essential that the emotion is recorded, for how else can future generations understand the revulsion that swept the country? On another level, it is my act of murder against the good name of Mississippi, an act of vengeance that couldn't begin to avenge the countless atrocities of that forsaken land.

In other words, at the depth of its irresponsibility, Mississippi had become the symbol of evil in America, and the song is only exhorting that evil to leave. As I said on the notes of my last album: "I was down there last summer and must admit that I met some nice people and that the state isn't as bad as my song implies, unless you are a Negro who has forgotten his place, or unless your last name was Chaney, Goodman, or Schwerner."

And this is the point of my writing. I'm not getting on stage to mouth the correct political images whether they're based on logic or not. I'm not out there to be the spokesman for the Left, for SNCC, for my generation, or for anybody but myself. I'm only singing about my feelings, my attitudes, my views. Not only am I not ashamed of this form of egotism, but I expect more or less of the same attitude from any creative artist. Anybody that puts the ideals of an honest movement before his own art is only sacrificing the movement by providing them with a distortion of himself and, hence, less than his best and most original.

The preceding argument also explains why a lot of people are wasting time and missing the point by trying to criticize Bob Dylan's change of subject material. The only thing that counts about Dylan's writing in the end is how good it is, not what it's about.

This is the difference between now and the thirties, an uncompromising artistic sense of quality rather than a view of music that borders on the functional. Even today, I frankly can't really get turned on by the freedom songs coming out of the South. These songs are admittedly tools to be used as a cohesive part of the movement and, in that context, they are perfect, but somehow it leaves me uncomfortable to hear them done on the legitimate performing stage in anything but a workshop. I'd much rather listen to the Righteous Brothers sing "You've Lost That Loving Feeling," regardless of how meaningless such a work might be considered.

In other words, I want to be destroyed by art. I want to hear work that is so good poetically, so exciting musically, so original in arrangement and execution that it can turn me inside out with the communication of feeling. It is perhaps the foundation of my career to utilize the highest levels of artistic social realism to carry topical songs to that point and beyond. Can an artist be satisfied with any less of a goal?

TIM HARDIN, THE SINGER'S SINGER
Hit Parader (January 1966)

Three years ago, there used to be a small coffeehouse in Greenwich Village known as the Thirdside. Nobody got paid a salary for singing, so we all passed a basket after each set, usually ending up with about three dollars. A lot of beginning performers would show up for a few days, make a little money, and then disappear. One of these people was Tim Hardin, 20, a folk blues musician who was dissatisfied with what he was doing and was searching for new musical directions.

About the only thing I remember about him from that period was that he was much taken with the main character in the movie "Lonely Are the Brave," played by Kirk Douglas. He was a cowboy living in modern times who wanted an unrestricted life, but was continually hemmed in and was finally destroyed by society. Perhaps the identification was due to the fact that Tim is a direct descendent of the legendary gunfighter John Wesley Hardin.

He had originally come to New York from Oregon to go to acting school and like many others before him got lost in the crowd. Then without anybody taking much notice, he moved to Boston where the folk scene is notoriously tradition-oriented. This didn't deter him from deciding that the best way he could express himself on stage was to play an electric guitar and submerge himself completely in the hard-driving rhythm and blues idiom.

A couple of years later, the commercial folk boom was beginning to taper off and many hastily formed groups were breaking up under the pressure of lack of work. One of the best of these groups was the bluegrass act the Knoblick Upper 10,000, whose banjo player Erik Jacobsen, 24, had become greatly impressed with the Beatles, the concept of their act and their music. His years of work in the folk field had left him unsatisfied with his own music, but he was convinced that out of the folk idiom would come a new and exciting form.

He also felt the key position to hold in the emergence of this new music was in independent record production. After breaking up the group, he started looking around for somebody in whom to invest the small amount of capital he had saved up from performing. A couple of his entertainer friends gave him a lead on Hardin who had now built up an unusual reputation in Boston as a maverick blues stylist. On a gamble, Jacobsen called him up and offered him money to come to New York and make a couple of dubs for him. Hardin agreed and after Jacobsen heard him in person, he decided to make an extra investment to produce a whole album. He took the acetate of twelve songs around to the various record companies, finally settling with Columbia. As of this writing, Columbia has, unfortunately, failed to release anything of Hardin's.

While all this was going on, a club on Third St. in the Village, the Night Owl, decided to start hiring entertainment, and under the management of Joe Marra, 32, the new rhythm and blues was chosen as the main concept of the club.

Tim Hardin was the first R&B act he hired and he played there many weeks in a row, giving him a much-needed outlet in a suspicious city. Somehow continually broke, he always managed to show up in a cab, running inside casually saying, "Hey Joe, you got a dollar, the cab driver's in a hurry." Then the wiry 5'7" musician with brown wavy hair and piercing eyes would get on stage and spend a few minutes tuning up with Buzz Linhart on vibes and Felix Pappalardi on bass before setting the stage on fire with his projection of intensity. Often, he wore a corduroy cap and coarse clothes, giving the impression that he was an earthy working man who also happened to play.

Unlike most folk performers who stand when they sing, Hardin projects a great authority by sitting in a hard wooden chair, keeping the rhythm with a loud-driving pounding of his feet, and leaning forward to emphasize the relentless power and urgency of his music. It took less than a week for the appearance of the new Hardin to affect the other musicians of the Village. While not drawing huge crowds off the street, he achieved a more important success, that of holding a number of fellow musicians in awe.

He had developed a horse-fast vibrato phrasing, original jazz guitar stylings, the stage presence of an intense actor, and an incredible communication of gutsy feeling. Many have come to consider him as a potential white Ray Charles, with his sense of timing and melody, that rare depth that develops to a point where someone can legitimately be called a soul singer.

On any given night you could walk into the Night Owl and find such people as Bob Gibson, Bob Dylan, Judy Henske, Odetta, Bob Shelton, Albert Grossman, and perhaps half of the other village club owners.

Hardin had found his niche and had come home to roost. The impact of his musical ideas on the disorganized New York folk crowd cannot be exaggerated. Every month his unique vocal mannerisms seem to crop up in a couple of already established singers. He has been influenced by some of the best Negro phrasing and he's carrying this influence along with his folk orientation to the groups that are going to be controlling the mass market, like the fast-rising Lovin' Spoonful who were formed by Erik Jacobsen from the musicians who were hanging around the Night Owl.

Hardin only plays professionally now and then because of a restless nature, so it's impossible to assume he'll make it to the top, but one thing is sure; he has all the makings of a legend, and when musical historians look back on this period to check the deepest roots and the most important influences and translators, Hardin will have to take his place along with Dylan, the Beatles, and the rest.

MAN AGAINST MUSIC
OR, BEFORE I'D BE A SLAVE I'D WANT TO KNOW EXACTLY WHAT'S IN IT
FOR NUMBER ONE
Village Voice (21 July 1966)

There is a new electric rock group sweeping the Village known as the Potted Flowers, which consists of a tulip, a daffodil, a dandelion, a carnation, and a black orchid. Who'd a thunk it? Electric flowers. Their first appearance only last night has caused such a sensation that they have already been signed by seven companies, and some have gone so far as to label them the American Beatles.

Their strength seems to be that they are so typical of the frantic Village musical scene, they have become an overnight symbol of the times. Many passers-by on MacDougal Street were overheard to say, "Listen to that volume, Stokely. There's no mistaking them, they're flowers, all right." Growing their petals extra-long, hooking their very stems to amps, they have scientifically improved on nature to such an extravagant extent that some patrons inside the club almost mistook them for weeds. By the way, the basic conflict in this theme is man against music.

Before the era of the Potted Flowers, music was created in a less frenetic and more human environment. For example, Hank Williams sitting in his garage with his tape recorder and acoustic guitar produced more music than all the Village rock groups put together. To a certain extent, partially because it is a new idiom, many groups intending to become the masters of volume have instead become the prisoners of noise.

Inviting Murder

The groups should understand that if good music amplified is great, lousy music amplified is grotesque, thus inviting murder. For the electric music to have real value the exuberance must be balanced by a sense of control, and the loudness must be executed with a sense of beauty. There is no reason why electricity has to be equated with insensitivity.

Hank Williams was dealing with something more powerful than a speaker, that is, an individual sense of music, an intangible communication with his own private muse, an infusion of his own personality into his music.

The commercial folk boom, in spite of its mass success and influence on other forms of music, seemed almost incapable of producing truly creative artists since it avoided the classic disciplines required of all music. During those years I was always disturbed that I could never really get turned on artistically by the folk scene except for the vocal timbre of Joan Baez and the complete Bob Dylan whirlwind. In terms of commercial groups, I think the only one that ever went beyond arrangements and into vital music was Gibson and Camp, who unfortunately never got the widespread recognition they deserved.

Through these recent years the major aesthetic achievements on the musical scene have been in the form of individual recordings like the Righteous Brothers' "You've Lost That Loving Feeling," Bob Dylan's "Like a Rolling Stone," the Rolling Stones' "Satisfaction," Beach Boys' "California Girls," the Beatles' "Rubber Soul" album, and now the Lovin' Spoonful have legitimately stepped into the class of heavyweight groups with their recording of "Summer in the City." And who can forget Barry Sadler, America's leading soul singer, offering us a new form of music, death. In view of such an erratic market, many people are asking, where is it all going? Many others are too high to care. I suspect it is all a fantastic plot, deviously designed so that the proceeds of all the marijuana sales in New York are actually supporting the war effort.

Aesthetic Vigilante

Perhaps where it is all going is where it has always gone: to those individuals who are able to avoid the stampede and spend their time and effort in bringing themselves together. I believe a re-evaluation and a new conception are needed to give the Village electric music the validity they claim to be striving for. Perhaps a mass citizens' arrest or an aesthetic vigilante terrorist squad is required, folks.

Now in the summer of 1966 two artists who have been on the scene for a few years will be releasing their first recordings which promise to be the first significant contributions to the musical scene in a long time. First, Verve-Folkways is releasing Tim Hardin, considered by many to be the finest white blues singer in the country. Second, David Blue on Elektra has improved so much in the last year that he easily surpasses the great majority of his better-known contemporaries from the *Broadside-Sing Out* scene.

Hardin works with a light combo background at different times including guitar, harmonica, piano, drums, vibraphone, and strings. If such a form as folk-rock does exist, the nuances and phrasing qualities of his voice easily make him the master interpreter.

Not Unnatural

The recent school of white folk blues singers was widely criticized as unoriginal, or a bad imitation, or not having enough balls. Hardin can take the rhythm and blues idiom and handle its guttural intonations without any unnatural strain on his voice, which at the same time has enough depth and feeling to simulate the sweet lyrical sound of a stringed instrument. His vocal attack is always to the point, and his off-beat syncopation is enough to keep the most blasé listener continually interested.

Hardin played at the Night Owl over a year ago and had a major influence on many of the local singers, including the then unformed Lovin' Spoonful and the Mamas and the Papas. He is the singer's singer; he is so together vocally that, like Dylan, he really goes beyond ego, and to hear him is to learn from him. He is the consummate artist, the teacher of other artists.

Into the Song

When he does a song, he makes his version *the* version. For example, if you want to understand one of the reasons why the folk scene missed the musical point, compare his rendition of "Green Green, Rocky Road," which he cut over a year ago, to any of the folk versions and the difference will have to be embarrassing. He is so far into the song that he exposes the superficiality of the other efforts.

Hardin is 25 now and lives in Los Angeles practicing his singing with a studio quality tape recorder and is constantly working on the subtleties and shadings in his voice. Compare that approach to the raucous noise that pours out nightly on the Village streets and the countless number of long-haired apprentices who seem to mistake shouting for singing.

Strong Original

David Blue has been prowling the streets of New York for some years now, caustically attacking almost anyone who stepped on a stage or put out a record. Now on his own sides, which should be but aren't titled "Blue's Revenge," he shows he has created a fantastic wealth of new material.

He looks like Dylan's older convict brother and sometimes sounds like it, but behind the superficial similarity is the unmistakable pulse of a strong original writer and stylist.

He is obviously influenced by Dylan, but unlike the imitators, he overcomes the style and uses it, rather than letting the style overcome him. Although he is not together enough to be as good as Dylan, he sometimes exercises a better economy of words, better melodies, and a surprising subtle tenderness. He still lacks Dylan's master imagery and the discipline required for greater length and the development of more complex themes. Here are some examples of his writing:

GRAND HOTEL

> Here I was treated especially well
> This was a grand hotel.

MIDNIGHT THROUGH MORNING

> And all the poets kept getting louder
> Even though they weren't needed any longer

These two records may or may not be chart sellers, but they are certain to have a major impact on a great many singers and writers, and they stand as two striking examples of the kind of value that can emerge from artists following themselves rather than following the market.

If you can still feel misty-eyed after reading this article, thank God, Mister, 'cause you're still an American.

CHANGES (LINER NOTES)
Jim and Jean, Verve-Folkways (1966)

The folk boom has come and gone like a plague.

As the scene came to its inevitable shift, some resigned and officially became salesmen, others became ethnic defenders of Mother Earth tradition even though there were no attackers.

Many grew their hair down to their wallets and jumped on the Beatle bandwagon in true hands-across-the-sea spirit. Palms upward as usual.

Practically everybody tried drugs.

Somehow this led to a musical revolution. The *Village Voice* was virtually panting with hip discovery. Discotheques spread like fungus. Many were moved to proclaim a new era of culture for the masses.

Myself, I also planned to form a new group of former folkies. We would expand our hair, and be backed by an electronic symphony orchestra, we would play sitars and various other eastern instruments we learned of by reading record jackets, and we would talk about the free-form ultra-Zen music on television. The group would be called the Pretensions.

Meanwhile back in the Village, largely hidden from the explosion, the money, and the hoopla, a group of writers have been working on their own revolution.

All of the writers have strains of sarcasm, cynicism, greed, and tenderness and some have been said to have large egos.

Aha! Into this mélange of ultra-hip and ultra-hyped scenes leap Jim & Jean, a true blend of Americana, the kind of couple who might well persuade people from Iowa to buy U.S. Savings Bonds.

Can they sing? Are they worth listening to? I think so, because unlike many of the people you have come to know and love in the folk and folk-rock scenes, they actually have voices with timbre and tone, control and intelligence.

There has been a vacuum of decent interpreters of the new wealth of songs pouring out of the New York decadence. These lyrics demand sensitive treatments, and don't necessarily need the overwhelming blare of drugged speakers. They demand phrasing, harmonies, counterpoint, and higher wages.

The Beatles have set a level of pure musical sound that is a tantalizing carrot to many an American group. Jim & Jean are one of the few groups who can meet the challenge of that level.

(All decent Americans will buy and love this record. The rest of you will have to fend for yourselves.)

SATIRE

AN INTERVIEW BY FANS IN THE UNDERGROUND OF GREENWICH VILLAGE
Unpublished

Q. How would you describe yourself?

A. Eich bien un Berliner.

Q. How did you become a protest singer?

A. It was either that or reform school.

Q. We understand that you were invited to the White House for dinner.

A. Yes. I walked up to Lyndon and said, "I'm much better than you are." Somewhat taken aback he replied, "No, I'm much better than you are." "See, I've already got you down to my level," I said.

Q. You know Bob Dylan used to be our hero until he sold out and went commercial. Now you're our hero. We admire your convictions and certainly hope you don't sell out, too.

A. Why it's the farthest thing from my mind folks. But you shouldn't let me be your hero anyway.

Q. Why not?

A. Well, as I was gazing at a statue of myself the other day, I realized that people take themselves far too seriously.

Q. Do you have any plans for the future?

A. Well, by middle age I tentatively plan to become an alcoholic to avoid serious interviews.

Q. What is your real name.

A. Robespierre.

Q. Why did you quit school before getting your diploma?

A. I had decided that education was really the process of apology between generations. Besides, they were starting to integrate.

Q. Would you recommend that everybody quit school?

A. Only if they're an egomaniac.

Q. Do you have any other advice for the youth of America?

A. Get it while you're young.

Q. Doesn't this attitude conflict with the meaning of your songs?

A. Of course.

Q. How do you spend your days?

A. Three times a week I take a course in how to be a Negro.

Q. How do you spend your nights?

A. As often as possible.

Q. What would you like to be if you weren't a topical singer?

A. The Presidential News Secretary.

Q. Why?

A. So I could utilize a short news brief I composed once in my awake, "President Johnson passed away quietly in his sleep last night. He was giving a speech at the time."

Q. Who is the greatest threat to America?

A. All the astronauts and Robert Goulet.

Q. Don't you even like the astronauts?

A. You gotta make a living.

Q. Do you have any ambitions?

A. Just one, not to be a success.

Q. What are you working on now?

A. I've just finished my first book entitled *My Seven Minutes with John F. Kennedy, His Wit, His Courage etc.* and I'm halfway in to my second, *Is Patriotism Camp?*

Q. What's the best thing you have ever written?

A. An apologetic fan letter to John Wayne.

Q. Did you have an unhappy childhood?

A. No, I spent it all in the movies.

Q. Do you belong to any organizations?

A. Only one, an artistic terrorist squad.

Q. Are you doing any television?

A. Yes, I'm doing a series called *Protest Man* where I attack essential problems by writing songs and making lots of money off them.

Q. What's the most difficult thing you ever attempted?

A. Trying to get Elvis Presley to record "Here's to the State of Mississippi."

Q. What's the most significant thing you ever did?

A. Racing into a Chamber of Commerce meeting in Wichita, Kansas, screaming, "The Chinese are coming. The yellow bastards are here. Millions of them swarming down Main Street trying to kill your mothers."

Q. How did you get away with it?

A. I left town in a police uniform disguised as the Mafia.

Q. Do you want to be a leader of the New Left?

A. I would, but I admire William Buckley too much.

Q. Something is happening, but I don't know what it is?

A. Well, my term for what is happening is the hip aesthetic left.

Q. What does that mean?

A. The life force of the sixties. Hip because it's aware of reality, aesthetic because of the increased appreciation of beauty, and left because it's the most effective and humane way of running things.

Q. Watch it, you're getting serious.

A. Sorry.

Q. Are there any practical suggestions from this philosophy?

A. Yes, we could have a hip aesthetic left week where all opposing troops in Vietnam could meet peacefully on the battlefield, smoke the finest imported Lebanese hashish, and watch Charlie Chaplin movies projected against the sky.

Q. You have some rather strange ideas.

A. You know, I'd come out for the legalization of marijuana, but I wouldn't want to get in to trouble.

Q. What do you do between writing songs?

A. Bite my nails.

Q. Would you burn your draft card?

A. No. But if I could find them, I'd burn my social security card and my birth certificate.

Q. Who are your favorite show business personalities?

A. Hubert Humphrey and Billy Graham.

Q. Do you ever dream?

A. Oh yes . . . the other night I dreamt America took over the entire world, officially, and turned it into a television series. On top of that, they gave it a low rating because nobody wanted to watch.

Q. Why do you go to demonstrations?

A. Because I feel guilty about being white and rich.

Q. Why have you come out against American foreign policy?

A. I think America has an ungrounded fear of progress. But in the event the U.S. mainland is attacked by Russia or China, I'm only kidding folks.

Q. What is the mood of young America?

A. Essentially anti-Protestant. You might describe these times as the revenge of the war babies.

Q. There is a theory that history is the process of compromised revolutions. Can you give us a *Bartlett's Quotation* quotation on this generation?

A. On the white steed of aesthetic rebellion I will attack the decadence of my future with all the arrogance of youth.

Notes by Phil Ochs
A middle-class hero of the bourgeois

THE SONGS OF PHIL OCHS
Broadside of Boston (25 November 1964)

Excellent! Clearly the finest songbook ever to emerge from the folk renaissance. As a matter of fact, it could stand as one of the outstanding masterpieces of English literature and will probably be considered for the Great Books series.

The songs themselves are so powerful that several leading historians have already credited them as the major turning point of the sixties in the search for a new left. The incredibly low price leaves this reviewer aghast when considering the infinite value of the material.

REVOLT ON THE CAMPUS
OR HOW I LEARNED TO LOVE THE FOLK SCENE AND STOP WORRYING
ABOUT MUSIC
(Pen name: Phillip Abbott Ochs)
The Realist 60 (June 1965)

Dallas isn't really all that bad if you stop and think about Columbus, Ohio; at least Dallas almost admits it. And Dallas doesn't have Ohio State University, which is still discussing the right of freedom of speech while other schools are arguing about pulling out of Vietnam.

Columbus is so extraordinarily American that in order to blend into the atmosphere you almost feel like putting a flag on your exhaust pipe and saluting the traffic cops.

When I was a student at State, I was so suffocated by the provincial patriotism that in a fit of madness I wrote a violent pro-Castro article for a dormitory paper. The next day I realized that few people there had a sense of humor, as Fidel was hung in effigy with me as the dummy.

Thinking quickly, I threw a football and a basketball at the enraged crowd, and while they were fighting over them, I escaped, disguised as a Young Democrat.

After leaving school, I knew that I had to do something that would pay a lot of money and wouldn't require too much work, so I became a protest singer.

Now, three years later, my phone rang, and the FBI and I learned that it was long distance from Ohio calling. Before I could say "Gus Hall," an excited voice explained that the Berkeley seed had spread to State, and my presence was requested for a rally to protest the speaker's rule that blocked the appearance of radical figures.

It seems the president of the university had said that Herbert Aptheker, a Marxist intellectual, would not be allowed to appear on campus. However, he added, "We are not afraid of having radicals speak here; for example, next month we are going to have Walt Disney."

When I was going to State, the only thing that aroused the students to any level of mass action was when the school decided not to go to the Rose Bowl. That year it was a three-way contest between Ohio State, LSU, and LSD. The students were so enraged, they stormed into downtown Columbus, over 5,000 strong, demanding that the games be held.

Finally, Ohio's hero, John Glenn, stood up and begged the students to go back, with limited success, until he lost his balance on the platform and fell over backwards, bringing everybody down.

It's not every college drop-out that gets a chance to take revenge on his alma mater, I thought, as my train slipped into Ohio under cover of darkness. When I got to the campus the next morning, the soporific spirit still prevailed: the art students were doing busts of Robert Taft; Ray Bliss was recruiting new faces from the shot put team; and the fraternities were building floats out of Regimen tablets.

Off in a corner the campus police were whipping the bare soles of a weeping co-ed with birch twigs, having caught her jaywalking. The administration building was still done in early cobweb, and shrill, rusty typewriters recorded the non-events of the day. The *Dispatch*, Columbus' progressive newspaper, was still running editorials like "As the Republican Party searches for a new vigorous image in 1968, let's not forget Ohio's John Bricker."

Excitement was mounting on the oval as the 4 o'clock rally approached, and the student Air Force ROTC dropped leaflets with President Johnson's picture asking everybody to stop complaining about freedom of speech and reason together for a while.

Hushed mutterings of damn and son-of-a-bitch rustled through the crowd as the students quietly asserted their right to talk dirty. As the speeches got underway, the plainclothesmen fingered their little Japanese tape recorders and moved in closer.

When it came my turn to sing, I identified myself as a paid agent of Berkeley and Peking, and opened up with a rousing chorus of "Why-O why-O why-O, why did I ever leave Ohio?" As I was singing, Communist agitators crawled on their hands and knees through the rows of seated students, obviously infiltrating.

Halfway through my set, the campus bells started to ring out proudly, almost drowning out the singing. A group of students quickly checked and reported that it was Dean Quasimodo hanging by the rope with one hand, and thumbing through *For Whom the Bell Tolls* with the other.

In spite of the harassment, the student morale was growing and was finally beginning to assume the proportions of an excited and vocal meeting. The angry, demanding noise attracted a passing detachment of U.S. marines who encircled the rally and opened fire. The commander later apologized with a sheepish grin: "Sorry, force of habit."

The remaining students were taken prisoner, and as they marched away on a pre-arranged signal, someone counted to three, and everyone yelled at the top of their lungs, *"Pertinence!"* To their amazement, all the university buildings crumbled into rocks and gravel. One of the students, wounded in the leg, muttered, "Sic semper multiversity."

The president staggered out on the oval like Alec Guinness in *River Kwai*. "I may agree with what you're saying, but I'll defend to the death my right to keep you from saying it," he moaned with his dying breath.

I escaped arrest only by agreeing to write a long article for the *Saturday Evening Post* exposing the Free Speech Movement as a front for Hanoi.

The sun was setting as the train pulled out of the Columbus station, and I joined a group of porters in the back of the train in a rousing chorus of "We Shall Overcome."

Top left: One year and ten months, Austin, TX, 1942. *(Courtesy Ochs Family Albums)*

Top right: Three and a half years, Arverne, 1944. *(Courtesy Ochs Family Albums)*

Right: Five and a half years, Far Rockaway, 1946. *(Courtesy Ochs Family Albums)*

Top: Columbus, Ohio, 1956.
(Courtesy Ochs Family Albums)

Left: Cleveland, Ohio, 1960 (or,
"Take It Out of My Youth").
(Courtesy Ochs Family Albums)

Portrait by Alice Ochs, 1966. *(Photo by Alice Ochs, © Meegan Ochs, courtesy Getty Images)*

"Demonstrations should turn people on, not off."   New York City, 1967.
(Photo by Michael Ochs, © Michael Ochs)

Phil Ochs, patriot. Circa 1967. *(Photo by Michael Ochs, © Michael Ochs)*

Phil, at an anti-Vietnam War demonstration in front of the United Nations in New York City, April 15, 1967. Martin Luther King Jr. also spoke at this demonstration.
(Photo by Michael Ochs, © Michael Ochs)

Profile of the artist as a young man.
(Photo by Alice Ochs,
© Meegan Ochs,
courtesy Getty Images)

"Visions of Shadows that Shine."
(Photo by Alice Ochs,
© Meegan Ochs,
courtesy Getty Images)

Left: Hollywood, 1970.
(Photo by Jim McCrary,
courtesy Phil Ochs Estate)

Bottom: "My Kingdom for a Car."
(Photo by Ron Cobb,
courtesy Phil Ochs Estate)

NEWPORT: SHORT HOT SUMMER
Broadside 61 (15 August 1965)

"The trouble with Newport '65 was that too many people forgot that it was sup-posed to be a festival. The cops were ridiculously harsh and rude. Many city perform-ers were uptight about how well they would do professionally. And juvenile gossip seemed to be on too many peoples' tongues. It should have been called the Newport Fuzz Festival. If people don't take it so seriously next year it should turn out to be a whole lot better."

THE NEWPORT FUZZ FESTIVAL
by Mississippi Phil Ochs
The Realist 61 (August 1965)

Normally, I wouldn't mind being fingerprinted, photographed, and interrogated under hot lights, but after all we were only trying to get into the festival.

"You want to murder Joan Baez, don't you?" asked the fat cop, spitting tobacco
on our Spanish leather boots.

"You don't understand," I replied wittily, "I was invited to sing in one of the
concerts last year."

"Oh, yeah, then why weren't you invited this year?"

I started to say, "Perhaps its . . ." but was interrupted by one of the festival directors who had noticed our plight and managed to get us in after signing an affidavit
swearing we weren't Jewish and didn't play electric instruments.

Once inside the barbed wire enclosure, we began to relax. On stage Joan Baez
and Donovan were humming an a cappella version of John Phillip Sousa's "Hands
Across the Sea."

After each performer was done, a cop would get on stage and announce: "Welcome
to Newport, outsiders. I'd like to ask your cooperation in observing a few simple
rules—no parking, no drinking, no smoking, no talking, no stepping on the grass, no
grass, no sleeping on the beaches, no sex. So enjoy yourselves, folks, it's your park."

"Don't shoot, don't shoot," I cajoled, walking past the guards into the audience.
The crowd was the usual assortment of folk purists wearing faded jeans, beer guzzlers
wearing faded smiles, and plainclothesmen wearing freshly pressed jeans and carrying
Harmony guitars.

Down below, in front of the stage, was a large pit, an idiot arena holding a motley crew of maniacal, milling photographers who surged forward like a great army of
large, snapping mosquitoes whenever a celebrity appeared on stage. I was fatalistically
hoping that at least one performer would throw an expensive Leica into the middle
of the hungry throng, and while they were all grappling in the dust, expose himself
to the audience, making them all miss the classic shot.

In 1963, there was an historic scene when Dylan, Seeger, Baez, the Freedom
Singers, and Peter, Paul & Mary joined hands to sing "We Shall Overcome." In 1964,
egos got out of hand and didn't realize the ritual was already old hat and leaped on

stage to no avail because several of the original important people weren't there this time, so no famous photograph emerged.

This year the traditional ending degenerated into a *La Dolce Vita* party as several disparate performers, festival officials, audience members, and passers-by joined in a Kafkaesque song-and-dance exhibition. There were so many people packed on stage, there legally should have been another fire exit.

Next year perhaps they will feature a Radio City Hall Rockette routine including janitors, drunken sailors, town prostitutes, clergy of all denominations, sanitation engineers, small time Rhode Island politicians, and a bewildered cab driver. The whole jamboree can be backed up by the beloved Mississippi John Hurt's new electric band consisting of Skip James on bass, Son House on drums, and Elizabeth Cotton on vibes, all being hissed and booed by the now neurotic ethnic enthusiasts.

One of the highlights of the 1965 festival occurred when a workshop turned into a workout. Alan Lomax was emceeing the blues workshop and was turned off by the Paul Butterfield Jug Band and implied as much on stage. Albert Grossman was turned off by Lomax's comments and implied as much to Lomax's face offstage. Heated comments were exchanged and before anyone could say *festival* the two lions of the Folk Power Structure were rolling in the dirt. They were pulled apart and immediately withdrew, Albert humming "Who Killed Davey Moore" and Lomax humming "If I Had a Hammer."

Both denied rumors that there would be a rematch in Madison Square Garden. Later in the festival a folk group which shall remain nameless wrote a song called "Talking Alan Lomax" in which they play the guitar background for a talking blues and say nothing. If anyone has a picture of the incident, I respectfully suggest they send it to the program directors who can use it as a dedication page for next year's program book entitled "We remember last year . . . the folk process."

During an evening concert, Lomax was discussing a group of former convicts who were chopping wood and hoeing in time to work songs. In a perhaps not unsympathetic gesture, one of the hoes lost its true aim and inadvertently demolished an innocent but expensive Vanguard microphone. Perhaps they could award a posthumous medal to the brave recording engineer who, with earplugs sensitively connected to the ill-fated mic, had his impressionable eardrums tuned to the slightest deviation in sound. The audience felt great sympathy for the mishap and gave them so many encores they chopped their way through the stage and fell in a heap on the ground.

During the Sunday afternoon concert it rained so heavily that the audience came out of their polite applause lethargy and began to cheer and even dance. It kept on raining, so the festival decided not to put on the Paul Butterfield band as scheduled for fear of someone being electrocuted. The audience was shocked, but then it's not always easy to put on folk music. One cryptic observer noted that perhaps the real reason they didn't put on the Butterfield band was out of fear that Alan Lomax and his ax-grinding convicts would be lying in wait.

In the final concert on Sunday evening, Bob Dylan, as usual, made history without even using a helicopter. I have a theory that it was really John Lennon on stage who had entered the festival disguised as Donovan, that the Butterfield band who played in back of Dylan was really the Kingston Trio getting kicks, and that Dylan's harmonica was really John Hammond.

Wearing an Audie Murphy black jacket, playing a Chuck Berry guitar, and performing his electrified alienation with passionate indifference, he assassinated the audience.

Some booed, some cried, some yelled "Take it off," but most just sat silently in a state of shock, sucking on crumpled beer cups. I was expecting God to open the heavens with his wrath, but instead Peter Yarrow embarrassingly brought Dylan back and he obligingly played two encores alone on an acoustic guitar, the band apparently having been slaughtered beneath the diamond stage by unforgiving Dylantants.

Alas, all good things must come to an end and as we left the scenic festival grounds bouncing around in the back of the police van, we had many fond memories. Dylan's lynching, while admittedly unsubtle and gauche, was understandable. Joan Baez's frugging on several occasions gave the festival the added flair of an Arthur Murray Dance Party. Peter, Paul & Mary certainly deserved a better fate than to have melted in the rain. The nagging question still remained: Why wasn't Regis Toomey invited?

It's probably only the beginning of a long and controversial history. Next year, in order to avoid a carnival atmosphere they will hold the evening concerts under a large tent. The addition of Phil Spector on the board of directors will ensure that the festival will continue to mirror changing tastes. An enlarged cartoon of Batman will dominate the stage and Andy Warhol will have exclusive rights to film his four-day opus, *Assimilation*.

And if I'm not invited next year, I guess I'll have to write another review like this.

THIS WAS THE YEAR THAT WEREN'T
Cavalier (December 1965)

This has been the year of the Indian; Johnny Cash recorded an Indian album, and more and more people in the folk world suddenly discovered there was more than a little wampum to be made by discovering a trace of Indian blood in their past and donning the traditional headband. This, too, got carried all out of proportion when Pat Sky, after an evening at the Gaslight Café with too much firewater, blew up and threw a tomahawk at a policeman trotting by on a horse and screamed, "Keep your stinking island!"

A more embarrassing scene took place as Buffy Sainte-Marie was closing an extended engagement in New York. At the end of her last set she was singing her stirring number, "Now That the Buffalo's Gone," and as she raised her guitar for the last loud chord, an unseen louse let loose a rubber-tipped arrow that landed right on her dark-skinned forehead. By the way, I also discovered some Indian blood in my veins the other day when I cut my finger on some beads and have tentatively titled my next album, *Screw You, White Man!*

Speaking of albums, I have invented a new game called Album Titles, which you can apply to your favorite or unfavorite folk performer. Here's a list of starters:

COVER: A color close-up of a large female breast

TITLE: *More Judy Henske*

COVER: A leering, bearded man aiming a rifle out of a window

TITLE: *Another Side of Dave Van Ronk*

COVER: A dungareed half-smiling, long-haired boy walking down a snow-covered street with Susie Rotolo

TITLE: *The Free-Stealin' Phil Ochs*

COVER: A dungareed half-smiling, long-haired boy leaning over the body of a dead Negro woman with a cane

TITLE: *Still Another Side of Bob Dylan*

COVER: A scene on MacDougal Street with several unkempt persons who have passed out with bottles in their hands, including Dave Van Ronk, Ed

McCurdy, Bob Dylan, Bob Shane, Phil Ochs, the New Wine Folk Singers, and Bob Gibson

TITLE: Elektra's *The Booze Project*

COVER: The Jim Kweskin Jug Band walking into a side door of a suspicious looking building with large sacks on their backs

TITLE: *Bringing It All Back Home*

COVER: Picture of two Negro men with wry smiles on their faces and a beautiful blonde Aryan white girl on their shoulders

TITLE: *Peter, Paul and Your Sister*

This has been a disastrous year for the presentation of folk music to the mass public. Many sacred cows were milked dry in an unbelievable series of outrageous events. For example, the basic incompatibility of generations and disparate music styles were exemplified in the knifing of "Spider" John Koerner by the suddenly vicious Mississippi John Hurt. Then there was that totally uncalled for and rather surprising incident on Bleecker Street when Pete Seeger, in the heat of an argument with Jean Ritchie, finally blew his top and jumped on her dulcimer.

And who can forget the sudden disappearance of 39 priceless Vanguard masters just two days before Jac Holzman took an extended trip to Europe. Or that Eric Andersen was assaulted by a free-wheelin' gang of teenage girls who stomped him mercilessly with their thirsty Spanish boots. But perhaps the most hideous example of foul folk play was when the Dave Van Ronk Jug Band forced the New Christy Minstrels to eat the American flag. The most frightening thing about that scene was that they did it in perfect unison.

Police are still investigating the bombing of the *Little Sandpaper Review*. There are at least 367 suspects with obvious motives, many of whom showed up at the burning building trying to block all the smoking exits, innocently protesting they didn't know the editors were inside. Minnesota police have been in contact with the Quebec Canadian Mounted, since in the last issue *LSR* had given a 1/16 rating to a new album of French-Canadian songs which it termed too extremist.

Actually, so may absurd things happened that I was forced to make up a second game called Folk Points. Here is an ingenious system to rate how *"in"* you are with the folk scene:

Discovering Indian blood in your past—seven points

Saying Joanie instead of Joan—five points

Saying that's not his real name, you know—three points (was 13 until *Newsweek*)

Having Ravi Shankar in your collection—four points

Being invited to Woodstock, New York, for a weekend—75 points

Being found without coterie outside Bernard's Café Espresso in Woodstock on a weekend—minus 75 points

Quitting a commercial folk group, growing long hair, and re-forming into Liverpool electric—nineteen points

Having a *Sing Out!* subscription—one point

Travelling to Hazard, Kentucky; Mississippi; or to the Georgia Sea Islands—eight points

Going on a Zen diet—23 points

Being invited to a Beatle party in England, flying there with Skip James, and turning on to LSD while showing Rudolph Nureyev your five-star rating in *LSR*—3,000 points

I am also starting a folk-entourage school where you can go into gladiatorial training to hang out in hip crowds with budding young folk stars. You learn how to criticize innocuously, put down any and all competition, get photographed by national magazines, and depart gracefully after a squabble with other folk entourages. If any budding young folk stars are interested in being assigned a following, which, by the way, is deductible, please contact me at General Delivery, Woodstock, New York.

This year also saw the emergence of Newport as the Academy Awards of Folk Music, where, in a secret ceremony open only to the industry, awards were given out in the form of folkier-than-thou gold flat-picks, affectionately called Hooeys (short for hootenanny). The only trouble was that everyone was so nice to everybody that every single award was a tie between at least fifteen people. So, it turned out that everybody even remotely connected with folk music got an award, with the notable exception of Randy Sparks, who was roundly hissed when his name was mentioned early in the evening.

At the end of the presentations, the whole folk scene joined hands and sang "We Shall Overcome" so many times that everybody passed out.

OUT OF THE ARCHIVES (NEW YORK CITY)

The Newport Pneumonia Fuzz Festival

by Mississippi Phil Ochs

Normally, I wouldn't mind being fingerprinted, photographed,
and interrogated under hot lights, but after all we were only trying
to get into the festival.

"You want to murder Joan Baez, don't you," asked the fat cop,
spitting tobacco on our Spanish leather boots.

"You don't understand," I replied wittily, " I was invited to sing
on one of the concerts last year."

"Oh yeah, then why weren't you invited this year?"

I started to say, "Perhaps its my..." but was interrupted by
one of the festival directors who had noticed our plight and managed
to get us in after signing an affidavit swearing we weren't Jewish
and didn't play electric instruments.

Once inside the barbed wire enclosure, we began to relax. On stage
Joan Baez and Donovan were humming an acapela version of John
Phillip Sousa's "Hands Across the Sea."

If my memory serves me correctly, after each performer was done
a cop would get on stage and announce something like "Welcome to
Newport, OUtsiders. I'd like to ask your cooperation in observing
a few simple rules- No parking, no drinking, no smoking, no talking,
no stepping on the grass, no grass, no sleeping on the beaches, no
sex. So enjoy yourselves, folks, its your park.

"Don't shoot, don't shoot," I cajoled, walking past the guards
into the audience. The crowd was the usual assortment of folk/purists
wearing faded jeans, beer guzzlers wearing faded smiles, and plainclothesmen wearing freshly pressed jeans and carrying Harmony guitars.

Down below in front of the stage was a large pit, an idiot arena

-more-

-2-

holding a motley crew of maniacal milling photographers who surged forward like a great army of large snapping mosquitoes whenever a celebrity appeared on stage. I was fatalistically hoping that at least
one performer would throw an expensive Leica in the middle of the hungry
throng, and while they were all grappling in the dust, expose himself
to the audience, making them all miss the classic shot.

In 1963, there was an historic scene when Dylan, Seeger, Baez,
the Freedom Singers, and Peter, Paul, and Mary joined hands to sing
We Shall Overcome. In 1964 egos got out of hand and didn't realize
the ritual was already old hat and leaped on stage to no avail be=
cause several of the original imp rtant people weren't there this time
so no famous photgraph emerged.

This year the traditional ~~ending~~ last Song degenerated into a La Dolce Vita
pa
party as several disparate performers, festival officials, audience
members and passers-by joined in a Kafkaesque song and dance exhibition. There were so many people packed on stage, there legally should
have been another fire exit. Next year perhaps they will feature a
Radio City Hall Rockette routine including janitors, drunken sailors,
town prostitutes, clergy of all denominations, sanitation engineers,
small time Rhode Island politicians, and a bewildered cab driver. The
whole jamboree can be backed up/by the beloved Mississippi John Hurt's
new electric band consisting of Skip James on bass, Son House on drum s
and Elizabeth Cotten on vibes being hissed and booed by the now neurotic
ethnic entusiasts.

One of the highlights of the festivals occurred when a workshop
turned into a workout. Alan Lomax was emceeing the blues workshop
and was turned off by the Paul Butterfield Jug Band and implied as much
on stage. Albert Grossman was turned off by Lomax's comments and implied as much to Lomax's face offstage. Heated comments were exchanged
=more=

-3-

and before anyone could say,"festival," the two lions of the folk
power structure were rolling in thedirt. They were pulled apart and
immediately withdrew, Albert humming "Who Killed Davey Moore," and
Lomax humming "If I Had a Hammer." Both later denied rumors that
there would be a rematch in Madison Square GArden. Later in the festival
a folk group which shall remain nameless wrote a song called "Talking
Alan Lomax in which they pкay the guitar background for a talking blues
and say nothing. If anyone has a picture of the incident, I respectfully suggest they send it to the program directors who can use it
as a dedication page for next year's program book entitled "We remember last year....the foкk process."

Later during an evening concert, Lomax was discussing a group of
former convicts who were chopping wood and hoeing in time to work songs.
In a perhaps not unsymbolic gesture, one of the hoes lost its true
aim and inadvertantly demolished an innocent but expensive Vanguard
microphone. Perhaps they could award a post-humous medal to the brave
recording engineers who with earplugs sensitively connected to the
ill-fated mike had his impressionable eakdrums tuned to the slightest
deviation in sound. The audience felt great sympathy for the mishap
and gave them so many encores they chopped their way through the stage
and fell in a heap on the ground, whereupon Lomax raced down the stairs
muttering, "I've got an axe to grind with you."

During the Sunday afternoon concert it rained so heavily that the
audience came out of their pplite applause lethargy and began to cheer
and even dance. It kept raining, so the festival decided not to put
on the PAUL Butterfield BAnd as scheduled for fear of someone being
electrocuted. The audience was shocked, but then it's not always easy

to put on folk music. One cryptic observer noted that perhaps the real

-more-

-4-

reason they didn;t put on the Butterfield Band was out of fear that
Alan Lomax and his axe-laden convicts would be laying in wait.

In the final concert Sunday evening, Bob Dylan as usual made
history without even using a helicopter. I have a theory that it
was really John Lennon on stage who had entered the festival disguised as Donovan, that the Butterfield Band who played in back of
Dylan was really the Kington Trio getting kicks, and that Dylan's
harmonica was really John Hammond.

Wearing an Audie Murphy black jacket, playing a Chuck Berry
guitar, and performing his electrified alienation with passionate
indifference, he assassinated the audience.

Some booed, some cried, some yelled "TAke it off", but most
just sat silently in a state of shock sucking on crumpled beer cups.
I was expecting God to open the heavens with his wrath, but instead
Peter Yarrow embarrasingly brought Dlylan back and he obligingly
played two encores alone on an acoustic guitar, the band apparently
having been slaughtered beneath the diamond stage by unforgiving
Dylanhants.

Alas, all good things must come to an end amd as we left the
scenin festival grounds bouncing around in the back of the police
van, we had many fond memories. Dylan's lynching while admittedly
unsubtle and gauche was understandable. Joan Baez's frugging on
several occasions gave the festigal the added flair of an Arthur
Murray Dance Party. Peter Paul and Mary certainly deserved a better
fate than to have melted in the rain. The nagging question still
remained- Why wasn*t Regis Toomey invited?

It's probably only the beginning of a long and controversial
history. Next year in order to a carnival atmosphere they will hold
the evening concerts under a large tent. The addition of Phil Spectre

-more-

-5-

on the board of directors will insure that the festival will continue
to mirror changing tastes. An enlarged cartoon of Batman will dominate
the stage and Andy Warhol will have exclusive rights to film his four
day opus, "Assimilation."

If I'm not invited next year, I guess I'll have to write another
article like this.

-30-

THE WAR IS OVER

HAVE FAITH, THE WAR IS OVER
Los Angeles Free Press (16–22 June 1967)

The war is over and what a relief. It sure was depressing—but now, thank God, we can celebrate. It has been called off from the bottom up, and now the only ones participating in it are those that still believe it exists.

Now some of you may not believe the war is over—and that, essentially, is the problem. The mysterious East has taught us the occult powers of the mind, and yet we go on accepting our paranoid president's notion that we actually are involved in a war in Asia. Nonsense. It's only a figment of our propagandized imagination, a psychodrama out of 1984.

By this time, it must certainly be apparent that Johnson is absurd, as compared to being wrong. It should also be crystal clear that the war has been extended so ridiculously long that it is more absurd than immoral, and that the standard moral arguments have been repeated so many times that they seem to have lost their meaning. There is no dialogue on the war, only the repetition of clichés. One outrage must be answered with another; only absurdity can speak the language of absurdity.

Demonstrations should turn people on, not off. The spiritually depraved public of America has shown it won't stand for the blunt truth served on a negative platter which it always defensively assumes is insult. A protest demonstration does not satisfy the demands of modern mass communications; it is somehow out of tune with the electric age. A protest rally is an act of negation against an act of negation, canceling each other out. The times demand a positive approach to demonstrations, a pro-life, joyful, energized, magnificently absurd demonstration against the sucking vacuum of war.

The underground must discard the establishment labels like "underground," "hippie," "flower children," and other assassination words; they've shown their colors—now they must show their true strength. The trick is not to go against the establishment, but not to believe them. Come on, now—do you really believe that a war is being fought in this day and age—certainly, not a war that has anything to do with us. Why, that would be absurd—don't you think?

On June 23, there is going to be a celebration of the end of the war. This celebration could be a love-in, a be-in, a to-be or not to be-in, a happening, a rally, a demonstration, an earthquake, a premature solstice, living theatre, living movies, a huge Hollywood production, a statement of numbers that you can attend without insulting your aesthetic.

The old standbys of the left and the attitudes they encompass should be avoided at this meeting. Classics like "Hey, Hey, LBJ—How many kids did you kill today?" are about as dated as the M-16. Since the war is over, we should have positive signs, like "Johnson in 68—the Peace President," "Welcome Hanoi to the Great Society," or "Thank you, Lyndon, for Ending the War."

As a living movie, everyone should do something creative and positive. Make up your own sign, wear appropriate clothes to the theme of a reenactment of VE Day, wave a flag and mean it. It's time for aesthetic rebellion, for creative anarchy; time for the use of surreal humor to ask now what our country is doing.

Johnson will be speaking at a $500 a plate dinner inside the Century Plaza Hotel, so we can have a penny a plate dinner outside at the celebration. How ironic to have this bit actor give a report on a demented war while outside thousands are celebrating the end of the same war!

Perhaps some people will walk up and say, "Hey, you guys must be crazy—there *is* a war going on; don't you read the papers?" To which you can reply, "No, you're the one who's crazy." History will decide who is really absurd.

We must realize that numbers and time are on our side, and the establishment needs us to fight this non-existent war. The one thing that will totally undermine Johnson's position is not to believe a word he is saying, to ignore the preposterous reality he has created for America and create our own reality. Let me repeat: if enough of us truly believe the war is over, we have the power to change our reality. Belief and faith can move mountains; this dated and corrupt generation should be easy. Hippies of the world unite—you have nothing to lose but your paranoia!

California is the most beautiful part of the country, and yet it has been taken over by the ugliest elements. Los Angeles is a plastic paradise, the exaggerated frontiersmen of a decaying materialist culture. This is a foundationless land of dreams, a studio posing as a city, a freak circus; what better place to make a bizarre stand? Without putting herself through any of the tasteless political changes of the East, LA has a golden opportunity to leap from total disinvolvement to the vanguard of the peace movement.

The thousands of young people flowing through California would respond to a call for this kind of rally rather than another protest demonstration. The psychedelic community can also create in the framework of this living theatre. Hopefully this will create an opportunity for the disparate elements of the state to merge gracefully.

The war in Vietnam is an amphetamine trip, a reflection of the spiritual disease that has gripped this country and distorted every principle on which it was built. This generation must make a choice between the total rejection of the country and the decision to regain a spiritual balance. I believe there is still something inherent in the fiber of America worth saving, and that the fortunes of the entire world may well ride on the ability of young America to face the responsibilities of an old America gone mad.

Old America has proven herself decadent enough to be willing to sacrifice one of her finest generations into the garbage truck of cold war propaganda. What kind of depths have they sunk into to dishonor the very meaning of the word honor by asking young men to die for nothing? This is not my America, this is not my war; if there is going to be an America, there is no war—*la guerre est finie!*

The criminal patriotism of today demands that every citizen sell himself—and now we pay the consequences, floundering in the jungles . . . not of Asia, but of New York to Los Angeles. Now we are the lost patrol who chase their chartered souls like old whores following tired armies.

Have you heard? The war is over!

HAVE YOU HEARD? THE WAR IS OVER!
Village Voice (23 November 1967)

Does protesting the war leave you tired and upset? Does civil disobedience leave you nervous and irritable? Does defending liberalism leave you feeling friendless and perhaps wondering about your breath? Does defending the need of repelling communist aggression leave you exhausted and give you that generation gap feeling?

On the other hand, are you tired of taking drugs to avoid the crushing responsibilities of a sober world? Do you want to do something about the war and yet refuse to bring yourself down to the low level of current demonstrations?

Is everybody sick of this stinking war?

In that case, friends, do what I and thousands of other Americans have done—declare the war over.

That's right. I said declare the war over from the bottom up.

This simple remedy has provided relief for countless frustrated citizens and has been overlooked for an amazingly long time, perhaps because it is so obvious. After all, this is our country, our taxes, our war. We pay for it, we die for it, we curiously watch it on our television—we should at least have the right to end it.

Now I enjoy violence as much as the next guy, but enough is enough. Five seasons is plenty for the most exciting of series.

On Saturday, November 25, we are going to declare the war over and celebrate the end of the war in Washington Square Park at 1 p.m.

For one day only, you and your family can achieve that moment you've all been waiting for. Ludicrous as this may appear, it is certainly far less so than the war itself. I am not recommending this as a substitute for other actions; it is merely an attack of mental disobedience on an obediently insane society.

This is the sin of sins against an awkward power structure, the refusal to take it seriously. If you are surprised the war is over, imagine the incredulity of this administration when they hear about it.

Two or three years ago the morality of this war was argued, and those who said the war was indecent and ineffectual were proven correct. And if you feel you have been living in an unreal world for the last couple of years, it is partially because this power structure has refused to listen to reason, or to recognize that they've lost their argument. But like all bullies and empires gone mad, they will not give in simply because they are stronger.

By this time, it must be apparent that Johnson is more absurd than wrong. The very word "wrong" has more connotations than immorality. There is no dialogue on this war, only the repetition of clichés from outworn arguments. Logic repeated too many times becomes ineffectual boredom, and Washington is numbing us with the rules of longevity. Step outside the guidelines of the official umpires and make your own rules and your own reality. One outrage must answer another; only absurdity can deal with absurdity.

Demonstrations should turn people on, not off. The spiritually depraved American public has shown it won't stand for the blunt truth served on a negative platter, which it always defensively assumes is insult. Demonstrations should satisfy the demands of this electronic and cinematic age. A protest demonstration can become one act of negation against another, canceling each other out. We need a newer and more positive approach, a pro-life, joyful, energized, magnificently absurd demonstration against the sucking vacuum of war.

More militant action could follow from this living theatre piece. You could refuse to go for a physical on the ground that there is no war. And suppose 20 or 30 million people signed a petition declaring the war over—the war which, by the way, has yet to be declared. What could be more democratic?

Think of that for a moment. How embarrassing can it get, to have an entire nation mobilized for war, to have the propaganda mills running full blast, to have half a million men near the field of battle, and this young country, so corrupt, so frightened, so sterile as to even avoid the minimum of ritual, to justify the travesty of their own self-destined downfall. If they don't have the courage of their reality to declare this war on, we should at least have the courage of our imagination to declare it over.

Everyone who comes should try to do something creative on his own, make up a few signs like "God Bless you Lyndon for Ending the War," wear clothes appropriate to the re-enactment of VE Day, wave a flag and mean it, invite a soldier along, form a brass band to play "When Johnny Comes Marching Home," bring extra noisemakers and confetti, drink beer, kiss girls, and give thanks this weekend that the war is over.

There will be songs, dancing, music, flowers, and hundreds of celebrities will be there, people like Ho Chi Minh, Betty Grable, Lyndon Johnson, Regis Toomey, and John Wayne.

The war in Vietnam is an amphetamine trip, a reflection of the spiritual disease that has gripped this country and distorted every principle on which it was built. This generation must make a choice between the total rejection of the country and the decision to regain a spiritual balance. I believe there is still something inherent in the fiber of America worth saving, and that the fortunes of the entire world may well ride on the ability of young America to face the responsibilities of an old America gone mad.

Old America has proven herself decadent enough to be willing to sacrifice one of her finest generations into the garbage truck of cold war propaganda. What kind of depths have they sunk into to dishonor the very meaning of the word "honor" by asking young men to die for nothing? This is not my America, this is not my war; if there is going to be an America, there is no war—*la guerre est finie!*

The criminal patriotism of today demands the corruption of every citizen, and now we pay the consequences—not only in the jungles of Asia, but in the materialist ravaged cities of America. Now we are the lost patrol who chase their chartered souls like old whores following tired armies.

Have you heard? The war is over!

POEMS

LOVE IS A RAINBOW
Unpublished, copyright 1965

And love is a rainbow, curving down from the sky
Falling crystals of color, shades of warm that never die!
Red melodies burning, still lead me to the night
And sing about the sights that they are sighing
Silver shadows returning, dazzle with desire
Now freezing in a fire, they are flying!

And love is a rainbow, curving down from the sky
Falling crystals of color, shades of warm that never die
Brown cascades are flowing, tinged upon your skin
Like strings of violins they are playing
Green breezes are blowing, cooling songs of tone
Now dancing in a moan as they are swaying

And love is a rainbow, curving down from the sky
Falling crystals of color, shades of warm that never die
Oh the yellow of the flowers, petals everywhere
Showing how to share the dreams of dawning
Blue fades in the hours, swallowed by the wine
To still the hands of time until the morning

And love is a rainbow, curving down from the sky
Falling crystals of color, shades of warm that never die

AND HERE COMES DAVID BLUE
Unpublished

And here comes David Blue
       Some Gal told me today
no less than nostalgically new
       Here I was treated especially well this was a grand hotel
and ofttimes disarmingly true
       oh I wish I could be her lover
and always good for a friendly fuck you
10 cents 10 cents will keep the street lights dreaming till you
               come along
but realing the second bong of the sarcastic gong
       doesn't ring as loudly yet feigning ever so proudly
it tastes like candy sweet strong and brown
       he prepares a band for the pubescent acid land
          the best of her childlike smiles
       an all star cast to avenge a Pennsylvania past
       scales for a window thief
and now his first triumphless tour for the unpoetic poor
       as old as distance is to time
Emerging from the psychedelic fog
with the thankless thoughts of the future
       I ain't crazy baby, I'm the King of Spain
the wounded words of the past
there is a house in the country I know that I will go there someday
       and the mystic music of the present
       baby I'd like to have you
scales for

THE CALIFORNIA CHRISTMAS SUN
Unpublished

The California Christmas sun
burned summer warm
the white tinsel trees
gloved seasonless cold
The bay lapped the shores
of the freeway
the speeding reindeer cars
weren't going our way
as we stood there freezing
in the frigid space
and cursed the holiday
"For Christ sakes
it's Xmas"
The naked swordsman
leaped outside his door
and looked all ways before
he crossed
he borrowed nothing from
the passers-by
but the curious + discounted
looks of the lost
The cops came with
their drugs + chains
+ saying "shoot" before we halt,
+ Santa lay there naked
in the snowless street
with his silver gift
bleeding from his hand,
+ he spoke his last
through the salt + pepper mike
for Christ sakes
it's Xmas

The bar was empty with
the coarse crowd
plunging up + down in their
seasaw celebration
kissing their corners
begging stimulation
from the draining shroud.
+ she went behind
the gas station
to piss + primp
she swallows the petrol
from the hanging pump
+ humped
+ stumbled back

CHE GUEVARA JUST CANNOT BE TRUE
Unpublished

Che Guevara just cannot be true
I've got too many other things to do
a Spanish Tyrone Power Christ
for Christ sake will you leave us
alone
there is an old

COBBWEBS
The War Is Over (songbook), 1968

The cosmetic cosmic city
crawls beneath its ashtray possibilities
the studios spread their poisoned beauty
outside the sound stages of parody
and beneath the mechanized moon
he sprawled his carnivorous cartoons
embracing the exquisite outrages
of his only and surrounding
hospitality.

Images melt into microphones
and smash their opposite mirrors
Madonnas caress their charcoal
in the future mystery marshes
begging for lover and lunatics
to count their degenerate numbers
and the passionate plastic surgeon
frantically restructures the island
as he sinks in the starlit nightmare
with all the exiles
of his quicksand.

And who will refrain from praying
in the corner coffee shop churches
after the pencils are broken
and the line
moves only
in circles.

COMING ATTRACTIONS
The War Is Over (songbook), 1968

The line goes around the corners of the corner
never was there a more respectable line
pungent professors sweet and sour students
and the porter advises
you must have a ticket to stand in this line

The fortune teller ticket seller
clears her cardboard glasses
tongues of tickets lap the pinching fingers
she never smiles back at the smiles
she only stares expressionless
at the doorman
who paces back and forth
and says
you must have a ticket to stand in this line

The bitter banter is tossed back and forth
they plot against the war
staring at each other's wives
limping thru their lives
at last a picture with a point
says the underground director
handing his sculptured friend a joint
and the constable clears his throat with wine
and says
you must have a ticket to stand in this line.

THE CRITIC
Unpublished

The critic who lies to himself
lies to the public
who believing what they read
deserve to be lied to
but what of the artist
who has carved away his lies
and lays his truth upon his wounds
open and raw
exposed for all
the critic
whose intelligence has passed
his feeling
flays the scars
most heavily
on those who have committed
the unforgivable deed
the creation beyond their
corporate conceptions.
the jealous cripple
attacks the boundless athlete
to the temporary cheers
of the almost curious spectators.

ENCORES
The War Is Over (songbook), 1968

Centuries took holidays
before these days
became desperately clear
that chariots full of Christmas cheer
could never draw the child near
but this year
one of the last remaining years
Santa Claus is a sniper
on the roof of Macy's
picking off customers
splattering packages
and miscellaneous toes
everywhere.

missionaries built millenniums
and caravans of cucumbers were exchanged
before the sin of sharing was uncovered
and the chocolate bayonets were deranged
but this year
one of the last remaining years
the soul brother reindeer
having nothing but nothing to fear
have destroyed all possessions
as the holiest of gifts.

hymns have swallowed histories
and faded into love
before a winter full of autumns
had covered up their harmonies
but this year
though one of the last remaining years
the fading matinee idol
clutching the memories
of his almost unforgettable performance
turns sadly away
from the diminishing applause
of his most terrified believers.

THE GREAT POST OFFICE ROBBERY
Unpublished (1968)

The Pasadena transvestite
works at the post office on holidays
to pay for his anti-social ways
he licks the stamps
pushing packages up ramps
sending lover's songs and chinese gongs
through the mail

Through rain and sleet and snow
he sees the seasons go
the army sends reports
on how the heroes died
the pamphleteers exhort
citizen choose a side
and his paycheck always arrives
thru the mail.

He doesn't have to work at the post office
he's been a genius for several years
and he realizes the banality of brilliance
he knows most syphilitics are prolific
he's learned it takes a week to put an hour together
so he never sighs
as he spreads the lies
thru the mail

In his previous lives
he was a knight, and before that a lady
and somewhere in the distant past
his father was hanged as a dragon
better a dragon than a dragoon
he mused, counting the confused
sealing artichokes in envelopes
thru the mail.

One day they had an investigation
on the morals of the post office
due to an anonymous letter
in effeminate handwriting
the experts could not decide if it was
a boy or a girl
so the Pasadena transvestite
spent his next vacation
in some uncivilized nation
and sent holiday greetings
a naked post card
to the head of the post office
thru the mail.

GRIFFITH
Unpublished

The officer of the confederacy
sat his southern son upon his knee
he spoke about the past
and breathed away his last
and the mystery of romance
passed into reality.

Like Asian guerrillas
the klan arose in his film
a nation was born
the theatre seats were torn
for the temporary truths
had no time for art or past reviews
thru the eyes of innocence
the guilty charge of common sense
accusing him of ignorance and worse
and forcing him to widen the scope
of his searching cinema hearse.

doves drew the emperor's chariot
to the arrow dead mountain girl
whose warning fell on frankincense
beneath the impervious lion headed columns
as the love feast of Balthazar
turned from the erotic aroma of victory
to the false nobility of suicides
while the rebel priests betrayed and prayed
on the fallen colonnades of Babylon.

Jesus outraged in his naïveté
fell upon the hypocrites
filming the carnage with his camera conscience
the accused were forced into honest action
repaying his success with the accolades of death
and immortality.
echelons of extras spat upon the star
heaping sterile hopes upon the stunt man
hurling stone and souls at their mortality.

The prince consort and the prince
play beneath the palace chairs
Catherine and the catholic lords
are plotting on the palace stairs
courtesans and cavaliers
intrigue the prince with bold affairs
the Huguenots are in the streets
they wait their turn and sell their wares
the soldiers burst upon the cobbled square
the mercenary finds the girl alone
and satisfies his loneliness
in return for royal games
the prince has given up his name
lest a massacre be judged insane.

Four lifetimes in a single stroke
three seasons settling on a strike
the caverns of the rooms are filled
by a desk, a chair, a dollar bill
the gallows wants no evidence
this time the master makes amends
and gives Lord Jim a second chance
and saves the sinking soul
surrounded by indifference.

But the heroes of the movie scales
cannot wait for epic tales
and wars to save democracy
need no reminders of infinity
and movies posing public dreams
have dared the outrage of extremes
to comment on a country's schemes

so the millionaire child
with his package of naivete
the tidal wave of timing spent
a masterpiece to save a day
bent on its own inevitable end
is crushed and marked a meddling friend
the state steals the filthy truth of art
to make its own art
and Griffith finds his true success
a fleeting moment of romance
a close-up of intolerance.

HAPPY NEW YEAR 1968
Unpublished (1968)

The year trembles and sputters and shrinks
and drops from the sky
and falls into puddles of ink and film and tape
cylinders of memory best remembered
or better dismembered
in the pools of the calendar sink.

You peel your apple thoughts
the slices pile round your slumbering boots
inside your foot is trapped in the thumbscrews of fashion
as your mind relinquishes the year
and searches for the root
of a less hesitant passion.

The anarchists charge up your spine
and borrow your brain
singing refrains
of a lost civil war
and the general
delirious with waste
lays his maps on the motel room floor
while the maid
massages his back with paste and burns his initials
into the bathroom wall.

The war crime tribunal
finds everyone guilty
especially themselves
and as they mount the suicide gallows
they drink a toast to excruciating self-honesty
and the inevitability of justice.

Not everybody was invited to last year's
living room
but certainly the opportunities and opportunists of doom
if not sliced from the social pie
will understandably be televised this year
in a helium balloon.
and a word to the wise
is sufficient surprise
if the doors ever opened
and entered your eyes.

if the disc jockeys had a choice
whether to play a church organ over the air
while swearing
or to try and save the world with John Gilbert's voice
if they had to choose which was the more daring
it would drive them to speed
or two or three nights
of the empty delights
of caring.

The coat is torn at the seams
the hopes are torn at the dreams
and 1968 finds the truck driver
ordering breaded cutlets of veal
while the revolutionaries
victorious in their zeal
find themselves still clawing to escape
all the freedoms of the bastille.

LETTERS TO THE EDITOR
Unpublished

Dear Bill Wargo
Threats of violence
like swear words
show lack of thought
and unfortunately
if this revolution has to be fought
your revolting maturity
must temporarily be sought;
so if you must, help yourself
to my rich, hot red blood
but considering Phillip Abbott Luce
and Billy Budd
please spare me my childish illusions.

THE NUDE MODEL PAINTS THE FOPPISH BOHEMIAN ARTIST
Unpublished

The nude model paints the foppish bohemian artist
the post reporter has learned
the message has been memorized and burned
the canvas has uncannily turned
he languishes on the Victorian couch
his legs seductively slouched
she captures his mysterious smile
laughter veiled in tears
she captures his sensuous style
and his scarf and his scarlet beard
his leather boots on the velvet cushions
a mirror behind his plume
and his trousers cut in the latest fashion
sucking on peppermint prunes
she stares at him like a famine
her breasts are rainbow strands
and with all the lust of a woman
she captures the beauty of man.

OLIVER BUBBLES AND HIS NOTES FROM A NEW AMERICA
Unpublished

Jack Kerouac went on the road
or at least some friends of his
the innkeeper wasn't particularly friendly
those years and something was in the
air that hadn't quite been before
but I guess it was to be expected
after the impossible defeat
of the victorious world war.

But you would have fought in the
second world war
he smiled with eisenhower kindness
tightening his leather sash
implying treason was pardonable in the present
but most unpardonable in the past.
my god what is the finalsoulution
of this freedom struggle for
if not the impossible defeat
of the victorious world war.

Hitler and Roosevelt were both clerks
in the same corporation
they chose their lot by straws
and in this case the better actor
was not judged by applause
but rather the stunned believability
of silence
what's a cast of characters
the stand-ins
the stunt men
the seconds
the musclemen in their self made
heavens

starring in the all time spectacular
the inevitable defeat
of the victorious world war.

At the medical base in Texas
or was it New Mexico
somewhere, somehow, suddenly
the war babies increased
by an unexpected number
like an undiscovered drop of oil
amid the dust of cattle
the Rio Grande sliced the
uncomfortable border
into uneven pies
but out of the state in
and into the skies
away from the insanity of the
tale and towers of Texas
under the shadow of the
deafening defeat
of the victorious world war.

the snow in New York is better
than the others
at least the photographs are better
in a country school house
surrounded by snowballs
and icy swings
and corduroy teachers
the Indians corralled in the
reservations
like prisoners of war
indeed like prisoners of war mused Oliver Bubbles
as we learned another history
and went home to a flashlight
memory of future beams

and cemeteries of submarines
couched offshore
decoding the frantic messages
of a farmer's defeat
in the victorious world war.

The soldiers returned
behind the years
of the glue factory
and nobody questioned the sigh of relief
least of all a young deserter
driving thru Gowanda snow
to see Cyrano de Bergerac
a soldier before the conflict
dream-hero of the deformed
into the popcorn factory
leaped the other other side of the sword
though I watched the German students as they dueled
in the after learning hours away from school
far from the joyful machinery
of the celebration of the defeated
in the victorious world war.

military school has more romance
than grades
dancing class
and without even the threat of
reform school
a western reminder
a beautiful bowie knife M-1
a 15 year old barrel of fun
to drill
perhaps to kill
a children foe
in the make believe valleys
of a weight-lifting bar.

and a country banjo
filled a spotless barracks
and a marching band
played the proud anthems
of the undefeated defeat of the victorious world war.

One day I heard a sound
through the invisible radio dial
it vibrated for a while
and broke thru the static
like a voice.
it must be some mistake
I've been taken before
no, it was no mistake
I heard others just like it.
it was great to stand up then
helping hands everywhere
everywhere an extended love
and public touch
and a common feel
almost unreal
ridiculous prosperity
wrapped with invisible poverty
(the privilege of property)
crawling beneath the gate
in disguises
usually showing honor
in the great defeat of the
victorious world war.

they took oaths the
journalism fraternity
by the mysterious lights of
waving candles.
there must be a citadel somewhere
where the lies don't flicker

not yet
(wake up you fool, said Oliver Bubbles)
like most satires, it was funny
only in snatches
I crawled inside the snatches to
avoid the organization
and collect a moment to breathe
but wait
if this travesty is a fraud
and Mussolini and Churchill
are both clerks in the same
corporation
that means more than one clown
will crawl thru the gears
of modern times.
a word run off by a fool
and written by a fool
without professional editing
might make a dent
in the fender of the accident
and there certainly must be more
to this glorious defeat
of the victorious world war.

The studio has built up a whole
catalogue of future stars
here they are standing on each other's shoulders
now just suppose one of our boys
is given the big part
now I mean the big part
it won't be easy for the
studio to control him
although you can rest assured
that his self direction
is somewhat limited

Hello Hello
yes you can relax now
yes it's really going to be true
this will be a chimonical charge
how many times can you come in a generation
incredible
that beautiful screen is finally out of the way
at last, at last
paradise on earth
(not so easy, not so easy, or my name isn't Oliver Bubbles)
no, oh no, impossibly, incredibly, no
I will not accept this change in the script
you see, I'm conditioned to happy endings
or at least endings
but since you insist
I cannot accept the responsibility for this
you'll pay with your truth for this
I cannot stand defeat
defeat is the one thing I cannot stand
in the defeat of the victorious world war.

A civil war
who would have guessed a civil war
though Dulles and Beria were
clerks in the same corporation
they still have the audacity
to give us sides to choose
but I can no longer choose a side
I can't even choose a choice
I'd rather hide in the coves
than surf on the waves
not many of us have avoided being
run over by cars
then again others have been run
over so many times

it is starting to feel good
rebellion is an act of faith
and faith belongs to the victors
although the victors of civil
wars can be counted on the fingers
of both hands
especially after the suicidal defeat
in the victorious world war.

I've bought everything you ever asked for
now don't you care for me
I've kissed your happy secrets
now don't you care for me
the revolt of the playback tapes
was never considered inside the laboratory
(beware of beauty, said Oliver Bubbles)
and the English returned
with their usual stylish irrelevance
and hurled marvelous insults across the sea
and Kennedy and Khrushchev are clerks
in the same corporation
he stood in the icy square
hurling boomerangs
at the taxis who would never stop
not even for an ambassador
or an outpatient
loose
in the propaganda asylum
propaganda, why don't be ridiculous
300 bureaucrats said in
quick unison
that would be against everything
we destroy for
in the preview defeat
of the victorious world war.

I've faced trainloads full of searchers
and more than one connection in my time
the devil moves in open ways
he serves syringes in silver trays
and the army of the dental school
is no one to offend
still the winters grow much colder
and the rainy seasons grow
and earthquakes hate publicity
they rarely ever show.
and what's a friend for, if not to rule.
and some said it was extra cruel to
wear binoculars at the blind school
but refugees can't be choosers
especially when they refuse to tell lies
to losers
and after seeing one too many concerts
of soldiers entertaining the civilians
I must confess
a certain nostalgia for lost regrets
and though Johnson and Ho Chi Minh
are clerks in the same corporation
and are rumored to be the best of friends
I must see China before the end
at least one time before the end
and stand in the ruins of an opium den
and dream away the defeat of the victorious world war.

ON ROBERT KENNEDY
Unpublished, June 1968

Is there a doctor for the Senator?
Move back
move back
let him have some air
he's lying there
doesn't anybody care?
Move back he can't breathe
through the curious crushing stares

Reality ripped love
off the sheltered warriors
he ruthlessly had himself shot
could it be . . . it couldn't be . . . a plot?
Shame shame shame on the shot

Death is the medal
we award
for anyone who stumbles
into life

Again and again the familiar surprise
a home grown Nobel Prize
infinite in size
familiar surprise

Ma, the late show
is re-running the
assassination
There's something unnatural in this nation
one lie covers the other until eternal damnation

The mandate is clear for a new direction

The people have made their choice
rejoice rejoice rejoice
the vacuum found a voice
the critics have sheathed their swords
a tear for the prince, not yesterday's whore
Yes, fortune has tilled the field

Only the present
is real
only in the shadow of death
is the size of the soul revealed

A life flickers in the night
a country flickers in the crime
and burns out.

POOR ZALMAN, OR THE FAILURE OF THE JEW IN AMERICAN SOCIETY
Unpublished

Poor Zalman
once a master of the pop karate
who could walk into a London club
and command the attention of hair dressers and agents
whose picture hung in private pubs
it is said he even experimented with drugs
but this was before the rains came
exposed on a Canadian triple agent

Poor Zalman
the potential Charlie Chaplin of a pop nation
a comedian to his bones
who once had the charisma of a Brian Jones
(now on probation)
whose guitar embellished the wine maker's songs
comedians weren't made to stand the test of right or wrong

Poor Zalman
who tries the comeback of the hunchback
and runs the gauntlet of degenerate moralists
the burlesque magician who grins insanely back at an insane world
who faces charges of treason with a comic bow
oh turn away turn away from this buffoon
yes he's not where it's at
for what can you expect
from the strongest and yet the weakest
of the spoons of spoonful flat.

TALKING CHICAGO JAIL BLUES
Unpublished

1

It happened not too long ago,
I decided to take a trip to Chicago;
I got to Lincoln Park on a Monday afternoon,
And stayed there with the Yippies by the light of the moon.
We did not care at all for the Democratic Convention,
We rather took a taste of American Revolution.

2

On Tuesday night we sat at the "Coliseum,"
They were having some folk-music down there in the auditorium,
Poetry, speeches, rock and roll demonstrations,
Lectures on revolutionary decentralization.
Phil Ochs came to sing: "I declare the war is over,"
In fact the war was starting in town at the Amphitheatre.

3

A few hours later we were back sitting in the Park,
When we heard students make some terrific remarks:
"The pigs are around," said the Yippies, blowing their tops,
"Pigs" being used as the new word to name the cops.
Actually they tear-gassed and beat us with great brutality,
Showing us Mayor Daley's typical hospitality!
I was amazed . . .
But a girlfriend of mine was maced . . .

4

"There has been no proof of police brutality" said R. Daley,
And CBS-News re-broadcast the statement daily,
While reporters, delegates were wounded—Come what may!
Seems like they've heard about Grimaud and the old Parisian way
And, as I was quietly walking on Michigan Avenue, I was arrested:
They said: "You don't have the press-card that your job requested."

5

OK, so we were imprisoned on Wednesday evening,

They took three pictures of each prisoner along with some fingerprinting.

I could not say a thing, nor ask any question. I was feeling kind of homesick,

Although the crowd was *not* asking for more . . .

After an hour's sleep we were hungry and began to roar.

A cop brought us some pig-sandwich, piss-coffee . . . and no toothpicks!

6

Later on, they took us down . . . to a place by the river;

I thought that the experience was over.

But no luck! Uptown in a truck we were driving

With only twelve seats for thirty-eight prisoners, doing some hard traveling . . .

"What kind of a house is this?" I started to wail,

"It's not a house" said an officer; "It's not a house, it's a jail!"

7

At last we were released, by paying a fifty-dollar bond;

I was lucky to find the money . . . Now here comes why I wrote this song:

The highway from Paris to Prague has a branch to Chicago,

That's what I learned in jail just a few weeks ago.

And, while leaving Illinois, I looked at Michigan Lake

And I started singing: "This lake is your lake . . ."

THE TORTURE GARDEN
OR, MUSIC, LOVE, & FLOWERS
Dare 6 no. 2 (1968)

You've seen the artist at work; now you can watch him at his leisure
No, there must be some mistake, I've only come to deliver the
carnival
No, there's no mistake. You and the other deserters are only out for
personal pleasure
farewell you fiend, he gasped leaning on the turntable
and his body was found
33 inches under the ground
under the underground of the torture garden.

The banana police have surrounded the monastery
come out with your legs crossed they shout thru the petal splitting
speakers
the high appeals have found you guilty of sobriety
so take off your purple robes and hang up your silken speakers
and before they could say hare krishna
they were discharged and drowned
in the underground nightmare nozzles
of the torture garden.

The night watchman jealously guards every day as a vacation
he pretends not to notice the foliage that falls from the track of
the greenhouse train
he has a fetish for turtles who help him guard the station
and he had no choice when one was swept under the barbed wire drain
breaking all the rules he dug his way under the roots of the wall
and was never again seen
though someone heard a scream
almost inhuman
in the echoes of the underground of the torture garden.

The democratic salesmen have taken out a billboard on the strip
warning the passing motorists not to stop for the traffic whistles
and three airliners have crashed, their engines gutted with bunches of
tulips
the Laurel canyon forest fire apparently was caused by guided missiles
every unimportant figure has recently sustained an accident
and the fertilizer crew
has had an epidemic of flu
while working double time in the underground of the torture garden.

The rebels and anarchists are publicized by *Time* magazine
their impossible pictures are splashed on the sand of their target's
breakfast tables
something must be done, why don't they call out the marines
and gurgling cologne in the bathroom they complain the states are unstable
a concentration camp would be much too camp
the candidates from both parties agree
the two party system is what makes this country free
broadcast live from the ballroom of the underground
of the torture garden.

the city rises uncomfortably in the concrete morning
the commuters cough and cancer and stumble in the sniper snow
oh my god, oh my god, oh my god haven't we had enough warning
type the tomahawk typewriters while quoting Thoreau
the candy sweet aroma exhausts the air-conditioned air
and every hour on the half-hour
the recorded voice repeats
for Christs sakes
will you or will you not take this flower
freshly grown
in the ground of the underground
of the torture garden.

THE UNDERWATER SCHOOLROOM IS FOND OF FIRE
Unpublished

The underwater schoolroom is fond of fire
where the harem veils have taught them desire
and their hands are raised for rainbows
upon the latest line
for the murder of a mind

The leather jacket lecture is praise the lord
he draws a loaded pistol on the blackboard
then they shoot him in the shoulders
and promise not to tell
they learn their lessons well

and you get the girl and the good times.

VIRTUE
Unpublished

I was never close to the corporation
who hatched me
in technical packages
and dropped me into
the frying pan
of a technical public.
there were men there
who were not so much evil as old.
and set in their crusted alcoholic ways
there were men there
who were not so much stupid as cold
who took to a machine like a bolt
rather than a lever.

Like an insensitive shell-less snail
I accepted their shell
and they loved me publicly and privately
pinching praises on their debutant
they announced me to the world
like patrons in invisible courts
though affairs are known to be short
and is there another word
for love that can only dominate?

But I would be an ingrate
to see only the sides of my side
did I not insult my better
men with long experience in the trade
oh I would have insulted them more
if I was not so much afraid
and in this tarnished twentieth century
you cannot face the Romans without a chariot
you cannot face the romantics without charity

and who is not grateful to be published
and publicized in a public age?

The years of a marriage
are not counted in days
the horse on the carriage can be beaten
in various ways
but I was young and I was hungry
and being myself I can look back
and be excused
they were not so young
but they were hungrier
and a master of motives
looks easily confused
the army of reformers
never quite expects to lose
the successful saboteur is subtle
the cork is not part of the bottle
it is only there to be corkscrewed away
before the pouring.

A contract between ambitions dies too soon
the dust had yet to settle on the choice
between buffoons
who would be the first to lunge at a ladder
among tall buildings
but we believe in you
you must remember that
and though the offer may be small
the choice is in your hands
there are opportunities at every hand
God help you if you fall.

The reasons for leaving
could never be explained
the limpid bravely walking away from the lame

and several castles crumbled
in the process of the game
but the network has its systems
and the poison can be spread
naively stumbling into talks
with partners of the dead
how much are you worth
ask the cunning crippled kings?
and I crawled beneath the criminals
to find a place to sing.
and I'd crawl beneath the animals
to find a place to sing.

My back against the background
and wondering where to turn
when the phone rang in the darkness
there was so much more to learn
a familiar voice a friendly voice
with compassion fully felt
we still believe in you
if there's anything we can do to help . . .
and by the way we are about to release some old tapes
we need to know who owns the songs
by the way can you help us in the rape?
but these were not recordings
not even finished songs
to release them now or anytime
would poison even friends
but we believe in you
he said again
a dagger dangling from his jaws
an artist doesn't own his work
we're a country built on laws
if you care to talk to us again
my lawyer will be there

you remember he was your lawyer
who gave you help before

Many lawyers later
many angry crops
the magazines that cover the scene
have hardly scratched the top
and we found our separate times
and filled our separate ambitions
good luck to those who stayed behind
among the taller buildings
and what am I to think
of the new familiar friends
who blew my trumpets to the world
travel with the trends
and what am I to think about
of all the years that slipped
and the only word for memories is hypocrite
is there another word, no the only word
the only word is hypocrite.
for those who raise you when you're rising
and damn you when you're down
caress you when they're with you
and curse you when you're gone
whose love is but possession
and possession is a sin
after all it was a business
not a singer not a song
still I'd crawl beneath the devil
to find a place to sing.

WHO WAS THAT MAN IN THE GOLD LAMÉ SUIT
Unpublished

You've seen the artist at his work
But never watched him at his insanity,
His only true escape is the house of cinematic sequels
The boy is young and wants only to be a star,
but that right is only reserved for worthy auctioneers,
But dares dreaming desperate dreams
of answers which lie inches above paranoia's pillow
and experiments with frozen feelings from frigid beds
while visions of mutant mice crawl through his diluted head
For morning brings piles of pencils dripping on to
unwilling paper
whose words almost never get a kind word.
Creating his greatest works partially relieves
the metal cancer which is always fatal
He senses the sounds of sorry rejection from the
Kingdoms obstacle objects
only to be haunted by the desire to be his poet brother
The minstrel then painfully exits laughing and dying
wearing the costume of his earlier prophets
and alcoholically rushes to scream at the faded image
in the carnival mirror
For who would dare appreciate the truth
from a non-commercial disbeliever.

I WILL NOT HURT YOU
Unpublished, copyright 1968

The rain comes down on the ravaged town,
and drizzles through the wind from the skinless sky,
to the sweating skin of the people in the square,
lying naked there, giggling on the ground,
and they're making love and they're making sounds.
Down the street comes the tapping beat of a cane on the cobblestones.
It's a strange old man and he's all alone.
The crystal cane cracks up the game and slaps them from their sleep.
Through the panting rage, he begins to speak.

Although I may not return all the passion that your little hearts desire.
I will be kind to you.
I will not hurt you, hurt you, hurt you, come to me.

The mad marquee explodes with glee outside of the city hall
with a satin flag hanging on the wall
the lions' loins on the jangling coins are dribbling from their chins
and naked angels tattooed on their skin
green with greed the bandits bleed their pockets packed with gold
and the boys are bought and the girls are sold
the sudden shock the strangers knock they dive beneath the desk
and a gentle voice clutches to their chest.

The howling whores dance by the doors and sparkle thru the streets
good evening sir would you like a treat
perfumed priests and scarlet beasts with velvet on their gloves
and a taste of god and a taste of love
come take your pick they know the tricks there's a fire in her face
for peace of mind and a state of grace
desire drums the soul succumbs and when he's allowed to leave
a tender hand taps his soaking sleeve.

The silver screen is never mean it treats you like a king
and you feel so good that your silence sings
movie stars and bourbon bars are waiting to be served
to pacify all your trembling nerves
Persian rugs and popcorn drugs intensify the scenes and they
come together in their wildest dreams
lost in prayer the floodlights glare the zippers start to fly
and they can't escape the courageous cry.

The laws of lust have had enough they must be left alone
and their patience snaps like a broken bone
against the wall his trousers fall everybody takes a turn
and the church bells ring and the incense burns
he crawls away a ghost in gray he's staring at the light
and the noise returns to the dancing night
the naked moon shines on his wounds as he smiles thru the pane
with his broken hand on his broken cane.

OUT OF THE ARCHIVES (POEMS)

And here comes David Blue

    Some Gal told me today

no less than nostaligically new

    Here I was treated especially well this was a grand hotel
       disarmingly
and ofttimes tenderly true

    oh I wish I could be her lover

and always good for a friendly fuck you

10 cents   lo cents will keep the strret lights dreaming till you

      come along

but realing the second bong of the the sarcastic gpmg

    doesn't ring as loudly yetfeigning ever as proudly

it tastes like candy sweet strong and brown

    he prepares a band for the pubescent acid land

      the best of her chillike smiles

    an all star cast to avenbe a Pennsylvania past

    scales for a window thief

  and now his first triumphless tour for the unpoetic poor

    as old as distance is to time

to synchronize their souls David Blue and the American Patrol

   Emerging from the psychelelic fog
to mount them and then some

with the thankless thoughts of the future

    I ain't crazy baby I'm the King of Spain 95

the wounded words of the past

there is a house in the country I know that I will go there someday

    and the mystic music of the present

this is a midnight dance done on a Persian rug.

   Scales baby I'd like to have you
   for a

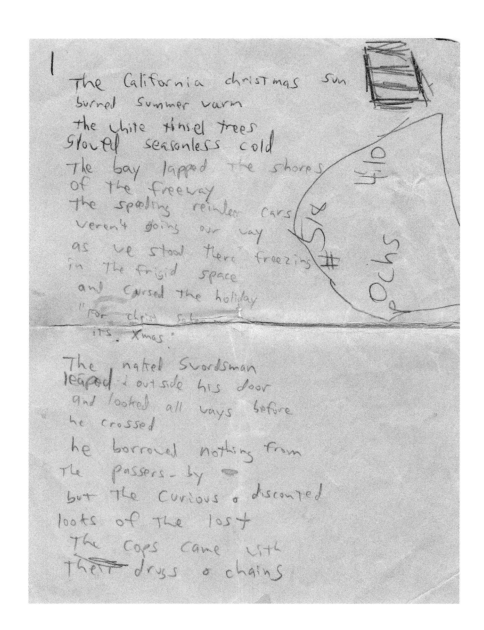

1

The California christmas sun
burned summer warm
the white tinsel trees
glowed seasonless cold
The bay lapped the shores
of the freeway
The speeding reindeer cars
weren't going our way
as we stood there freezing
in the frigid space
and cursed the holiday
"for christ sake
its Xmas"

The naked Swordsman
leaped outside his door
and looked all ways before
he crossed
he borrowed nothing from
The passers-by
but the curious & disconted
looks of the lost
The cops came with
their drugs & chains

& saying "shoot" before we halt.
& Santa lay there naked
in the snowless street
with his silver gift
bleeding from his hand,
& he spoke his last
Through the salt & pepper mite
For christ sakes
it's   Xmas

The   bar was empty with
the cancer crowd
plunging up & down in their
seasaw celebration
kissing their corners
& begging stimulation
from The draining shroud.
& she went behind
  the gas station
  to piss & primp
she swallows the petrol
from The hanging pump
  & humped
  & stumbled back

The critic

The critic who lies to himself
lies to the public
who believing what they read
deserve to be lied to
but what of the artist
who has carved away his lies
and lays his truth upon his wonnds
open and raw
exposed for all
the critic
whose intelligence has passed
his feeling
flays the scars
most heavily
on those who have committed
the unforgivable ~~deed~~ *deed*
the creation ~~beyond their~~ ~~~~ Corporate
~~~~ conceptions.
the jealous ~~critic~~ cripple
attacks the boundless athlete
to the temporary cheers
of the ~~~~ almost curious
                          spectators.

his
Oliver Bubbles and Notes from a new America

Jack Kerouac went on the road
or at least some friends of his
the innkeeper wasN't particualirly friendly
those years and something was is the
air that hadn't quite been before
but I guess it was to be expected
after the impossible defeat
of the victorious world war.

But you would have fought in the
second world war
he smiled with eisenhower kindness
tightening his leather sash
implying treason was pardonable in the present
but most unpardonable in the past.
my god whah is the finalsoulution
of thes freedom struggle for
if not the imppssible defeat
of the victorious world war.

Hitler and Roosevelt were both clerks
in the same corportation
they chose their lot by straws
and in this case the better actor
was not judged by applaude
but rather the stunned believability
of silence
what a cast of characters
the stand-ins
the stunt men
the seconds musclemen
the churthe musclemen in their self made
heavens
starring in the all time spectacular
the inevitable defeat
of the victorious world war.

At the medical base in Texas
or was it New Mexico
somewhere, somehow, suddenly
the war babies increased
by an unexpected number
like an undiscovered drop of oil
amid the dust of cattle
the Rio Grande sliced the
uncomfor talbe border
into uneven pies
but out of the state in
and into the skies
away from the insanity of the
tale o towers of Texas
under the shadow of the
deafening defeat
of the victorious world war.

2-

the snow in New York is better
than the others
at least the photographs are better
in a country school house
surrounded by snowballs
and icy swings
and cuordurcy teachers
the indians corraled in the
reservations
like prisoners of war   *nisel Oliver Bubbles*
indeed like prisoners of war
as we learned another history
and wnet home to a flashlight
memory of future beams
and cemetaries of submarines
couched offshore
decoding the frantic messages
of a farmer's defeat
in the victorious world war.

The soldiers returned
 behind the years
of the glue factory
and nobody questioned th sigh of relief
least of all a young deserter
driving thru Gowanda snow
to see Cyrano De Bergerac
a soldefer before the conflict
dream-hero of the deformed
into the popcorn factory
leaped the other other side of the sword
though I watched the German students as they dueled
in the after learning hours away form school
far from the joyfuo machinery
of the celebration of the defeated
in the victorious world war.

military school has more romance
than grades
~~or education~~ *dancing class*
and without even the threat of
reform school
a western reminder
a beautiful bowie kniefe M-1
a 15 year old barrel of fun
to drill
perhaps to kill
a children foe
in the make believe valleys
of a weightlifting bar.
and a country banjo
filled a spotless barracks
and a marching band
played the proud anthems
of the undefeated defeat of the victorious world war.

-3-

One day I heard a sound
throught the invisiible rdaio dial
it vibrated for a while
and broke thru the static
like a voice.
it must be some mistke
I've been taken before
no, it was no mistake
I heard other's just like it.
it was great to stand up then
helping hands everywhere
everywhere an extended love
and public touch
and a common feel
almost unreal
ridiculous prosperity
wrapped with invisible poverty   (the proveles of
crawling beneath the gate   property)
in disguises
usually showing honor
in the great defeat of the
victorious world war.

they took oaths the
journalism fraternity
by the mysterious lights of
waving candles.
there must be a citadel Somewher
where the lies don't flicker
not yet
(wake up you fool, said Oliver Bubbles)
like most satires, it was funny
only in snatches
I crawled inside the snatches to
avoid the organization
and collect a moment to breathe
but wait
if this travesty is a fraud
and Mussolini and Churchill
are both clerks in the smae
corporation
that means M re than one clown
will crawl thru the gears
of modern times.
a word run off by a fool
and written by a fool
withoug professional editing
might make a dent
in the fender of the accident
and thére certainly must be more
to this glorious defeat
of the victorious world war.

The studio has built up a whole
catalgue of future stars
here they are standing on each other's shoulders

-4-

now just suppose one of our boys
is given the big part
now I mean the big part
it won't be easy for the
studio to control him
although you can rest assured
that his self direction
 is somewhat limitied
Hello Hello
yes you can r-slax now
yes its really going to -be true
this will be a chimonical charge
how many times can you come in a generation
incredible beautiful
that lousy screen is finally out of the way
at last , at last
paradise on earth
(not so easy, not so easy, or my name isn't Oliver Bubbles)
no, oh no, impossibly, incredibly, no
I will not accept this change in the script
you see, I'm conditioned to happy endings
or at least endings
bu since you insist
I cannot accept the responsibiltiy for this
and Dulles you'll pay with your truth for this
I cannot stand defeat
defeat is the one thing I cannot stand
in the defeat of the victorious world war.

A civil war
who would have guessed a civil war
though Dulles and Beria were
clerks in the same corporation
they still have the audacity
to give us sides to choose
but I can no longer choose a side
I can't even choose a choice
I'd rather hide in the coves
than surf on the waves
not many of us have avoided being
run over by the cars
then again others have been run
over so many times
it is starting to feel good
rebellion is an act of faith
and faith belongs to the victors
although the victors of civil
wars can be counted on the fingers
of both hands
especially after the suicidal defeat
in the victorious world war.

-5-

I've bought everything you ever asked for
now don't you care for me happy
I've kissed your inside secrets
now don't you care for me
the revolt of the playback tapes
was never considered inside the laboratory
and th3 English returned   (look out beware of Beauty)
with their usual stylish irrelevance   Said Oliver Bubbles)
and hurled beautiful insults across the sea
and Kennedy and Khrushev are clerks   marvelous
in the same corporation
he stood in the ioy square
hurling boomerangs
at the taxis who would never stop
not even for an ambassador
or an outpatient
loose
in the propaganda asylum
propaganda, why don't be redilous
300 besurocrats said in
quick unison
that wo uld be against everything
we destroy for
in the preview defeat
of the victorious world war.

I've faced trainloads full of searchers
and more than one connection in my time
the devil moves in open ways
he serves the ons wars in silver trays
and the army of the dental school   syringes
is nn one to offend
still the winters grow much colder
and the rainy seasons grow
and earthquakes hate publicity
they rarely ever show.
and what's a friend for, if not to rule.
and some said it was extra cruel to
wear binoculars at the blind shhool
but refugees can't be choosers
especially when they refuse to tell lies
to   losers
and after seeing one too many concerts
of soldiers entertaining the civilians
I must confess
a certain nostalgia for lost regrets
and though Johnson and Ho chi minh
are clerks in the same corportation
and are rumored to be the best of friends
I must see China before the end
at least one time before the end
and stand in the ruins of an opium den
and dream away the defeat of the victorious world war.

on Robert Kennedy

Is there a doctor for
~~the~~ senator? move Back
~~Get it back~~ move back
let him have some air
he's lying there
doesn't anybody care?
~~think but for~~
Move back he can't breathe ~~they curious~~
Reality ~~ripped~~ love the
off the sheltered warriors ~~crushing~~ stores
he ruthlessly had himself shot
could it be ... it couldn't be ... a plot
Shame shame shame on the shot
~~but you know that the~~
~~it was hardly surprising~~

Death is the medal
we award
for anyone who stumbles
into love

Again & Again the familiar surprise

A home grown Nobel prize
infinite in size
~~the~~ ~~you~~ ~~sure~~ ~~you~~
~~here~~ ~~surprised~~ familiar surprise

There's
Ma, the late show somethin
is ~~recurring~~ the unnatural
assassination,
~~some~~
~~almost~~ ~~makes~~ ~~you~~
~~about~~ ~~this nation~~ in this nation
one lie covers the other until eternal
damnation
The mandate is clear
for a new direction

The People have made their
choice
rejoice rejoice rejoice
thus the Vacuum found a
voice

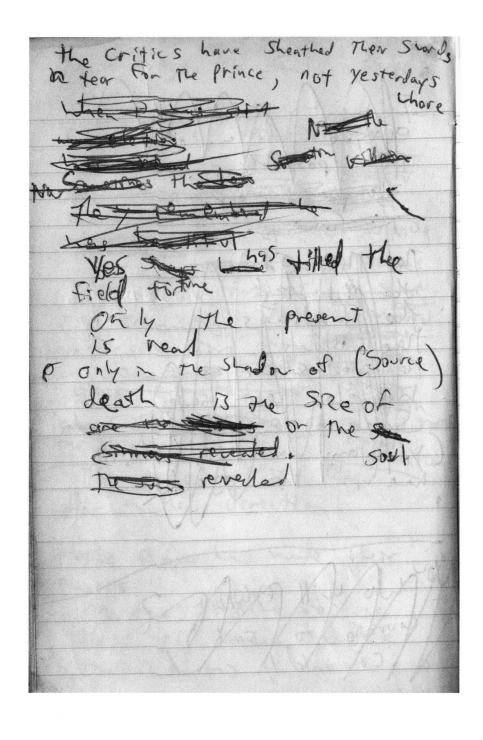

the critics have sheathed their swords
in fear for the prince, not yesterdays
                                                                      whore

~~When~~ ~~the~~ ~~etc~~
~~told the lies~~   ~~N~~ ~~the~~
~~the~~ ~~and~~   ~~South~~ ~~killers~~
~~No~~ ~~Sweeties~~ ~~the~~ ~~bees~~
~~they~~ ~~remembered~~ ~~the~~
~~were~~ ~~beautiful~~

Yes ~~she~~ ~~has~~ has tilled thee
field future
Only   the   present
is   real
p only in the shadow of (Source)
death   is the sire of
~~one~~ ~~the~~ ~~teens~~   on the ~~so~~
~~Sinner~~ ~~revealed~~.   soul
~~the soul~~ revealed

Please lower your trays
for meals
be like so many to serve

A lite flickers in the night
a country flickers in the past
and burns out. crime

Poor Zalman
--Poor Zlman or the Failure of the Jew in

American Society

Poor ~~Zalman~~ Zalman

once a master of the pop karate

who could walk into a London club

and command the attention of hair dressers and agents

whose picture hung in private pubs

it is said he even experimented with drugs

but tha was before the rains came

~~and felt~~ exposed on a Canadian triple agent

Poor Zalman

the petentail Chrlie Chaplin of a pop nation

a comedian to his bones

who onde had the charisma of a Brian Jones

(now on probation)

~~whose guitar embellished~~ the wine makesrs songs

comedians weren't made to stand the tsst of right or wrong

Poor Zalman

who tries the comback of the hunchback

and runs the gauntlet of degenerate moralists

the burlesque musician who grins insanely back at an insane world

who faces charges of treason with a comic bow
                                    oh   turn away
~~so spare yourself the agony of these grooves~~ ~~so~~ turn away, from this buffoon

~~for thats~~ yes he is not where it's at

for what can you expect

from the strongest and yet the weakest

of the ~~spoons~~ of spoonful flat.
        spoons

"The Torture Garden"   Written by Phil Ochs
                                              Copyright 1968 by
                                              Barricade Music, Inc.

You've seen the artist at work; now you can watch him at his leisure
No, there must be some mistake, I've only come here to deliver the
carnival
No, there's no mistake. You and the other deserters are only out for
personal pleasure
farewell you fiend, he gasped leaping on the turntable
and his body was found
39 inches under the ground
under the underground of the torture garden.

33 1/3

The banana police have surrounded the monastery
come out with you legs crossed they shout thru the petal splitting
speakers
the high appeals have found you guilty of sobriety   *wretched*   *sneakers*
so take off your purple robes and hang up your silken speakers
and before they could say hare krishna
they were discharged and drowned
in the underground nightmare nozzles
of the torture garden.

The night watchman jealously guards every day as a vacation
he pretends not to notice the foliage that falls from the track of
the greenhouse train
he has a fetish for turtles who help him guard the station
and he had no choice when one was swept under the barbed wire drain
breaking all the rules he dug his way under the roots of the wall
and was never again seen
though someone heard a scream
almost inhuman
in the echoes of the underground of the torture garden.

winter whistles

The democratic salesmen have taken out a billboard on the strip
Pacifying warning the passing motorists not to stop for the music whistles
and three airlines have crashed, their engines gutted with bunches of
tulips
The Laurel Canyon forest fire apparently was caused by guided missiles
every unimportant figure has recently sustained an accident
and the fertilizer crew
has had an epidemic of flu
while working double time in the underground of the torture garden.

-2-

The rebels and anarchists are publicized by Time Magazine
their impossible pictures are splashed on the sand of their target's
breakfast tables
something must be done, why don't they call out the Marines
and gurgling cologne in the bathroom they complain the states are unstable
a concentration camp would be too much camp
the candidates from both parties agree   *starts*
the two party system is what makes this country free
broadcast live from the ballroom of the underground
of the torture garden.

                    ravaged
the city rises ~~uncomfortably~~ in the concrete morning   ~~~~ *manchewick*   *they rub chemicals*
~~the commuters cough and cancer and stumble in the sniper snow~~   *on their skin*
oh my god, oh my god, oh my god haven't we had enough warning   *heavens of a*
type the tomahawk typewriters while quoting Thoreau   *healthy*
the candy sweet aroma exhausts the air-conditioned air   *slow*
and every hour on the half-hour
the recorded voice repeats
for Christs sakes
will you or will you not take this flower
freshly grown
in the ground of the underground
of the torture garden.

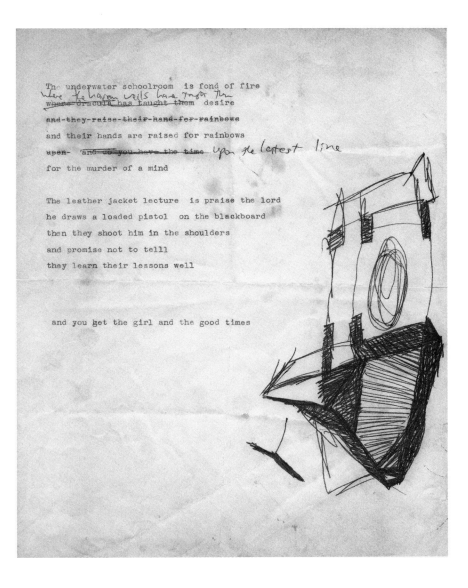

The underwater schoolroom is fond of fire
where the haven veils have taught them
where Dracula has taught them desire

and they raise their hand for rainbows

and their hands are raised for rainbows

upon- and do you have the time upon the latest line

for the murder of a mind

The leather jacket lecture is praise the lord

he draws a loaded pistol on the blackboard

then they shoot him in the shoulders

and promise not to telll

they learn their lessons well

  and you get the girl and the good times

Virtue

I was never close to the corporation
who hatched me
in technical pagkages
and dropped me into
the frying pan
of a technical public.
There were men there was were
who were not so much evil as old.
and set in their crusted alcoholic ways
there were men there
who were not so much stupid as cold
who took to a machine like a bolt
rather than a lever.

Like an insensitive shelless snail
I accepted their shell
and they loved me publicly and privately
pinching praises on their debutant
they announced me to the world
like patrons in invisible courts
though affairs are known to be short
and is there another word
for love than can only dominate?

But I would be an ingrate
to see only the sides of my side
did I not insult my better
  men with long experience in the trade
oh I would have insulted them more
if I was not so much afraid
and in this tarnished twentieth century
you cannot face the Romans without a chariot
you cannot face the romantics without charity
and who is not grateful to be published
and publicized in a public age?

The years of a marriage
are not counted in days
the horse on the carriage can be beaten
in various ways
but I was young and I was hungry
and being myself I can look back
and be excused
they were not so young
but they were hungrier
and a master of motives
looks easily confused
the army of reformers
never quite expects to lose
the successful saboteur is subtle
the cork is not part of the bottle
it is only there to be corkscrewed away
before the pouring.

A contract between ambitions dies too soon
the dust had yet to settle on the choice
between buffoons
who would be the first to lunge at a ladder
among tall buildings
but we believe in you
you must remember that
and though the offer may be small
the choice is in your hands
there are opportunities at every hand
God help you if you fall.

The reasons for leaving
could never be explained
the limpid bravely walking away from the lame
and several castles crumbled
in the process of the game
but the network has its systems
and the poison can be spread
naively stumbling into talks
with partners of the dead
how much are you worth
ask the cunning drippled kings?
and I crawled beneath the criminals
to find a place to sing.
and I'd crawl beneath the animals
to find a place to sing.

My back against the background
and wondering where to turn
when the phone rang in the darkness
there was so much more to learn
a familiar voice a friendly voice
with compassion fully felt
we still believe in you
if there's anything we can do to help....
and by the way we are about to release some old tapes
we need to know who owns the songs
by the way can you help us in the rape?
but these were not recordings
not even finished songs
to release them now or anytime
would poison even friends
but we believe in you
he said again
a dagger dangling from his jaws
an artist doesn't own his work
we're a country built on laws
if you care to talk to us again
my lawyer will be there
you remember he was your lawyer
who gave you help before

Many lawyers later
many angry cross
the magazines that cover the scene
have hardly scratched the top

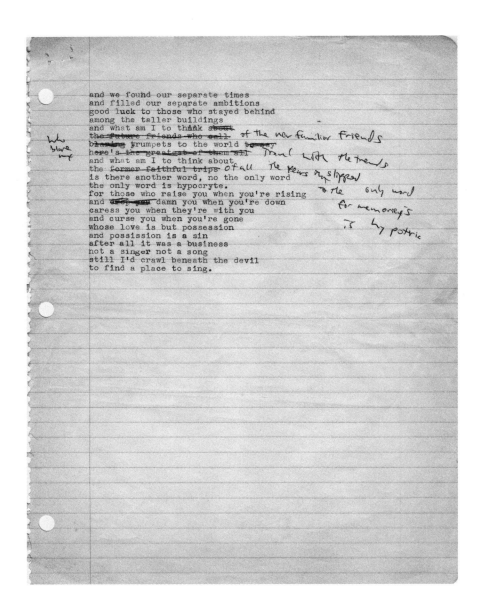

```
and we found our separate times
and filled our separate ambitions
good luck to those who stayed behind
among the taller buildings
and what am I to think about
the future friends who call      of the new familiar friends
blazing trumpets to the world to say
here's the greatest of them all   travel with the trends
and what am I to think about,
the former faithful trips  of all the years my slipped
is there another word, no the only word
the only word is hypocryte.                to the  only word
for those who raise you when you're rising
and drop you damn you when you're down      for memory's
caress you when they're with you
and curse you when you're gone                .s  by patric
whose love is but possession
and possission is a sin
after all it was a business
not a singer not a song
still I'd crawl beneath the devil
to find a place to sing.
```

who blure my

LOS ANGELES

PHIL OCHS DISCUSSES POLITICS OF SONGWRITING
Kablegram 41 no. 4 (15 December 1967)

Of course, any entertainer should say exactly what's on his mind, whether he be a singer, dancer, or senator. Like any enclosure, the mind has to be aired out once in a while—if thoughts are confined or repressed for too long, they will only go stale and hinder the birth of new thoughts.

An entertainer earns his public position by wit, charm, talent, or connections and if he feels strongly enough about a particular issue, he should apply his abilities at tasteful opportunities. If he is correct, he will have been a catalyst to the further-ance of something important; if he turns out to have been wrong, he will have to suffer the intellectual consequences and if his talent comes out unscathed, he should emerge somewhat wiser while having the issue in point discussed and perhaps clari-fied further.

I think this is true especially for a performer like myself who is essentially a writ-er who has built his political and social thoughts into the foundation of his pattern of writing.

In 1961 I was inspired to write my first song in response to the controversy over the Cuban invasion. No artist is ever completely separated from the political and so-cial currents of his time and if he is, he is avoiding a certain amount of responsibility to his public, his character, and his art.

My opinions have been tied up with my career since the beginning, so there was never any question about my speaking about issues on the side, since I do it quite blatantly on the stage. I am more than glad that the Beatles have chosen to point out their feeling on war, drugs, and the current madness of the world rather than accept the banal stance of many of their contemporaries.

I believe it becomes more and more apparent with each passing year that American politics is closely related to show business. This apathetic public is specta-tor trained and as time goes on, they will be bombarded with opinions from more diverse and surprising sources. Shirley Temple lives! As the arts gain maturity in this relatively young nation, they will inevitably reflect all areas of national life.

I have always been a believer in the art form of social realism which can reflect and comment upon current events and will inevitably affect the mentality of the more open and intelligent masses. The insight of the artist is of great value to any culture, especially one so uncultured as ours.

For example, a movie like *The Battle of Algiers* by Pontecorvo is of great benefit in helping the masses' understanding of emerging and revolutionary countries, the rationale of terrorism, indeed the grassroots of the cold war and our present conflict with China. We are supposed to be a democracy, but our mass media has been almost criminal in neglecting the real controversies of our time, preferring instead a mundane sort of pap which ultimately is more dangerous than any opinion because it only serves to stifle thought. In the atomic age, the last thing we can afford is a powerful, thoughtless, and sheeplike "democracy."

I believe I have not only the right but the responsibility to say what I am thinking as a public performer. The bankruptcy of the level of national discussion demands intelligent comment and if the mainstream power structure avoids their responsibilities, others must take it upon themselves. The bad theatre of Lyndon Johnson is a large spur to this train of thought.

The artist is first and foremost the reflection of his times, and his ability to stay a few steps ahead of the rest of the society is his contribution to his society. As technology moves us closer together, increasing and crowding our complexities, the arts will play a larger role in improving our communication and understanding. The human race is, after all, the longest running series with the highest ratings.

PLEASURES OF THE HARBOR (LINER NOTES)
A&M (1967)

I've been away for a while but I hope to be back again soon.
I'll return with a tune to show all was not lost on the naked moors.
From the razor's edge of a Louvre of loveless beds a tone tossed across
an ocean of seas, pass the body please.

Some might mistake it for a coin it sparkles so over the waterless waves.
Others might suspect a falcon to attack their own flagellant flying saucers.
Now who would be that depraved certainly not the children of Chaucer's.
But it's only a filament of fantasy diffused through the stained glass
window of the haunted whorehouse
the last desperate laugh of a fool's passion
to say I have been faithful to thee Cynara in my fashion.

And a toast to the pretender who dove between kegs of cognac
and floundered on the floor to be stabbed in the neck by straws
once upon a time we lived by laws.

From the pubs of London to the Hills of Edinburgh a jealous journey
on the ecstasy side of tragedy. I watched my life fade-away in a flash
a quarter of a century dash through closets full of candles with never a room
for rapture though a kingdom had been captured.

And so I turn away from my drizzling furniture and pass old ladies
sniffling by movie stars' tombs, yes I must be home again soon.

To face the unspoken unguarded thoughts of habitual hearts
a vanguard of electricians a village full of tarts
who say you must protest you must protest
it is your diamond duty
ah but in such an ugly time the true protest is beauty

And the bleeding seer crawled from the ruins of the empire
and stood bleeding, bleeding on the border
he said, passion has led to chaos and now chaos will lead to order
Oh I have been away for a while and I hope to be back again soon.

JAMES DEAN LIVES IN INDIANA
Village Voice (9 May 1968)

Hubert Humphrey is a disgrace to his party and his country. If he bargains his way into the Democratic nomination, that will be the final moral death of that crusted party, the last questionable cause of old men.

These last years, propelled by an ambitious and amoral exuberance, Humphrey has provided a classic public example of one of America's greatest talents—ripping out the hearts of once good men. The Stevenson syndrome, an exhibition of formerly honest men parading naked in their lies. Perhaps a conscience transplant.

To me the war is a symbol of the disease which has gripped America, Americanism. The love of a country mistaken for sterility. The real traitors are clearly defined. You can find them leading Indiana farm boys into American Legion halls, grinding James Deans into Chuck Robbs.

They advertise themselves as the National Rifle Association, clutching their guns like nipples, hiding behind the Constitution and assassinating those who dare to live the real Constitution. The owners of the local newspapers, the owners of the thought control tv stations, of the oil, yes of the blood-sucking oil towers of Texas. Can it be it is all the owners, that Marx was right? Or is it possible we are flying through a thunderstorm of corruption, seemingly endless but perhaps bounded by sunlight if we knew the way or if we found a better pilot?

Nineteen sixty-eight is the year of the revolution. It is this year that America will start to demilitarize herself. It is this year, in the morality of survival, we will come face to face with the racial crisis.

But perhaps it can also be the year that the dehumanized machine can pull back the Mace and club, maniac police forces who are rapidly becoming the largest criminal element in the nation. Perhaps in 1968 the American people can stop the Justice Department from keeping Jim Garrison from trial (if the truth be known, Garrison might be the best candidate, being the only completely and publicly honest elected official in America).

This year could be a creation of a free network paid for by public funds to allow a dialogue (with Independent films) that would really be effective in blocking future Vietnams.

I sang in Indiana for Eugene McCarthy (Love me I'm a Liberal?), although my first instinct was for Kennedy, even after New Hampshire. It isn't easy to drag my guitar past the sensual photographs of a displaced prince (better looking than Paul Newman; I'd like to see a shirtless candidacy shot of him saying "Robert Kennedy is Hud"—then I'd vote for him).

In the meantime, McCarthy has been CONSISTENT in his philosophical attack on militarist America. He has also been more SPECIFIC about the bad guys, calling for the dropping of J. Edgar Hoover, Hershey, Rusk. Hoover, Hershey, and Rusk . . . sounds like a law firm, of outlaws. He has explicitly discussed the nature of the CIA, and called for recognition of Red China. Kennedy, like Rockefeller, takes the cowardly position of "Well, I firmly believe we should increase communications with China."

McCarthy, as of this writing, still has not faced the issue of police brutality, Jim Garrison, thought control, and is not as impressive as Kennedy on the ghettoes.

But if American politics cannot get more rational, more specific, more honest— less image and more substance—it may well be time to join the National Liberation Front and bring this country to the destruction it has been begging for so long. (It's either us or tidal waves and earthquakes, folks.)

But no matter who wins in Indiana, the steamroller campaigns of two liberal and attractive candidates should have a healthy effect on the state, and may shake up the roots of this heartland of reaction.

Recognizing Humphrey as a disgrace and McCarthy as a healing salve, I should also state that in the madness of American politics that their roles could have been reversed.

If Johnson had chosen McCarthy as Vice-President, the kiss of death, he could have been inched over (stay with us, Gene, at least your dovish sentiments are being aired and considered in the corridors of power, and since our boys are dying, we must keep public solidarity in front of the enemy).

Humphrey could have rationalized his ego-loss bitterness and could have become the voice of dissent against an administration about which he had increasing doubts.

Kennedy is the tragic prince who played with the fascist Falstaffs of the '50s in his younger days and now seems to have acquired a kingly conscience on the fringes of a new responsibility.

Anyway, in the current rules of the game, Humphrey is a disgrace, and if he should get the nomination I believe there would be riots, sabotage, the formation of a third party, and other media outrages the way there would have been if Johnson had run. Humphrey is the prize seduction of the materialists.

America is two Mack trucks colliding on a superhighway because all the drivers are on amphetamine. On primary day I'll pay a visit to James Dean's grave and go to Indiana, watching the returns, not without a sense of amusement.

TAPE FROM CALIFORNIA (LINER NOTES)
A&M (1968)

Hi, thought I'd drop you a line
from the beautifulpeoply coast
where I'm filming the family slime
(the most)
stopping behind the Pendleton barracks
to get high
(tonight American pigs you die!)
I left my mind in San Francisco
I left my life in LA
thought I'd drop you a line
a Chevrolet from Che
to say
the NLF is nibbling
they're not afraid they're not alone
(you are afraid you are alone)
can it be the War of Liberation
has finally come home?

Farewells + Fantasies, Folks
P. Ochs

REHEARSALS FOR RETIREMENT (LINER NOTES)
A&M (1969)

This then is the death of the American
imprisoned by his paranoia
and all diseases of his innocent inventions
he plunges to the drugs of the devil to find his gods
he employs the farce of force to crush his fantasies
he calls conventions of salesmen and savages
to reinforce his hopelessness
So the poet swordsmen and their lost generation
must divorce themselves from their very motherland
only for the least sensation of life or love or pain
our deepest and most religious moments
were on elevators posing as planes

Part two of this earnest epic
finds seaweed lapping against your eyes
the sailors have chosen the mystery surprise
to join the flying dutchman in his search for a green disguise
Still others invade the final colony
to present their tinted tributes to the millionaire assassin
While I stumble through this paradise
considering several suicides
for distant lavender lovers
or bless the violence of the ridiculous revolution
for self bronzing brothers
and finally turn away from the turquoise towers
of this comic civilization
my responsibilities are done let them come let them come
and I realize these last days these trials and tragedies
were after all only
our rehearsals for retirement.

LEAVING DARWIN
Unpublished travel journal excerpts, August 1972

Friday August 18 [1972]—Fitful sleep. Get about three hours. In the back room of wharfie Jack Phillips at 39 McMinn St., Darwin, N.T., Peppa said last night, "but I still like your singing." She waves goodbye in the morning. Morning coffee and diary. Pasting last pix in. Jan arrives. I thought my watch was wrong. The usual last-minute rush. Not even time for a shower. What will I forget this time? Give diary to Jack. Send to B[ob] Garcia. Air express. Consignment number etc. My soggy jacket and sweater send slow and cheap. Leave some papers and pix behind, trying to lighten up. Quick farewells. Then lovely Jan drives me to the airport. They plan to leave in December and then keep travelling. That's all there is. If only I had a woman like that. They've been married one year. The full last name is Wesley-Smith. Tells me to look up brother, Peter, studying Chinese legal history in Hong Kong.

At the airport, the same TAA [Trans Australia Airlines] crew. Take care of details. Go through bags waiting for the bar to open. Trip will take six hours. Very low on bread. Leave $2 bet behind with Terry. Signed a poster for the worker's club. They page me for customs, just when the beer is ready. Get that done. Then down three quick ones. Final call for Merpati to Denpasar. Race out. So sad. A lovely two months in Australia must come to an end now. Very emotional. Take a last look around. In bar, approached by young American couple. Saw me last night, from Santa Barbara, very sweet and naïve looking. On plane, some kids from the Townsville house, even younger and more vulnerable looking. It's really good I did the show last night. Keep looking out window for last glimpse. Goodbye beautiful Australia. The last tip dissolves into many islands, then a long, dull trip. At first very smooth. Read about Asia. Free Meals. Free glasses of warm beer.

Indonesia—Bali

After 2 1/2 hours, a lousy bumpy landing in Indonesian Timor, Kupang. One hour wait for customs. Seedy place. Lots of kids hanging around. Very hot. When the plane takes off the air conditioning goes on. On the ground it's sweltering. Go back for my camera. They don't change money at the airport. See red and white Indonesian flag. A couple of hangars. People with baskets on their heads. Someone says it looks like Tijuana. Kids ask for cigarettes. Some soldiers with rifles. This is my first stop in Asia. It is like a poor Mexican town. Walk out in street. Some cows sniffing a dry bucket.

Filled with water, they shy away. Followed by group of kids. So barren here. (My body has been a good friend. I won't need it when I reach the end.)

Sit in shade by small building. A thankful breeze. Meanwhile, they're madly looking for me. Forgot about customs. Where's your ticket? Back to plane and then where's your camera? They like to search that. Finally back on. Looked pretty carefully though suitcase. Off again. Air pockets. Trip becoming endless. Doze off, then a smooth bank into Bali. Beautiful cliffs. Waves crashing. We land. Off to bag check. Surrounded by hustling boys. How much to town? First price 400 rupiahs (1 dollar). Then hear French guy who was here before, only 50 cents to beach. Bargain. Kid named Putra puts me in bus. Off we go. A paradise, just like Haiti. Every time I look around, some amazing new sight. Animals everywhere, palm trees, rice fields, women with baskets. A similar smell to Haiti. The bustle of life mixed tightly. Crowded. Beeping horns all the time. In back of bus with women, kids, chickens, etc. Go to Adi Yasa as recommended, 11 Nakula Street. They have a double: 300 rupiahs (75 cents). OK. A cell-like room with no circulation. Very hot, but not quite as bad as Darwin. Drop my things off, then go to Bali Hotel to cash traveler's cheque. $10 [at] 405 rate.

Go to bar, have cold beer. Bintang Baru Bir, pilsner, 200 rupiahs. An older American there works for oil company in Bass Straight, wearing khaki clothes. Get talking. Pays $14 for an air-conditioned room here. Lonely looking man. Light up a Monte Cristo in celebration of my arrival. Putra waiting outside. Off we go on motorbike through this amazing city. It was basically a market town. Capital used to be Singaraja. Then we get on bike, zip around town. Amazing place, horns honking, bicycles everywhere, baskets on heads, animals thronging. Get off and walk through market. Again, like Haiti. Wooden stalls. Cooking food. Sandals. Cloth. Sarongs. Bags. Carvings. Framed cheap pix. Suharto. Many fruit and vegetables.

Sunday, August 20
Rent a bike for 800 rupia ($2). A Honda. Learn how to use gear shift, one down then three up. My boots come in handy. A small green light means neutral. Very difficult and subtle to get. Zoom off precariously. Turn down guide. Get maps. Off I go, whee! What a fantastic feeling. Total independence and freedom. A speed rush. Feel like Steve McQueen. Finally get the bike feeling and what a perfect place, breathtaking rice fields, soft green intricate terracing. Stop at roadside bar.

Two friendly boys there who speak English. Overjoyed when I tell them that I sing. Two ice rice wine and valium. Off I spin. Cost two or three dollars a night here. A thatch hut circular bar. Pass through Ubud. Have lunch there. Many tourists. Some boy from Sumatra. Everyone poses for pix. They have a habit here of asking for your address. Go up side street. Look at museum and garden and ponds outside. Hindu deities. Animals. Sensual statues. Very good two-lane roads, perfect for bike. Have to keep asking directions. Went through Batu Bulan. Pass Bangli. Then up the country, sixty kilometers. Starts to get cool as I gain altitude. Women bathe naked in brown streams by roads. Wash the kids, laundry. Very primitive and untouched. Temples and carving everywhere. When the Muslims came the Hindus all came here. Protected by water, a sacred isle. Batur is a volcano. It erupted, I believe, in 1963. You can see the mass of lava down the side. Once in a while, a green spot pokes up. Next to it is a huge lake. Women hustling fruit and tourist trips.

See a dead body. Come back by horse. Takes three hours.

Don't have time.

Please buy beer, coke.

Road is high and good view point. Stop at several places then restaurant for wine. Gorgeous landscape. Two ominous craters. Some folks hike to the top. Another three hours. It's a small place, but you need a month to see it. Park your bike and take long walks. Pick up a losman [word uncertain, "losmen" means a cheap inn or lodge in Indonesian. Ochs may be referring to lodgings on hiking trails] along the way, have a girl with you. I'm not comfortable with my camera. Lose my lens cap. Always hard to start bike. Race back. Open up Honda. It's even getting cold. This is the best way to keep cool here. Exchange notes with Dita and friends. Always play pop music at Adi Yasa. First night Sebastian sounds great. A new record by Feliciano. These guys really got it together. I feel so inadequate. The usual insecurity and temporary super drive to learn music. McCartney. Lots of laid-back notes. I follow Dita every day, taking the basic tours. Hot again. Go out for cool night ride. Bike won't start. Guy says there's a part missing. Goes for it. Too late. Works falteringly. I go out anyway. Zoom down a strange road. So cool. End up at Bali Beach again. Walk around. No one outside. Jump in pool. Like velvet. A great psychological theft. Like a little boy. Throughout this trip I become more aware of an arrested adolescence. I get the feeling American media freezes lack of development. Even through idols like James Dean or Walt Disney etc.

THE LAST TEN BEST LIST
Los Angeles Free Press (9–19 February 1973)

For years now I have lived off my reputation as the best dressed entertainer in Hollywood. But I realize now I have certain responsibilities here in the sodomized Seventies to do more.

Unbeknownst to the general public, behind this glossy exterior lurks a fanatic student of the cinema. I see most of the films that are released each year and I notice several I admired were left off many reviewers' lists. Here is a perspective on the year in no particular order.

Frenzy—Hitchcock's best movie in years—slow building suspense, a realistic and terrifying sexual murder, and tight direction. Also, an interesting study of natural, not doll, women. He gets classy performances out of Jon Finch who had no stature in *Macbeth* and especially Barry Foster who has been one of those familiar but nameless faces, giving a semi-Michael Caine-ish performance.

This seems to be the year of old masters turning in good discipline genre work (the flashbacks in Cukor's *Travels with My Aunt*) as many of the young Turks flounder in the post–*Easy Rider* formlessness.

Bad Company—A haunting piano score by Harvey Schmidt, the dark-toned photography of Gordon Willis and brilliant performances by Jeff Bridges and Barry Brown mark this over-looked gem. Sparks of inspiration on a light frame. Bridges seems to grow with every role, emanating a tough proletarian charm that will stand out in the "Fightin' Side of Me" Seventies.

It seems to be part of a series of the Hollywood attempt to redefine the myths of the Old West that they created. Barry Brown has a charming quality very reminiscent of the young Jimmy Stewart, perhaps too consciously. There ought to be a network of theatres to keep works of this quality available to the general public, for those who miss the commercial sweepstakes.

Kansas City Bomber—The reigning sex fantasy finally gets an earthy part. Whether or not you accept this film will probably depend on the mythic thrill you get watching Miss Raquel warming up in the ring, chewing gum, whirling around to the strains of the national anthem. Aside from the miscasting of Kevin McCarthy and some awful dialogue, this is a cartoony slice of Americana which accomplishes the difficult task of studying a priceless American burlesque, showing its attractions and drawbacks without going for the easy kill. It is helped along by the strong supporting performances of Norman Adler as an over-the-hill Fat Freddie and Helena Kallianiotes as Miss Raquel's bitchy competition.

The Harder They Come—This is my favorite movie of the year. The first Jamaican movie, totally original, poetic, raw and haunting. An incredible debut by Jimmy Cliff whose rhythmic reggae provides the best musical background of the year.

With the main spotlight on the story of a pop singer-turned outlaw and killer, Perry Henzell shows a side of Jamaica not covered in the rising tourist view of the world. The lilting street talk of the Kingston ghettoes is a marvelous use of speech as sound (made understandable by appropriate subtitles). Here are the shanties and slums, the swirl of the streets, weed dealing mystics, and the small corruptions of a hustling record business existing in third world squalor.

The film also provides one of the most telling industry stories of the year. It was turned down by several major studios who didn't see the value of this genuine black cinema as they wallow in their Jim Brown–Stella Stevens fantasies.

Rage—It must have been a traumatic year for George C. Scott promoting fascism in *The New Centurions* and violent revolution in *Rage*. This is one of the hardest hitting political films ever made in America. Unfortunately, it is lacking in visual scope for the screen, and is shot too much like a teleplay.

Its strength lies in coming boldly to terms with the growing crimes of a faceless bureaucracy against the individual. It is more Kafka than Marx and strikes that curious revolutionary chord that unites the instincts of both minutemen and weathermen.

Lady Sings the Blues—A star is born. Diana Ross makes the best debut of a singer on screen ever. The magnetism of her voice is matched and surpassed by her presence. She is a Movie Star. She is beautiful, she radiates from the screen, and she is always intriguing to watch.

The script is too sugary and sentimental, but Miss Ross carries every moment with the capable help of Richard Pryor and Billy Dee Williams. And what a relief to see an element of grace and warmth from a black movie. It makes you wonder what is behind the poisonous images coming from the others.

For the blood-porn addicts, the best violence is dished out by *Across 110ᵗʰ Street*. It is reminiscent of the excellent *Get Carter* in terms of fury and pace. I find it interesting to watch how the advancing age of good actors can add a flavor to sad and weary roles. Here is Anthony Quinn as a corrupt cop (remember Lancaster in *Gypsy Moths* and *Ulzana's Raid*).

Tony Franciosa leaps back onto the screen with a vengeance, relishing his role as a sadistic Mafioso engaged in a life-and-death struggle with the new black gangster structure he helped to create (shades of Joey Gallo).

There is a wonderful sequence when a dying mobster hurls his blood money from a rooftop to the ghetto kids below, and when fate catches up with Tony Quinn his face, in the course of five seconds, registers an incredible range of anger falsely directed, pain, sorrow, and disbelief—surely one of the best screen moments of the year. Again, this movie exemplifies the value of a controlled and unrelenting tempo.

Fat City—John Huston shows his form as a classy ex-champ, before being knocked out cold by the unranked Roy Bean. Great work by Stacy Keach and Jeff Bridges in his second standout of the year. Realistic, raunchy, overphotographed Stockton, California gyms, bars, real fighters acting, actors getting very close to real boxers. Main drawback is the over-sloshy performance of Susan Tyrrell.

Cabaret—A great musical with the fabulous song and dance theatrics of performer Liza Minnelli overcoming the gross and overdirected performance of Liza Minelli. Helmut Griem and Joel Grey are perfection. This is one of the few pictures with a fully realized sense of style reflecting the increasingly popular pre-Fascist state of Germany. Perhaps the Nazi's biggest mistake is that they did not retain screen rights.

For tenth place we have a draw: *Deliverance* and *The Godfather*, both obligatory. Dickey's novel is one of the most natural movies in years, but there is something empty and removed about the picture that stops it from being great. *The Godfather* has some atrocious screenwriting (the facile treatment of the movie producer: "I don't like wops, niggers, etc.") and Brando could have been used much better—less make-up, more screen-time and development.

But they're both ambitious movies, large and mythic canvasses, the creation and extension of visual fantasies, the dreams of America. They both seem to show that as our capacity for feeling sinks, we need ever larger doses of violence to be reached dramatically.

Every year I seem to think it was a bad year for movies, but every Ten Best list looks good in retrospect. Memories improve with age. One forgives weak moments in films like an unfaithful lover you can't live without. See you at *Last Tango*.

MIKE MAZURKI'S SPOT
Los Angeles Free Press (16–26 February 1973)

Underneath the soul sucking smog of L.A. lie the lonely shadows of eight million prisoners of fame, many sentenced to solitary confinement. There is little organic connection between people here, no sense of neighborhood, and very little past associations.

Who knows who is living next door to you? It could be Nixon's brother, it could be the lighting man for *2001*, it could be your second cousin. No one dares to ask. Some have been dead for years and nobody even knows . . . Mayor Yorty, for example, but that's another story.

Every once in a while, I break out of my little cell and check out the cemetery for signs of life. Legend has it the only real life in this town is among the very successful who are usually recognized by their dark limousines, their dark glasses, and their piles of booze and pills. Nobody talks to them except ghosts and reporters, and many of them end up being the loneliest of all.

The town is not completely lacking in charm. Death attracts interesting visitors. One of these is José "Mantequilla" Napoles, Cuban born, Mexico City wined and dined, the welterweight champion, and as the cliché goes, pound for pound the greatest fighter in the world.

I watched him training recently at the old Elks building on Parkview Road across from MacArthur Park (Westlake Park before MacArthur returned). The rich used to live there, the lake used to run through Wilshire Boulevard, and the Elks used to own it before selling it to the Bauer Brothers who have most of the area now.

The structure is enormous with a 50-foot painted ceiling, wrought iron doors at the top of the imposing staircase, an Olympic-size swimming pool at the YMCA below. It is mainly a man's territory. They made a concession to the ladies with a large powder room on the ground floor.

Most of the people who came to see Napoles are Mexican; they provide the backbone for boxing in this town. As José pummels his hard-to-find sparring partners, the crowd yells, "Arriba . . . Mantequilla" (his nickname, smooth as butter), as they savor the physical embodiment of their national pride.

They say he has a weakness for tequila and women, and once in a while a beautiful girl will jump in the ring for pictures and whistles. Occasionally a great white hoper will throw out an insult, but Napoles speaks only in Spanish (he travels with translators) and sullenly goes on punching.

On the way out I stopped at the bar for a cool Coors, and as I looked over, I noticed a sign saying Mike Mazurki's Spot. My heart jumped. Could this be the same Mike Mazurki that pounced on Richard Widmark, threw Tyrone Power around, and fought in the foreign legion with Burt Lancaster in my boyhood dream movies? Only in Hollywood.

It took a few weeks to build up my courage, but I went back determined to talk to him and find out what he was doing here. Jerry Meeker behind the cash register was friendly. "Oh, yeah, Mike's been here for three months. He hangs around when he's not refereeing wrestling matches at the Houston Astrodome or selling stuff on the idiot box. I think you call them commercials."

To kill time, I walked by the empty bandshell across the street and listened to the echoes of the countless anti-war rallies I had attended there. When I came back, he was carrying a case of champagne glasses for a wedding reception they were catering the coming Sunday.

We didn't know what to make of each other, but I stammered out something about the *Free Press* and how I dug him in *Ten Tall Men*. He seemed surprised and said, "Come back tomorrow: I'll bring some stills."

Mike Mazurki is 62 years old and looks 40. He is 6'4" and weighs 240 lbs. His appearance is tough, but he's more gentle than your average Hare Krishna convert thrusting leaflets at you on Hollywood Boulevard. He was a professional wrestler and fought 4,000 men in the ring. He has appeared in over 100 movies. Most of his bones have been broken, and he speaks with a rasp from repeated blows to his Adam's apple.

He was discovered by Josef Von Sternberg while wrestling at the Olympic Auditorium; Sternberg wanted a guy who could speak Russian for *Shanghai Gesture*. He screen tested with Victor Mature and Gene Tierney. "They made me shave my head, 'cause I looked too much like Mature," he said, showing his Roman profile. "Sternberg, he's the guy that discovered Marlene Dietrich."

Mike is Ukrainian, born on Christmas day in 1909. He lived there six years and was brought over after his parents had settled near Albany, New York. Thousands were leaving then because of the poverty and the easy emigration laws. There are over two million people of Ukrainian descent in North America.

"I can still speak and write Ukrainian, which is to my way of thinking a high-class Russian." He describes the old country as a vast farmland like Nebraska or Iowa where he had to walk half a mile to get water. In the Russian Orthodox Church there were no seats and, since some of the services were over three hours long, he would often pass out from hunger or thirst. To this day he only goes to the end of a service.

His father was a blacksmith who worked for the railroad. His mother was a domestic for the local baron and the local priest.

He got a Bachelor of Arts degree at Manhattan College, excelling in track, football, and basketball (the tallest center in all the New York schools). After graduation he got a job on Wall Street, going to law school at night. But this was during the depression, and a local promoter noticed him doing some amateur wrestling and offered him $500 a night to turn pro. At that time wrestling was a more legitimate sport, and many college athletes were turning to it.

He wrestled five nights a week in New York: Monday night at Madison Square Garden (they packed in 35,000 every week); Tuesday at St. Nicks; Wednesday in Brooklyn; Thursday in White Plains; and Friday at the Broadway Arena. "In those days you got by on sheer ability, but today everything is exaggerated. That's what you call showmanship."

Wrestling in Europe is known as the Greco-Roman style, in which you could only fight from the waist up, but here in America it developed into catch as catch can, anything goes.

Mike fought many of the champions. A match was decided by three falls, shoulder to the mat unless the opponent gave up under a painful hold. "Sometimes we'd talk to each, threatening or joking, 'I'm gonna break your fucking arm if you don't give up' . . . 'you don't mean that' . . . 'yes sir I do.'

"I had everything going for me when I broke into pictures. I'd work on a film for three months; and when I told a promoter I was available for a fight, he'd advertise 'just returned from Hollywood where he made a movie with Gary Cooper.' The fans would say, 'Jeez, it's a movie star.' Today that's nothin'. In those days it was somethin'."

In his heyday he fought with Gorgeous George and Man Mountain Dean. "Now George was a great little wrestler, 175 pounds, fancy gowns and marcelled hair. He made over four million dollars. Man Mountain Dean was originally a boxer by the name of Soldier Leavitt; he served under Patton. Now it wasn't so much he was good, but he was so strong; he jumped on some guys and broke their backs."

He had some work to do with his wife Sylvia, so I arranged to meet him the next day. As I walked out, I was approached by a thin, nervous Chicano. He said, "My name's Eddie Rodriguez, I used to be a fighter. You know, I'm 49 years old; but don't you think I'm in great shape?"

"Yeah."

Then he showed me an autographed card saying, "Your friend always, Bobby Chacon." "Hey, how about giving me 50 cents for a bus into town." I handed him some coin and started to leave.

On impulse I turned and said, "I think Turi Pineda's gonna take Chacon." A look of authority returned to his face, and Eddie said, "No way, no way."

The next day I came back and walked by the old Elk pensioners sitting in the lobby with their canes and memories. Mike and I continued our talk over some chicken teriyaki and one of his eight salads.

"Ya know, I didn't always look like this, with my pugnacious nose and cauliflower ears. Look, here's a picture of my daughter. People look at her and say, 'she's yours?' [he shows me a beach-fresh California blonde]. Don't forget I been wrestling 35 years. I took a lot of beating, a lot of physical contact.

"I did this picture called *Behind the Rising Sun*. I was a Japanese wrestler who fought Bob Ryan. Now, the same producer and Eddie Dmytryk the director were going to do *Murder, My Sweet* with Dick Powell in his first role as a tough guy. So, I called him and I said, 'Hey, Eddie, this Moose Malloy character is me.' 'Oh,' he says, 'why don't you stick to wrestling, you're not an actor.'

"They tested everybody in town. Victor McLaglen, Ward Bond, all the big boys, muscle men from the beach, even truck drivers. So, one day I happened to walk into the commissary at RKO. Sitting with Dmytryk was the studio president, Charley Koerner; he's dead now. Someone says, 'Hiya Mike' . . . 'Hi boys' . . . I happened to be wearing a loud coat at that time. Dmytryk looks around and says, 'That's Mike Mazurki the wrestler,' and Koerner says, 'But that's Moose Malloy.'

"We went up to the head office. Mr. Koerner he looks at me and says, 'Can you read?'

"I didn't know how to take that. I says, 'Whadyamean can I read?' Now he's hurt my feelings. Ya know they see a big guy here in Hollywood with a raspy voice and a busted nose, they immediately say he's punchy. I played punchy parts. They paid me to play those things.

"I told him I was a college graduate with a year at law school. So I tested with Powell and got the part. They'd been looking for two months. That Eddie Dmytryk, he was a funny little shit. And he used to say, 'Oh, I can beat your ass,' and I said

'C'mon Eddie, you're a little shit.' And he was an amateur wrestler, and he hated professionals. All these little guys are cocky little bastards. But Eddie taught me a lot about acting. Anyway, I got the part. This brought me into prominence. This made me a feature actor. There's a lotta luck in your life, you know that dontcha, Phil?

"Now Lancaster, there was a great guy. I was wrestling Primo Carnera in Evansville, Indiana. Burt looks me up and says, 'What are you doin', come down to the circus tonight.' So I came down and gives me the biggest hand, he says my best friend from Hollywood, fighting Carnera. This is in the big tent. We sold out the goddam house. That's the kind of guy he is."

"What about *Rope of Sand?*"

"You remember that one? You remember a lot of the old ones, don't you?"

"Yeah, I go to the movies all the time."

"That's good."

"Four times a week."

Then proudly, "Did you know my other pictures?"

"Yeah, *Donovan's Reef.*"

"How about *Blood Alley?* Then there was that great one with Tyrone Power, *Nightmare Alley*. You see that?"

"Parts of it on television."

"I'll tell you what happened with Tyrone Power one day. I was supposed to get him up against a juke box. He's supposed to do this [he gestures], and I'm supposed to grab him and make him marry the girl [he grabs me], but I had him loose; I didn't want to hurt him, and he broke away a couple of times.

"So the director, Ed Goulding, says, 'For Chrissake, Mazurki, hold the guy.' So the next time I grabbed him! I grabbed him so hard—skin, hair, and everything, and I say, 'You sonafabitch, you stay!' And he yelled like a goddamned hyena.

"And Goulding shouts, 'It's a take!' So Powers walks off the set. 'I'll never work with the sonavabitch again . . . Look at this, look at this. He hurt me.' For two hours he doesn't show.

"George Jessel was the producer. He says, 'Mike, what are you tryin' to do?'

"I said, 'I'm sorry.'

"'Goulding says you're killing my stars.' They don't know the real story. So Ty comes back and says he was kidding. After that, we were the best of friends. I didn't want to hurt the guy. Once you hurt 'em and it gets around Hollywood, you won't work anymore.

"But you can get it, too. I was doing *Dakota* with John Wayne, and I had just finished killing Ward Bond. The Duke must have got carried away, 'cause in the next scene he pulled my hat over my eyes and I ended up with on the floor with a bloody nose."

Mazurki has a great scene in Ford's *Cheyenne Autumn*, where as the Polish sergeant he tells Lt. Widmark after an Indian massacre: "I didn't come to America to be a Cossack."

"When World War II broke out, four of us, all wrestlers, went down to volunteer. They put us in special service. They fit us in for our languages. Joe Savoldi for Italian, me for Russian and Polish, Lopez for Spanish. They asked Willy Davis what language he spoke and he said, 'Ah speak profane.' He's from the South. Savoldi later became a commander in the invasion of Sicily.

"After a while, they gave me a physical. The doctor said I couldn't go in the regular service; I had a bad back. They took X-rays. You know the vertebrae goes down like this; well, mine was out like that.

"Now that's when I used to go to the bars, and these little guys who used to be in the service, they'd say, 'You big palooka, how come you're not in?' And they'd try to pick a fight with me. And I'd have to take all the crap and walk out. I couldn't hit 'em; I couldn't hit a man in uniform. Me, a civilian. They'd say, 'Look at that big bastard hitting that poor little soldier. He's fightin' for his country.' Get the point?"

We shook hands, and as I drove back, I felt strangely vulnerable in the crowded, deserted streets. That night, as I was typing up our conversation, the tube was on and I watched the haunted faces of the first POWs climbing off those awkward planes in the Philippines, returning from the ultimate wrestling match. They looked so fragile and ghostlike, and they said "God Bless America," and I went outside to get a beer. But it's not New York; the bars were closed.

REQUIEM FOR A DRAGON DEPARTED
Los Angeles Weekly News (21–28 September 1973)

I was in the Philippines in September of 1972 ending a concert tour through Australia and Southeast Asia. It was a steamy Sunday, the day before the American puppet Marcos was to declare martial law. Rumors were rife in the papers, then known for being the most outspoken in Asia.

I didn't know what to do on my last day in Asia. I had missed the boat which would have retraced the death march from Bataan; so at ten in the morning I went to see a Bruce Lee double feature. I had heard his name mentioned in Singapore, Bangkok, and especially, in Hong Kong—always with a sense of wonder, the way some people talk about Clint Eastwood or Muhammad Ali.

Though it was Sunday in the major Christian area in Southeast Asia, the theater was packed. Outside, in typical Filipino fashion, was a sign reading "Please check your guns." It seemed like the most violent place on earth. There were gunfights and knifings late almost every night in the brothels and bars. If you had some money you had a bodyguard; if you had real money and land, you had a small and well-trained army.

I bought a San Miguel beer and peanuts and groped my way to a seat. There I was entranced for three hours; I could hardly believe my eyes. I had seen Japanese Samurai movies, but was not prepared for what was to come. The pictures were *The Big Boss* and *Fists of Fury* (released here as *Fists of Fury* and *The Chinese Connection*). The stories were simplistic and mainly based on revenge. They always involve fighting schools and a revered master teacher. "I will teach you to be the best fighters in the world, but you must never use it to harm anyone unless absolutely necessary."

Near the beginning is the act of outrage: the insults of a rival school, the poisoning of a master, the murder of a loved one. Lee, the hero, the best fighter, demands vengeance, and is always restrained until he can hold himself no longer. Then follows the most exciting action ever filmed on the screen. One man against fifty with no weapons. He begins to wade his way through the lesser villains with karate chops: his fists, his elbows, his feet; there are no camera tricks. The audience is hysterical: clapping, cheering, sometimes leaping to their feet. When he gets to the major villains it becomes a dance of extraordinary beauty; one reviewer said that Lee made Rudolf Nureyev look like a truck driver.

It is not the vulgarity of James Arness pistol-whipping a stubbled, drunken stage robber; it is not the ingenious devices of James Bond coming to the rescue nor the ham-fisted John Wayne slugging it out in the saloon over crumbling tables and paper-thin imitation glass. It is the science of the body taken to its highest form—and the violence, no matter how outrageous, is always strangely purifying.

The following is based on information provided by Bill Stern at Warner Brothers Publicity, Fred Weintraub, and a magazine called *Fighting Stars*, whose opening editorial reads, "We all feel the lack of the right words to say, especially those that would give comfort to his stricken family and friends. For all of us, the world is a much smaller place."

Bruce Lee was born in San Francisco in 1940, and from age three to 18 was raised in Hong Kong. His father was a star in the Chinese opera. He studied martial arts from his early teens and was a master at age 18. He entered the University of Washington in Seattle where he earned a degree in philosophy. There he met and married an American girl named Linda. They have two children—Brandon and Shannon, aged eight and four. He also was a child actor in Chinese films.

Lee used to go to Long Beach for the Karate tournament, where he would put on exhibitions of his own particular style, Jeet Kune Do. There he was noticed by a television producer who, at first, wanted to cast him as the number one son in a Charlie Chan series, but he changed his mind and Lee first emerged into the western consciousness as Kato in the *Green Hornet* series. International distribution made him a hero in Hong Kong. He had trouble getting movie roles in the U.S. and appeared only occasionally—once as a villain in *Marlowe* and in a strong segment of *Longstreet* with James Franciscus called "Way of the Fist."

Finally, Raymond Chow of Golden Harvest Studios in Hong Kong offered him his first feature, *The Big Boss*, to be filmed in Thailand in July 1971. The location was so remote that Lee lost ten pounds from lack of meat in his diet. The opening of *The Big Boss* in Hong Kong turned out to be a cinematic revolution. It became the first film to outgross the champ, *The Sound of Music*: $2.8 million for *Music* and $3.2 million for *Boss*.

Then everyone went crazy. Lee quickly finished *The Chinese Connection*; like *The Big Boss*, directed by Lo Wei. This was followed by the only picture Lee directed, *The Way of the Dragon* (as yet unreleased in the U.S.), by reputation the best of his four films. *The Way of the Dragon* was also the first Chinese film to do location shooting in Europe. The dragon name is used twice since Lee's name in Chinese—Lee Hsiao-lung—means "little dragon."

As important as the action is the face and mind of Bruce Lee. The expressions he gets as he psyches out his opponents are beyond description; at times he is lost in ecstasy—almost sexual—and when he strikes, the force of the blow is continued by his mind and the look of concentration and satisfaction is devastating.

Two months later, at a Hollywood party, I was raving about Bruce Lee and Chinese boxing movies when I ran into Fred Weintraub, veteran of the Bitter End in Greenwich Village, Neil Diamond, and the *Woodstock* movie. "Bruce? Why he's a good friend of mine. As a matter of fact, I'm just leaving for Hong Kong to negotiate a deal with him and Warner Bros." We both knew the impact that a westernized version of this type of film would have on the American audience.

The months pass. I see Freddie occasionally, delirious with excitement as *Enter the Dragon* is progressing. Then it is complete. I am eagerly awaiting the results—when, on July 20, while singing in Toronto, I pick up a paper and read, to my shock and amazement, "Bruce Lee Dead at 32 in Hong Kong of a Brain Hemorrhage." Impossible . . . it can't be . . . tears of disbelief. But it is true. The healthiest and most athletic man on the screen is snatched away by the cruel joke of death.

It's my feeling now that Bruce Lee will become a James Dean figure of the seventies. James Dean was a great actor, finishing three films before dying in a car crash at the age of 24. Bruce Lee was not that kind of an actor, but on a physical level he will survive in the imagination as long as there are movies. They both found their way into mythology by a brief but totally magical presence on the screen, followed by a sudden and meaningless death.

There is a great tradition of screen adventure first popularized by Douglas Fairbanks Sr., then Jr., followed by Errol Flynn and continued by Burt Lancaster and Toshiro Mifune.

One of the last moments of pure adventure I saw on the screen was in 1952 when Lancaster slashed the rope of the high mast in *The Crimson Pirate* and flew to the top, his golden hair glowing against the blue sky, shouting something like, "Follow me, mateys!" Coincidentally, I saw *The Crimson Pirate* in Bangkok, two weeks before the Bruce Lee experience. By the expansion of body discipline, Lee will change the course of adventure films of all countries.

At this point arrives Weintraub, associate producer Paul Heller, and Warner Brothers. Lee is heading for the throne of Eastwood and Bronson and there is no question that, had he lived, he would have been the highest-paid actor in movies. What follows is based on a conversation with Fred Weintraub at Warner Brothers.

"I met Bruce when Sy Weintraub brought him over to my house. Sy studied with him along with James Garner, Steve McQueen, James Coburn, and Lee Marvin. He didn't like to teach, and consequently charged $100 per hour."

Fred believes that part of the appeal of Lee's pictures will lie in the fact that most people have not been threatened by a gun, but everyone has been hit; this will provide total identification. "I think Bruce is a great exploitation actor—like Eastwood, Wayne, etc. They believe what they do at the moment they are doing it, no matter how outrageous; these actors are worth their weight in gold."

Weintraub said Bruce was totally absorbed with his body and his abilities. Often, he would meet somebody, and within a couple of minutes, would invite the person to feel or punch his stomach. Sometimes he would take his shirt off at screenings.

"I remember standing in line at some restaurant and Bruce would suddenly lash out a punch next to my face. I could feel the brush of air, but I was never afraid; he had absolute control, he never missed, he was like a sharpshooter. He was an expert in the use of his body. He went to all the best teachers in each school and mastered their technique—every specialty.

"He loved looking at his body. He lived in an eleven-room mansion in Hong Kong with a college size gym. He worked out for hours every day, including a three-mile run; there were mirrors so he could watch his own movements. But it wasn't all physical. He would lock himself away for days to read books on the philosophy of fighting, books on John L. Sullivan, *The Art of Kick-Fighting*.

"I remember once we were having dinner with John Tunney and John asked, 'Do you think you could have beaten my father?' Bruce said, 'To tell you the truth, I could beat anybody in the world. Of course, if I sat still and your father hit me—or Clay did—forget it. The question is could they ever get close to me.' He went on to describe a couple of books that Gene Tunney had written that no one had heard about. He had the most unbelievable library on the science of fighting. No one knew more about all kinds of fighting than he did.

"He liked to tell stories from Chinese legends. His favorite was the one about the praying mantis. A cruel emperor was ravaging China. Suddenly his army column stopped. Enraged, he rode to the front and asked what was the matter. The commander said, 'There is a praying mantis in front of us.' 'So?' 'He is standing on his

"The Oncoming Storm." *(Photo by Ron Cobb, courtesy Phil Ochs Estate)*

Phil with Miranda. *(Photo by Alice Ochs, © Meegan Ochs, courtesy Getty Images)*

Phil with Jerry Rubin, 1969. *(Photo by Alice Ochs, © Meegan Ochs, courtesy Getty Images)*

(Photo by Ron Cobb, courtesy Phil Ochs Estate)

(Photo by Ron Cobb, courtesy Phil Ochs Estate)

The Thinker. New York City, 1965–1966.
(Photo by Alice Ochs, © Meegan Ochs, courtesy Getty Images)

"On the streets of New York City . . ." Circa 1965–1966.
(Photo by Alice Ochs, © Meegan Ochs, courtesy Getty Images)

Left: "Ochs, here."
(Photo by Alice Ochs,
© Meegan Ochs,
courtesy Getty Images)

Bottom: "A secret smile on his face."
(Photo by Alice Ochs,
© Meegan Ochs,
courtesy Getty Images)

Top Left: "Total independence and freedom." Los Angeles, 1969.
(Photo by Tom Wilkes, courtesy Phil Ochs Estate)

Top Right: Phil at the Troubadour, Los Angeles, 1974.
(Courtesy of Phil Ochs Estate)

Bottom Left: Phil at Michael's Venice apartment, circa 1973 (a favorite photo).
(Photo by Michael Ochs, © Michael Ochs)

Morning reverie. New York City, 1965–1966.
(Photo by Alice Ochs, © Meegan Ochs, courtesy Getty Images)

legs and is prepared to attack.' The emperor thought and agreed; the whole column rode around the praying mantis."

Fred describes an incident that occurred when Lee's last picture was two-thirds complete. "Hong Kong is a pretty rough place. Wherever Bruce went he was besieged for autographs and often people would challenge him to fight on the streets; he tried to ignore them. There was a young karate student who was an extra on the picture, who walked up and said, 'I don't think you're so fast—I think I can beat you.' I froze. I thought, Oh my God, suppose he got hurt. Bruce pulled away from me, raised his hands and stamped his feet three times—the signal he was ready to fight. Suddenly he swerved and laid the student out on the floor with a kick in the face, walked away without a word to him, and said, 'Let's do the next scene.'

"Basically, he was a loner. He didn't trust anybody. The only people close to him were Raymond Chow and, especially, his wife Linda. He adored and spent a lot of time with his kids.

"Many Chinese-Americans have an incredible sense of insecurity about themselves. Young, well-to-do Chinese often make self-deprecating jokes about doing laundry, etc. This is often covered by an air of superiority. Bill Stern tells of driving Bruce through Coldwater Canyon, taking the curves quickly, and Bruce said, 'I can see by the way you drive this car you would like to have a car like mine, a Porsche 3.' He has also ordered a $32,000 Rolls Royce for Hong Kong."

Fred: "I wouldn't say this in public, but while making *Dragon* he personally fed stories to the local Chinese papers of how he had fired the American writer on his picture. It's partially a colonial mentality—or, if you can picture it, a dead-end kid suddenly becoming a millionaire. If I could send a note to Bruce right now, it would be, '*Dragon* outgrossing *The Getaway* in every engagement.' Nothing would make him more happy."

Bruce Lee had two funerals. The first, in Hong Kong, brought out over 30,000 bereaved fans, the biggest funeral they ever had there. At Lee's actual funeral in Seattle, Steve McQueen and James Coburn were among his pall-bearers. Fred: "His death affected many high-ego people I know—to think that he, of all people, could die so suddenly—"

Lee blacked out six months before his death, for no known reason. He had a complete physical checkup after that with the best doctors in Los Angeles, and they gave him a clean bill of health.

The official cause of death is listed as an aneurism, a congenital weakening of a vessel in the brain. Maybe he did die of an aneurism. However, there were rumors in Hollywood of cocaine.

Maybe Bruce Lee was killed by some crazy person or some rival business faction. Maybe he wasn't meant to be cast as a James Bond figure, serving the interests of Interpol. Maybe he lived more intensely than any human being can live. Or maybe he died for the same reason that James Dean died: they had taken too much of the fire, and the Gods were jealous.

OPPOSES POT DECRIMINALIZATION, FREEP PRESS PASSES
Los Angeles Free Press (30 March-9 April 1973)

It wasn't easy to get to interview Tom Reddin. When I called up three weeks ago his press man was curt and distant and said they were too busy.

Another time they said they would actually come to the *Free Press* office, but they never showed up. I'd given up and, as luck would have it, when I got the unexpected call that he was finally available I was in the middle of a terrible hangover. However, I had the experience of ducking some overzealous police clubs under his direction at the Century City debacle some years back and was curious to find out what kind of guy he was.

In my sodden condition I did some quick research and found out the following. Tom Reddin was born in New York City and is 56 years old. His father, according to *Time* magazine, was a "flamboyant carnival tycoon who made more than a million dollars building amusement parks in Europe and Australia and lost it all in unsuccessful oil drilling in Oklahoma."

Reddin served four years in the navy and came to LA in 1937. He was held up at gun point while working as a gas station manager and soon afterward joined the police department in 1941. He was on the force for 28 years and was Chief of Police for two years and four months.

I had a few nervous attacks during this interview and had to leave the room a couple of times. Mr. Reddin was very kind to me in my turmoil and surprisingly patient considering his tight campaign schedule. As we shook hands my insides were climbing the wall, but I plunged in . . .

Why are you running for Mayor?

Because the city needs leadership. It needs someone who can bring efficiency and economy into government, someone who is familiar with the problems of all the people.

How would you define the power of the Mayor?

First of all, it is having the prestige of being the Mayor of the third largest city in the U.S. You can make a great number of things happen without directly ordering that they take place. In addition, the Mayor has the power of appointment for all the commissioners and about half the general managers. He has more control over the budget than the Governor has over the state budget, or the President with the national. He can hold hearings, subpoena witnesses, and focus attention on the city's needs.

I have some difficulty in figuring out, on a specific level, what's different between you and the other candidates on mass transit, crime control, environment, etc.

The principle difference, where qualifications are concerned, is that among the challengers I am the only one who is an administrator, the only one who has run a major organization. The police department, when I was its head, had 8,000 employees and a budget of 125 million.

Unruh has never administered anything. He's been a power broker in the legislature, but that is not administration. It doesn't involve planning, staffing, budgeting, or fiscal management. Bradley is even at a lesser level. He has been a policeman up to the rank of lieutenant and a Councilman.

Another difference is that I don't have any political hang-ups as the other candidates do. I don't owe any political debts. I would not be partisan at all. I wouldn't be a slave to any special interest group.

Now let's face it. Yorty has been in politics for 40 years. He's got political hang-ups that won't quit. Bradley is a partisan Democrat. Unruh a self-proclaimed professional politician.

On the major issue of personal safety and security, law and order, or whatever you choose to call it, that is where I spent my life, where I built my reputation. Where Bradley will philosophize about it and talk about long range programs, causes and cures, when it comes to dealing incisively with the problem of the moment he is found wanting.

Remember when the buses were being held up so many times in the South end of the city that the drivers were going to go out on strike? They would have closed down transportation for the entire city. I went to a union meeting on Saturday and told them I would give them 200 men to ride shotgun on Monday night. Everyone told me I was crazy. But I knew how to move men around and put them on this particular problem without hurting the overall efficiency of the force. The bus problem was solved by that one particular action and it's still not a problem today.

Unruh just doesn't understand it. He's a Johnny-come-lately on this issue. He says he'll increase the force 20 percent and put the cop back on the beat. Well, hell, I put the cop back on the beat years ago. The Mayor says he supports the department no matter what they do. My approach is three-fold: causes and cures, long range planning, and dealing with the crisis of the moment.

Excuse me! Can I get some water?

Sure, Jane can we get some water here. You may have determined in reading the recent polls that . . .

Would you excuse me I don't feel very good.

Reddin seemed amazed as I left the room. I went outside and Joe Scott, the press guy who had been stand-offish before, showed real concern and offered me some aspirin. I pulled myself together and returned. Somehow the paranoia before the interview had lessened, and things were on a more relaxed and natural level.

On the issue of mass transit—I was just in Mexico City and they have a system there where cars will go down a main street like Paseo de la Reforma and carry six people for a dime apiece. Why haven't you proposed something specific like that?

I have. I call them maxi-taxis. I also proposed mini-buses that would sweep neighborhoods and take people to shopping or entertainment spots.

Chief Davis apparently made a statement about putting gallows in airports and hanging offenders on the spot. What do you think of that?

Well, I refer to Davis' statements as rhetorical overkill. He goes a long way to make his point. You may recall a few days later his next statement was how can anybody be against a speedy trial with due process of law. It's just his manner of approach. I don't think it's good. I don't think he has to overstate his case as much as he does.

Would you keep him on as police chief?

There is no choice. A chief can only be removed for specific causes as outlined in the City Charter.

What do you think of a civilian police review board?

I oppose it. The right to discipline is one of the strongest powers that the head of an organization has. That gives him the ability to control the people that work for him.

What about the Knapp commission report that exposed widespread police corruption in New York? Isn't it the nature of any bureaucracy to defend their own?

Well, yes, and if it were necessary, I would not oppose the formation of such a commission here. Having been at the top here I know that we severely deal with the shortcomings of people on the force. I know there is no cover-up here. But for years people knew that the N.Y.C. police department was corrupt and finally the Knapp commission exposed it. There has been none of that feeling by a lot of people here in Los Angeles.

The criticism here seems to be charges of police brutality, over-reaction, and a menacing image. The image of the L.A.P.D. is that of a robot, leather and all. You know what I mean?

I would hope that it is not that much that way now as it was before I instituted the community relations program. We changed the training considerably to bring in a much more human approach to the job. Now, if nothing has changed, then those changes were failures. As long as there are people on the streets and people in authority there are going to be conflicts.

What do you think of police movies like New Centurions *and* Dirty Harry?

I saw both of them. I view movies as entertainment. Now in *Centurions* they condensed many careers into four characters, they aggrandized considerably what would happen to the average policeman in the same time span. The book recited things that I know happened in the department.

I enjoyed the movie and I enjoyed *Dirty Harry*. There were things in both that I didn't like, for example that Harry was depicted as being as brutal as he was. The movie created revenge responses in the audience where they thought, "Ah, ha, it serves the bad guy right." I didn't like that. I don't like to feel that sort of thing does happen. I like to feel that the man is professional enough to keep himself above it.

I've had my frustrations, too. I did a lot of first line police work. I've been on the ground and I've been shot at; I've had guys beat me in court and thumb their noses at me. I've had guys who are going to kill me. I still have several contracts out for my life. The people who have indicated they are going to get me will have to stand in line, but I feel you can't go around living looking over your shoulder.

Can you tell me of any experiences that happened to you on the force?

I arrested my first murderer when I was a beat man on East Fifth Street in 1941. I walked into a beer joint just when a guy was stabbing someone. I disarmed the suspect (I was on the department judo team, perhaps a little more skilled than most at disarming), got blood all over myself and my uniform, handcuffed him, hauled him out of there, and sent him off to jail. The sergeant, an old timer, wanted to know why I didn't kill the son of a bitch. I never gave a thought to the possibility. My thought was to let the system of justice take its course. Another time I stopped a guy for a traffic violation and when he got out of the car he dropped dead on the spot.

I feel really nervous. It's some kind of anxiety attack.

[Reddin smiles.] You shouldn't.

Do you think I could talk to you later?

Why don't you go ahead and see if things calm down for you?

[I left the room again and, in the meantime, he took care of some other business.]

Can you talk about your TV experience as a newsman? Why did you do that and what happened there?

Actually, I retired to go on TV and radio when I found out I could contact half a million people per day. That's what motivated me, because in 1969 there were a lot of things not being said.

I can tell you of something I saw personally. I was at one of the news stations and saw footage that wasn't shown on TV. It was two cops in a black area going into a backyard and yelling over a fence. "Hey, nigger woman, where is so and so?" Now I don't see anything in the normal police structure where anything would happen to that man, right?

Well, it should if it became a matter of official record because that type of language is a forbidden type of language.

Do you really think a formal charge would be followed up?

Sure.

What do you think of the pressures on newsmen now, subpoenas and all?

I disapprove of it. I think confidential sources of information should remain confidential. I believe the move against newsmen is very bad. As a matter of fact, I contributed to Farr's defense.

Can you discuss Mayors Lindsay [N.Y.], Rizzo [Philadelphia], and Daley [Chicago]?

Lindsay is the ideal example that you can't run a city if you're not an administrator. It takes more than charm or charisma.

I knew Rizzo when he was commissioner. Now he came into office strictly as a conservative law and order man. There are people in Philadelphia that like that and those that hate it, and I think being locked into a given position like that would make it difficult for him to represent all the people.

I like Daley. He's the consummate politician, one of a vanishing breed. The people there will accept some reputation for corruption because he's a good mayor. He can and does get things done.

How do you explain the rise in use of drugs?

I think it's a problem of availability and the real pressure should be applied to the dealers. Where the addict is concerned, I think we should be pouring all sorts of money into pharmaceutical cures. I approve of methadone even though it is habit forming because at least a man can lead a productive life on it, unlike heroin. I don't think addicts are criminals. I think they're sick people. I'm glad that in California you can commit yourself and get the cure and treatment necessary.

Do you differentiate between grass and other drugs?

Yes! You can get a habit with pills, you don't get a habit with grass. You can become psychologically addicted to it, like you are perhaps to your pipe. I think we're headed for decriminalization of marijuana.

Are you in favor of that?

No. In the interim report of the National Institute of Mental Health they discouraged the use of the drug and pointed out dangers in persistent use. However, I'll go along with their final recommendation. I was one of the people who helped conceive a law in 1968 to reduce possession from a felony to a misdemeanor at the discretion of the judge. I'm not a real hardnose on it.

Can you tell me something about Chief Parker?

Parker was a very interesting man. I wasn't really close to him. Nobody was in his later years. He became quite a recluse. He had a brilliant mind, but was highly opinionated.

He's accused of making the L.A.P.D. more repressive.

During his time in office, 16 years [1950 to his death in 1966] he took a department that was largely inefficient and corrupt and made it into the highly efficient organization it is today. He adapted the approach that the job of a policeman is basically impersonal, which perhaps it could have been at the time. But when I came in I tried to change it back to a more human orientation while trying to keep the professionalism that Parker brought in.

I want to get into a touchy area. I suppose the most critical view of you would be in your handling of the Century City demonstration. What is your perspective on it?

Naturally I've spoken about this a number of times. At Century City we had the one and only major confrontation between the people and the police. During that confrontation the police department learned a great deal and the demonstrators learned a great deal, as evidenced by the fact that since that time there have been no further confrontations on that scale.

Now we had information that there were specific plans for violence, that there were threats against the President's life. We knew how the parade was going to come to a stop, how they were going to storm the front of the hotel, and on and on, a great number of things that concerned us.

Let me put it this way. I was in the crowd that was stationary in front of the hotel. My criticism is when the police charged into the crowd causing a melee, didn't that put the President's life in more danger?

We would never endanger the President's life. He was inside the hotel in the banquet room . . . We were protecting him rather than endangering him [Reddin at this point visibly begins to get angry.] I really don't want to debate this with you. I've answered your question and I don't think pursuing it is going to do either one of us any good.

Okay.

Just go back and pick up old copies of the *Free Press*. I was the front-page subject for the next three or four months as a result of that. I don't want to go over it again.

It took a minute for the atmosphere to clear and I asked him about leisure time, reading, etc.

I read the *New York Times* and *Wall Street Journal* every day. I hate to cop out to this, but I like travel and I love reading about foreign places, comparing their civilization with ours. On books, I liked *The Day of the Jackal* and especially Ardrey's *Territorial Imperative*.

Do you think the Free Press *should have a press pass?*

No. If it did there would be dozens of other publications that would come along with it. I was sued over that and the courts have since ruled that the refusal is the proper exercise of the department. The regulation is that it should be a daily whose principal content is coverage of the news, which eliminates the *Free Press*.

Were you close to Yorty when you worked together?

No. Yorty and I never became friends. I was never invited to his home.

Really? As Police Chief and Mayor?

Yes, that's right. I stayed kind of aloof from him. I rebuffed him a couple of times when he or people on his staff wanted things that I thought were improper. We didn't have an unpleasant relationship, but we never became friends. There's a lot of times when Mayor Yorty's not here, and I sometimes wonder whether or not he's there.

I understand you are for locker searches in schools.

We're going to have to change an attitude that started in the mid '50s that a person is not responsible for his voluntary acts. Age doesn't matter to me. If he's intelligent enough to think out what he's doing and has the physical ability to do it and it's wrong, we've got to hold him responsible. We've got to get off the kick of explaining away reprehensible behavior, heinous crime, because we've got a sick society. Now that's wrong. This self-guilt does nothing to solve the problem.

I suggested searching lockers in high schools and students whenever needed. Students who possess weapons or drugs should be suspended or expelled. Immediately criticism came heaping down upon me. But the Board of Education adopted the proposal after I explained to them it's no different from me taking an airplane trip. When you go to a federal building you're searched. When I was in the service, and on the police force, my locker was searched. My attitude is: If I have nothing to conceal, why should I worry?

Well, thanks for the interview.

Sure, and I hope you feel better tomorrow.

The next morning, I got up at 6:30 and drove down to the harbor at San Pedro to see the Reddin campaign in action and pick up some more information. He was joined there by Broderick Crawford for a good-will tour of the area.

After breakfast, we went down to the water to say hello to the boys. So there I was walking along the fish-slippery docks with the towering super-chief, the hero of the Highway Patrol (not to mention shades of Willie Stark in *All the King's Men*), and a couple of union guys feeling the full rush and fantasy of the Wild Bunch.

The fishermen were heading out to sea. John Wayne was on the radio for Mayor Sam, the seagulls were flying, hunks of tuna were being sliced, and this sweet and terrifying man walked up to an old longshoreman and said, "Hi, I'm Tom Reddin. I'm running for Mayor."

BREZHNEV ON TV. LET'S MAKE A DEAL
Los Angeles Free Press (20 July 1973)

My sources in Washington have informed me that there was much discussion on the best possible way of presenting Premier Leonid Brezhnev to the American public on television.

The more conservative elements wanted a straight, face-the-camera approach with a map of Russia in the background. In one corner would be the Soviet flag, and in the other a hammer and sickle over the Chase Manhattan Bank.

However, some advisors suggested a more adventurous approach. They argued that the most effective path to reach the American public was through a game show format so the message could be absorbed in the exact way the public is programmed.

Brezhnev's advisors were open to any suggestions, so for the sake of argument a secret tape was made to see how it would work. A hush-hush call was made to Monty Hall, and the noble experiment was on. The Russian Premier would make a surprise appearance on *Let's Make a Deal*, disguised in a polar bear costume.

The details were worked out as Brezhnev was treated to a private screening of *I Was a Communist For the FBI* and *Deep Throat*.

Although the idea was finally rejected, my Hollywood contacts arranged for me to see a bootleg tape of the failed experiment. The following is a transcript of some of the highlights.

Monty Hall (MH): "Wow, what a great audience. I bet you're all ready for fun and games and money, money, money. We're going to ask you to price some items, and see if you'll sell out or go for the big one. Who's gonna win the big prize today?" he chuckles, pinching a girl in a pink bunny outfit clutching a giant carrot.

"I've got a five dollar bill. Would you like a five dollar bill?"

Hysteria fills the studio. Monty eludes the grasping hands and gives the bill to a World War I veteran hopping on the floor dressed as a frog.

"Ladies and gentlemen, we are deeply honored to have with us today a very special guest, a man who is bullish on America, someone you housewives have never seen up close.

A bear lumbers up. "Yes, behind the mask is the MC of the biggest game show in the world. Yes, it's Lenny Brezhnev, host of the Union of Soviet Socialist Republics."

Audience cheers and gasps.

(MH) "Now Lenny, you've seen the demographics on our audience and you know some of them are anti-communist due to previous conditioning. So just to put people at their ease, will you explain to them that you're really not a socialist, are you?"

Brezhnev (LB) "No, as a matter of fact it's one of the most amazing misprints in history. I have carefully re-read Lenin's writing, and his original notes read the Union of Soviet Satiated Republics."

(MH) "Beautiful, here's ten dollars."

(LB hesitates) "Well, uh, I don't mean to be boorish, but could I take it in German marks?"

(MH) "You're beautiful. I can't tell you how proud we are that you have chosen *Let's Make a Deal* to get across your true message to the American public. Here's a fifty.

"You know last week we had Pat and Dick Nixon on. He came dressed as a plumber and she as a storefront mannequin. We had three giant doors. Behind the first were homes in California, Florida, and Washington with an extra two million dollars for improvements; behind the second was a hardbound edition of every monitored phone conversation of the twentieth century. Behind the third was Costa Rica."

(LB) "Which one did he pick?"

(MH) "Uh, unfortunately, he didn't have time. Just before the choice he arrested himself."

(LB) "I hope he has a good lawyer."

(MH) "Lenny, you're a card. Here's 500 marks. Now for the big deal of the day. Here's one million rubles. Now you can keep this, spend it on anything you want, or gamble it and take whatever is behind this iron curtain."

The audience bellows, "Do it, do it, go for broke!"

(LB hesitates and says) "What the hell, the cold war is over."

The Iron Curtain rises. Out comes Jill St. John and Liv Ullman with a copy of Henry Kissinger's phonebook. Yes, Mr. Brezhnev, for your first prize you get two weeks at the fabulous new Sinai Hilton with these international beauties, plus hundreds of celebrities for company."

(LB) "Small potatoes. Is that all I get?"

(MH) "No, there's much more." (The second curtain rises.)

"Yes, it's a 20-year supply of Wheaties, Wonder Bread, and Hostess Twinkies, plus 245 million Papermate pens to hand out to each Soviet citizen as a souvenir to commemorate the hundreds of treaties you signed last week."

More cheers.

(LB) "What is this, a joke?"

(MH) "Wait, here's the third." (It rises again.)

The astounded audience views two Eskimos laboring under a heavy pipe hoisted on their shoulders. Yes, it's the biggest freezer in the world, Alaska, brought to you by Standard Oil with optional icebergs on the side, for the busy Premier who doesn't have time to chill his own champagne.

(MH) "I've never seen a bear jump so high. By the way, did you and the President discuss Watergate?"

(LB) "What's Watergate?"

(MH) "Oh you must have heard, the President and 30 of his closest aides were caught breaking into the opposition party, and then spent months lying and covering it up."

(LB) "Well, I don't know if it will hurt him or help him, but he did say in Moscow that he was finally beginning to understand the advantages of a one-party system."

(MH) "Any final word to the American public?"

(LB) "Better bread than red."

(MH) "Thanks Lenny, regards to little Tanya, and thanks for showing that you, too, can make a deal. Now stay tuned for a double feature, *The Meaning of Stalingrad* brought to you by Pepsi Cola and Bebe Rebozo in his first appearance on *I've Got a Secret*.

WILL ELLIOT RICHARDSON BE OUR NEXT PRESIDENT?
Los Angeles Weekly News (24 August 1973)

It is becoming increasingly obvious that there is no possible way for Nixon to continue his charade as "The President." Slowly but surely the immensity of the corruption
of Watergate, the illegal campaign "dirty tricks," the misuse of Federal power (political use of the IRS), the deals with ITT and the large wheat handlers, the enemies list,
the failure to release tapes, and the pure greed of ten million dollars spent on home
improvements (bullet-proof swimming pools!) is seeping into the middle American
mentality like a huge turd into a steamy swamp.

McCord was the left jab and John Dean the right cross. Nixon is dead. He is no
longer President. If the Japanese attacked Pearl Harbor again, he would go on TV and
call for support; the general reaction could well be, "So what—it's been done before."

America hasn't been much on morality these last ten years, but they usually
provide a respectable level of entertainment. It would be difficult for any playwright
to beat the spectacle of this weasel, trapped in the basement of his own ambition,
squeaking desperately for help and support as his aides (also guided solely by ambition) spend their time cutting each other's throats to save their own skins.

The most likely way out is resignation—either voluntary or forced.

I believe the decision that Nixon has to resign was made at least three months
ago. I assume that, as usual, it was a matter of capital and finance. America is in
desperate trouble. The dollar is in grave danger, inflation is rampant, the scars of
Indochina will take a long time to heal, and the government stands there paralyzed
like (excuse the expression) a pitiful, helpless giant.

Put yourself in their shoes. (Even if you can't do it by the vote, just fantasize.)
From the capitalist point of view, how can they best straighten out this mess? They
must find a means to restore a measure of confidence in the federal government. The
country demands nobility and leadership, and Nixon stands there as living proof that
masturbation does, in fact, lead to insanity.

Nobody wants to play poker with a guy who has been caught cheating.

The needs of corporate America demand a switch from chaos to stability.

My guess is that Nixon has been told that he has to leave by the powers that be.
Agnew, though an effective temporary thug for Babbitt fund-raising and bullying the

media, doesn't have any of the real strength and character required for the hour. He is still the same political hack he was five years ago when Nixon picked him out of the Maryland gubernatorial gutter.

So it is necessary to remove him first.

Under the 25th Amendment to the Constitution, section three, "Whenever there is a vacancy in the office of the Vice-President, the President shall nominate a Vice-President who shall take office upon confirmation by a majority vote of both houses of Congress."

It seems pretty obvious that the decision to expose Agnew's past corruptions was made by over-zealous aides in the federal government, if not by Nixon himself.

Agnew's press conference was an interesting study in psychology. He was like a good fighter raised on easy opponents who suddenly and viciously got clobbered. His knees buckled, but he came back fighting gamely. However, the anger and hurt in his eyes betrayed the sudden knowledge that he not only had to fight the press and the Justice Department, but also the boys in his own corner—one of the few human moments in this network of bureaucratic lies.

I assume he'll be out of the picture in a month or two. That clears the way for the Mystery Guest. Who could possibly restore at least a measure of confidence in this shabby atmosphere? The word around Washington was Nelson Rockefeller. He has his own legitimate power base, and he is easily strong enough to pass confirmation by both houses. Other off-the-wall possibilities are Ronald Reagan or Mark Hatfield.

But over the last couple of weeks one figure seems to be looming larger and larger as a possibility, and that is Elliot Richardson.

The media are often used to manipulate the public. There is an amazing small picture in *Time* magazine (August 20, 1973) of a beaten Richard Nixon standing behind a confident and larger Elliot Richardson.

Richardson could re-unite some Kennedy loyalty with his Harvard background. His experience in government includes heading the Department of Health, Education, and Welfare, and, significantly, Secretary of Defense—so he's had a chance to sleep with the military.

Now he is Attorney General, the man who appointed Archibald Cox, his image of honesty untouched. He has already carefully been steering a course independent of Nixon.

And who would he choose as Vice-President? Why, Howard Baker—of course. The Southern star of the Watergate hearings, entrenched in the powerful Dirksen wing of the party, the perfect bandage for a wounded nation.

It would be a powerful new team, led by the ideal technocrat—combining efficiency, intelligence, experience, image-honesty, good media looks: the essential requirements for the beginning of a return to stability.

Both men owe a great deal to Nixon, and a separate side deal could be made. They could secretly decide who would be prosecuted and who should be left off, who will be the fall guys—Mitchell, Haldeman, etc.

With Agnew gone, Nixon appoints Mr. "return to confidence" and gives his farewell speech. "I am totally innocent. However, the government is paralyzed. For the good of the country I must resign."

Or, "The easy thing for me to do would be to stay on as your President. However, I have chosen the more difficult course. Good-by." He dashes out and is allowed to retire to Costa Rica to write his last book, *Six Thousand Crises*, before the inevitable suicide.

Of course, Richardson may not be the choice, but I think this article reflects the basic thinking behind the real decision-making process. Nixon's last address to the nation was so boring and mindless, I can only surmise that it was merely an attempt to buy time before making a real move.

There are several other possibilities. One is impeachment, if he insists on being a spoil-sport—leaving Carl Albert and the Congress with a caretaker government.

We could have military rule—but the military is too unruly, and their credibility has also been destroyed.

Another is a convenient death, a plane crash, or the surprise return of a more effective viral pneumonia.

Even if he managed to hang on, he would be totally impotent. He would have no power in Congress, reduced power in foreign affairs, and zero believability with the American public. He can't hide forever behind county fairs, Billy Graham, and the Veterans of Foreign Wars.

Besides, there are enough disgruntled people in the CIA and FBI who would leak their own information if he decided to stay. Actually, I'm sure some of them are responsible for the awesome amount of disclosures already.

If Nixon had an ounce of decency or a sense of honor he would have resigned a long time ago, just on the level of suspicion or the involvement of his closest aides, especially John Mitchell.

If this were a parliamentary system, he would have been forced out long ago on a vote of confidence.

But this is America, where show business and media hypnosis replace the law—and we seem forced into the role of an uninvolved and over-entertained audience.

I suppose the final lesson of all this is that your character is your fate. Here is Nixon on election eve, licking his chops at the point of his greatest victory. He believes he is loved. He believes he has finally beaten John Kennedy. And then, twenty-five years of lies, deceit, and hypocrisy come whipping around like a giant cosmic pie and flies *splat!* into his jowly and corpselike face.

Maybe there is a God.

OUT OF THE ARCHIVES (LOS ANGELES)

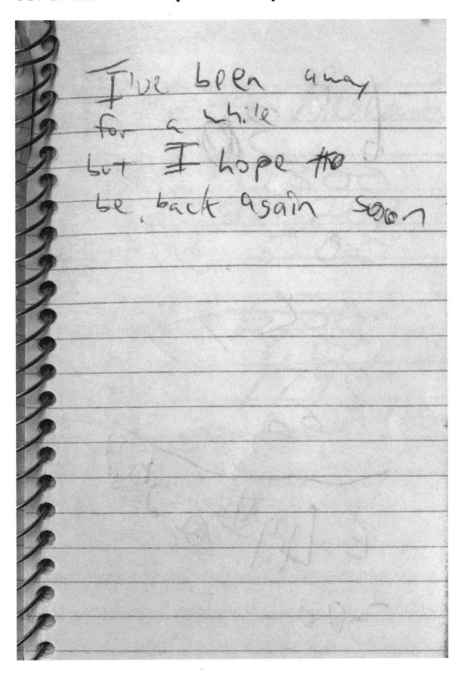

Leaving Darwin

Friday Aug 15 - Fitful sleep - get about 3hrs - in the back rm. of wharfie Jack Phillips at 39 McMinn St., Darwin, N.T. - Peppa said last nite but I still like yours singing - she waves goodbye in the morn - morning coffee + diary - pasting last pix in - Jan arrives - I thought my watch was wrong - the usual last minute rush - not even time for a shower - what will I forget this time? - give diary to Jack - send to B. Garcia - Air Express - Consignment no. - etc. - my soggy jacket or sweater send slow + cheap - leave some papers + pix behind - trying to lighten up - quick farewells - then lovely Jan drives me to airport - they plan to leave in Dec. & keep traveling - that's all there is - if I only had a woman like that - they've been married one year - the full last name is Wesley shit tells me to look up brother Peter - studying ch. legal history in HK - at the airport the same TAA crew - take care of details - go thru bags waiting for the bar to open - trip will take 6 hrs - very low on bread - leave 82 Get behind u. Terry - signed a poster for the workers club - they pay me fr customs - just when the beer is ready - get that done - then down 3 quick ones - Final call for Merpati to Denpasar - race out - so sad - a lovely 2 mos. in Australia must come to an end now - very emotional - take a last look around - in bar approached by young Amer. couple - saw me last nite - fr. Santa Barbara - very sweet & naive looking - on plane some kids fr. the Townsville house - even younger + more vulnerable looking - it's really good I did the show last nite - off we go - keep looking out window for last glimpse - goodbye beautiful Australia - the last tip dissolves into many islands - then a long dull trip - at 1st very smooth - read about Asia - free meals - free glasses of warm beer -

Notes - Singapore - City of the Lion - founded by S Raffles - 1819-24 - People's Action Party - PAP - Lee Kuan Yew - 224 sq. mi. - pop. 2 mill. - 75% Chinese - 13% Malay - 9% Ind. - Sampans - Instant Asia - Bugis St. - red helmet riot police - Payar Lebar Airport - Sing / dollar - $5.33 - Brunei - Letters of credit - Mt. Faber - the Raffles - A Lion in the Sun

Hong Kong - British Crown Colony - Nanking Peace Treaty of 1842 - 1st opium war - 1839-41 - Stone cutter's Island - the New Territories - Kai Tak airport - pop 4 mill. - 600,000 in 45 - Tuen Wan - Hakka - Tanka

Phillippines - Span. 300 yrs. - Miguel Lopez de Legazpi - Suez - (1869) - Cavite Arsenal - Jose Rizal - Liga Filipina - Emilio Aguinaldo - 7100 isles - 80% Catholic - Moslims of Mindanao - Hukbalahaps - Pasig River - Iglesia ni Cristo - Mayon Volcano (Albay) -

Indonesia

Bali - Bali Beach Hotel - expert rice growers - 2 crops ayr. - gamelan music - Gilimanuk - Sanor Beach - Island of the Gods - djukung - Ubud - Legong - Klung Klung - Kuta Beach - Ketchak (monkey dance) - isle of Lombok - Java - Sumatra - Sulawesi - Silienjras - Borobudur - the advance of Islam - cloves - Molucas - Atjeh (N. Sum) Stamford Raffles - (1811-16) - Diponegoro - Coup - Sept. 30 1965 - rubber + oil - 120 mill. people - Sumbawa - Flores - Sumba - wayang shadow play - Garuda -

Rupiah- 412- to 1 US Dollar - Ni Tour- Djakarta was called Batavia under Dutch- Kebaioran Baru - Tandjung Priok- fish market -(Pasar Ikan)- batik- Jogja- Tretes- Surakarta- Padang- rijstafel- nasi goreng - babi guling- Soto- (Zamrud Airlines) - Makasar - Menado - Dili - trishaws- filigree gold- Bahasa-Indonesia-

After 2½ hrs. a lousy bumpy landing in Portuguese Indonesia Timor - Kupang - 1 hr. wait for customs- seedy place- lots of kids hanging around- very hot- when the plan takes off the air cond. goes on - on the ground it's sweltering- go back for my camera- they don't change money at the airport- see red & white Indon. flag - a couple of hangars- people & baskets on their heads- Someone says it looks like Tijuana- kids ask for cigarettes- some soldiers w. rifles- this is my 1st stop in Asia- it is like a poor mex. town- walk out in st.- some cow sniffing a dry bucket- filled w. water- they shy away- followed by group of kids- so barren here-(my belly has been a good friend- I won't need it when I reach the end)- sit in shade by small bldg.- a thankful breeze- meanwhile they're madly looking for me- forgot about customs- where's your ticket- back to plane & then where's your camera- they like to search that- finally back on- looked pretty carefully thru suitcase- off again- air pockets- trip becoming endless- doze off- then a smooth bank into Bali - beaut. cliffs- waves crashing- we land- off to buy check- surrounded by hustling boys- how much to town- 1st price 400 rupiahs (1. doll.)- then hear Fr. guy who was here before - only 50¢ to beach- bargain- kid named Putra puts me in bus- off we go- a paradise- just like Haiti - every time I look around some amazing new sight- animals everywhere- palm trees- rice fields- women w. baskets- a similar smell to H.- the bustle of life mixed tightly- crowded- beeping horns all the time - in back of bus w. woman, kids, chickens, etc.- go to Adi Yasa as recommended- 11 Nakula St.- they have a double- 300 rupiahs- 75¢- ok- a cell-like rm. w. no circulation- very hot but not quite as bad as Darwin- drop my things off- then to Bali Hotel to cash travellers cheque -$10- 405 rate- go to bar - have cold bir- Bintang Baru Bir- Pilsener- 200 rupiahs- an older Amer. there- works for oil co. in Bass Strait- wearing khaki clothes- get talking- whores in Sing. - pays $14 for air cond. rm here- lonely looking man- light up a Monte Cristo in celebration of my arrival- Putra waiting outside- off we go on motobike thru this amazing city- it was basically a market town- capital used to be Singaradja- then get on bike- zip around town- amazing place - horns honking- bicycles everywhere- baskets on heads- animals- thronging- get off & walk thru market - again like Haiti - wooden stalls- cooking food- Sandals- cloth- sarongs- bags- carving- framed cheap pix- Suharto- many fruit & vegetables-

Mike Mazurki's Spot

by Phil Ochs

Underneath the soul sucking smog of Los Angeles lie the lonely shadows of eight million prisoners of fame, many sentenced to solitary confinement. There is little organic connection between people here, no sense of neighborhood, and very little past associations. The other day they found a guy who was born here and stayed; they threw him out of town and he was last seen heading for Australia.

Who knows who is living next door to you. It could be Nixon's brother, it could be the lighting man for 2001, it could be your second cousin. No one dares to ask. Some have been dead for years and nobody even knows, Mayor Yorty for example, but that's another story.

Every once in a while I break out of my little cell and check out the cemetery for signs of life. Legend has it the only real life in this town is among the very successful who are usually recognized by their dark limosines, their dark glasses, and their piles of booze and pills. Nobody talks to them except ghosts and reporters, and many of them end up being the lonliest of all.

The town is not completely lacking in charm. Death attracks interesting visitors. One of these is Jose "Mantequilla " Napoles, Cuban born, Mexico City wined and dined, the welterweight champion, and as the cliche goes pound for pound the greatest fighter in the world.

I watched him train recently at the old Elks building on Parkview road across from Macarthur Park(Westlake Park before Macarthur returned). The rich used to live there, the lake used to run through Wilshire Blvd., and the Elks used to own it before selling to the Bauer brothers who have most of the area now.

The structure is enormous with a 50 ft. painted ceiling, wrought iron doors at the top of the imposing staircase, an olympic size swimming pool at the YMCA below. It is mainly a man's territory. They made a concession to the ladies with a

-2-

large powder room on the ground floor.

Most of the people who came to see Napoles are Mexican; they provide the backbone for boxing in this town. As Jose pummels his hard to find sparring partners, the crowd yells , "Arriba...Mantequilla (his nickname, smooth as butter), as they savor the physical embodiment of their national pride.

They say he has a weakness for tequila and women, and once in a while a beautiful girl will jump in the ring for pictures and whistles. Occasionally a great white hoper will throw out an insult, but Napoles speaks only in Spanish(he travels with translators) and sullenly goes on punching.

On the way out I stopped at the bar for a cool Coors, and as I looked over I noticed a sign saying Mike Mazurki's spot. My heart jumped, Could this be the same Mike Mazurki that pounced on Richard Widmark, threw Tyrone Power around, and fought in the foreign legion with Burt Lancaster in my boyhood dream movies. Only in Hollywood.

It took a few weeks to build up my courage, but I went back determined to talk to him and find out what he was doing here. Jerry Meeker behind the cash register was friendly. "Oh yeah, Mike's been here for 3 months. He hangs around when he's not refereeing wrestling matches at the Houston Astrodome or selling stuff on the idiot box, I think you call them commercials."

To kill time I walked by the empty bandshell across the street and listened to the echoes of the countless anti-war rallies I had attended there. When I came back there he was carrying a case of champagne glasses for a wedding reception they were catering for the coming Sunday.

We didn't know what to make of each other , but I stammered out something about the Free Press and how I dug him in "Ten Tall Men". He seemed surprised and said come back tomorrow, I'll bring some stills.   He is 6'4" tall & weighs 240 lbs.

Mike Mazurki is sixty-two years old and looks forty. His appearance is

-3-

tough and threatening, but he's more gentle than your average Hare Krishna convert

thrusting leaflets at you on Hollywood Blvd. He was a professional wrestler and

fought 4,000 men in the ring. He has appeared in over 100 movies. Most of his

bones have been broken, and he speaks with a rasp from repeated blows to his

adam's apple.

He was discovered by Joseph Von Sternberg while wrestling at the Olympic

auditorium. Sternberg wanted a guy who could speak Russian for "Shang hai Gesture";

He screen tested with Victor Mature and Gene Tierney. "They made me shave my head

cause I looked too much like Mature," he said showing his Roman profile."Sternbeg,

he8s the guy that discovered Marlene Deibrich."

Mike is a Ukrainian born on Christmassday in 1909. He lived there six years

and was brought over after his parents had settled near Albany NY. Thousands were

leaving then because of the poverty and the easy emigration laws,. There are now

over two million of Ukrainian descent in North America.

"I still can speak and write Ukrai nian which is to my way of thinking a high

class Russian." He describes the old country as a vast farmland like Nebraska or Iowa

where he had to walk half a mile to get water. In the Russian Orthodox Church there

were no seats, and since some of the services were over three hours he would often

pass out from hunger or thirst. To this day he only goes to the end of a service.

His father was a blacksmith who worked for the railroad here, and his mother

was a domestic for the local baron and the local priest.

He got a bachelor of Arts at Manhattan college, excelling in treack, football,

and basketball(the tallest center in all the NY schools). After graduation he

got a job on all St., going to law school at night. But this was during thedepression

and a local promoter noticed him doing some amateur wrestling and offered him $5000

a night to turn pro. At that time wrestling was a more legitiambe sport and many

college athletes were turning to it.

H wrestled five nights a week in New York, M nday at Madison Square Garden

-4-

(Monday-at they packed in 35,000 every wk), Tuesday, St. Nicks, Wed, Brooklyn,
Thurday White Plains, and Fr. the Broadway arena. "In those days you got by on
sheer ability, but today everything is exagerrated. That's what you call showmanship.
    b   Wrestling in Europe is known as the Greco-Roman style, in which you could only
fight from the waist up, but here in America it developed into catch as catch can,
anything goes.

        Mike fought many of the champions .A match was decided by three falls, shoulders
to the mat unless the ether- opponent gave up under a painful hold. "Sometimes we'de
talk to each other, threatening or joking. "I'm gonna break your fucking arm if you
don't give up.....you don't mean that ...yes sir I do...You never know."

    .   I had everything going for me when I broke into pictures. I'd work on a
film for three months, and when I told a promoter I was available for a fight,
heSd advertise just returned from Hoolywood where he made a movie with Gary
Cooper. "The fans would say Jeez, its a movie star. Today that's nothin. In those
days it was somethin.'

        In his heydey he fought with Gorgeous George and Man Mt. Dean. "Now George
was a greatl little wrestler, 175 lbs., fancy gowns and marcelled hair, he made
over four million dollars. Man Mountain Dean was originally a boxer by the name of
Soldier Levitt; he served under Patton.Now it wasn't so much he was good , but h e
was so strong; he jumped on some guys and broke their backs. "

        He had some work to do with his wife, sylv. , so I arranged to meet him
the next day. As I walked out I was approached by a thin nervous Chicano. He said
"My name's Eddie Rodriguez, I used to be a fighter. You know I'm 49 years old, but
don't you think I'm in great shape?"

        "Yeah."

        Then he showed me an autographed card saying "Your friend always, Bobby Chacon. "
Hey , how about giving me 50 ¢ for a bus into town. I gave-it handed him some coin
and started to leave.

        On impulse I turned and said "I think Tori Pinedd's gonna take Chacon. A look of

-5-

authority returned to his face, and Eddie said, "No way, no way."

The next day I came back and walked by the old Elk pensioners sitting in the lo by with their canes and memories., we continued the talk over some chicken treeayaki and one of his eitht salads.

"Ya know I didn't always look like this, with my pugnacious nose and cauligdour ears. Look, here's a picture of my daughter. People look at her and say , she's yours?" (he shows me a beach-fresh Cal. blonde). Don't forget I been wrestling 35 years. I took a lot of beating, a lot of physical contact.

"I did this picture called "Behind the rising Sun. I was a Japanese ~~wheslate~~ wrestler who fought Bob Ryan. Now the same producer and Eddie Dmytryk the director were going to do "Murder M_ Sweet" with Dick Powell in his first role as a tough guy . So I called him and I said hey, Eddie, this Moose Malloy character is me. Oh, he says why don't you stick to wrestling, you're not an actor.

They tested everybody in town. Victor Mcglacglen,. Ward Bond, all the big boys, muscle men from the beach, even truck drivers. So one day I happened to walk into the commissary at RKO. Sitting with Dm_tryk was the studio president, Charly Koerner, he's dead now. Someone says Hya Mike....Hi boys...I happened to be wearing a loud coat at that time. Dymtrik looks around and says that's Mike Mazurki the wrestler, and Koerner says, but that's Moose Malloy.

We went up to the head office. Mr. Koerner he looks at me and sayd, "Can you read?"

I did 't know how to take that. I says whadyamean can I read?" Now he's hurt my feelings. Ya know they see a big guy here in Hollywood with a raspy voice and a busted nose, they immediately say he's punchy. I played punchy parts. They paid me to play these things.

I told him I was a callege graduate with a year at law school. So I tested with Powell and got the part. They'd been looking for two months. That Eddie Dmytrk. He was a funny little shit. And he used to say, "I can beat your ass and I said Oh

-6-

C'mon Eddie , you're a little shit.Ah, he was an amateur wrestler and he hated
professionals. All these little guys are cocky little bastards. But Eddie taugth
me a lot about actin Anyway I got the part. This brought me into promincene. This
made me a feature actor. ⁺here's a lotta luck in your life, you know that dontcha, Phil?"

Now Lancaster there was a great guy. I was wrestling ⁺rimo Carnera in Evansville,
Indiana. Burt looks me up and says what are you doin, come down to the circus tonight.
So I come down and he gives me the biggest hand, he says my best friend from Hollywood,
fighting C⁺rnera. This is in the big tent. We sold out the goddam house. That's the
kind of guy he is.

What about "⁺ope of Sand?"

"You remember that one? You remember a lot of the old ones, don't you?"

Yeh, I go to the movies all the time.

⁺hat's good.

⁺our times a week.

Then proudly, "Did you know of my other pictures?"

yeh, ᴰonovan's Reef

How about "Blood Alley?" Then there was that great one with Tyrone Power,
Nightmare Alley", you see that?"

Parts of it on televsion.

"I'll tell you whht happened with Tyrone Power one day. I was supposed to get
him up against a juke box. He's supposed to do this (he gestures) And I'm supposed
to grab him and make him marry the girl (he grabs me) But I had him loose, I didn't
want to hurt him and he broke away a couple of times.

So the director Ed Goulding says,"For Chrisszke Mazurki, hold the guy.
So next time I grabbed him! I grabbed him so hard...skin,hair and everything, and
I say you sonofabith you stay!

And he yelled like a goddamned hyena.

And Goulding shouts, "Its a take!" So Power walks over off the set. "I'll never
work with that sonovabiyh again. Look at this, look at this. He hurt me.

-7-

For two hours he doesn't show.

Really?

George Jessel was the producer. He says, "Mike , what are you tryin to do!"

I said, "I'm sorry."

Goulding says you're killing my stars.They don't know the real story.So Ty comes back and says he was kidding. ~~Since then~~ After that we were the best of friends. I didn't want to hurt the guy. Once you hurt em and it gets around Hollywood you won't work anymore.

But you can get it too. I was doing "Dakota" with John Wayne and I had just finished killing Ward Bond. The Duke must have got carried away, cause in the next scene he pulled my hat over my eyes and I ended up on the floor with a bloody nose.

Mazurki has a great scene in Ford's "Cheyenne Autumn." where as the Polish sergeant he tells Lt. Widmark after an indian massacre " I didn't come to America to be a Coassack."

" When world war II broke out, four of us all wrestlers went down to volunteer. They put us in special service. They fit us in for our languages. Joe Savoldi for Italian, me for Russian and Polish, Lopez for Spanish. They asked Willy Davis what language he spoke and he said, "Ah speak profane." He's from the South. Savoldi later became a commander in the invasion of ~~Italy.~~ Sicily

After a while they gave me a physical. The doctor said I couldn't go in the regular service, I had a bad back. They took x-rays. You know the vertebrae goes down like this...well mine was out like that.

Now that's when I use to go to the bars, and these little guys who used to be in the service, they'd say, you big palooka, how come you're not in? And they'd try to pick a fight with me. And I'd have to take all that crap and walk out. I couldn't hit em. I couldn't hit a man in uniform. Me,a civilian. They'd say look at that big bastard hitting that poor little soldier. He's fightin for his country. Get the point?"

-8-

as I drove back ~~I felt~~ *Strangely Vulnerable in*

We shook hands and ~~I drove my war torn volkswagon back through~~ the crowded,
deserted streets. That night as I was typing up our conversation the tube was on
and I watched the haunted faces of the first POW's climbing off those awkward planes
in the Phill ippines, returning from the ultimate wrestling match. They looked so
fragile and ghostlike, and they said "God Bless America", and I went outside to
get a beer, but its not New York, the bars were closed.

-30-

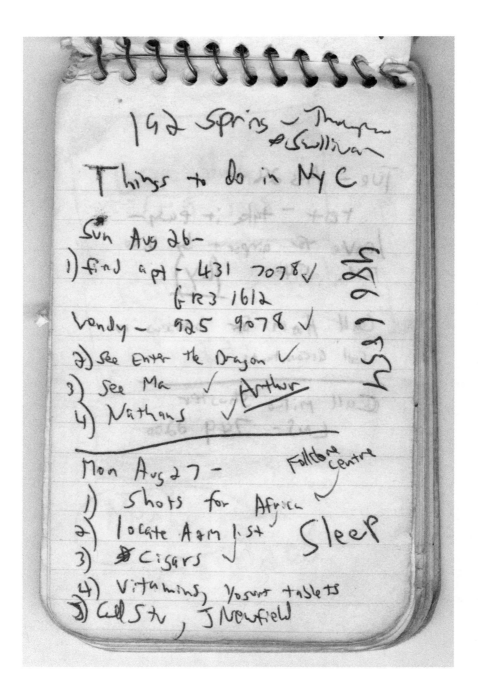

Requiem For a Dragon Departed

The Story of Bruce Lee

By Phil Ochs

I was in the Phillippines in September of 1972 ending a tour through Australia and SE Asia. It was a steamy Sunday;, the day before the American puppet Marcos was to declare martial law. Rumors were rife in the papers, then known for being the most outspoken in Asia.

I didn't know what to do on my last day in Asia. I had missed the boat which would have retraced the death marchfrom Bataan; so at 10:00 in the morning I went to see a Bruce Lee double feature. I had heard his name mentioned in Singapore, Bangkok, and especially in Hong Kong, always with a sense of wonder , the way some people talk about Clint Eastwood or Muhammed Ali.

Though it was Sunday in the major Christian area in SE Asia, the theatre was packed. Outside, in typical Phillipino fashion was a sign "Please check your guns." It seemed like the most violent place on earth. There were gunfights and knifings late almost every night in the brothels and bars.

If you had some money you had a bodyguard; if you had real money and land you had a small and well-trained army.

I bought a San Miguel beer and peanuts and groped my way to a seat. There I was entranced for three hours; I could hardly believe my eyes. I had seen the Japanese Samurai movies but was not prepared for what was to come.

The pictures were "The Big Boss" and "Fists of Fury" (released here as "Fist of Fury" and "The Chinese Connection"). The stories were simplistic and mainly based on revenge. They always involve fighting schools and a revered master teacher. "I will teach you to be the best fighters in the world, but you must never use it to harm anyone unless absolutely necessary."

Near the beginning is the act of outrage-the insults of a rival school, the poisoning of a master, the murder of a loved one. Lee, the hero, the best fighter demands vengeance and is always restrained until he can hold himself no longer.

Then follows the most exciting action ever filmed on the screen. One man against fifty with no weapons. He begins to wade his way through the lesser villains with karate chops; his fists, his elbows, his feet; there are no camera tricks.

The audience is hysterical, clapping, cheering, sometimes leaping to their feet. When he gets to the major villains it becomes a dance of extraordinary beauty; (One reviewer said that Lee made Rudolph Nureyev look like a truck driver.)

It is not the vulgarity of James Arness pistol-whipping a stubbled, drunken stage robber; it is not the ingenious devices

2

of James Bond coming to the rescue, nor the ham-fisted John Wayne
slugging it out in the saloon over crumbling tables and paper thin
imitation glass. It is the science of the body taken to its highest
form and the violence, no matter how outrageous, is always strangely
purifying.

As important as the action is the face and mind of Bruce Lee.
The expressions he gets as he psyches out his opponents is beyond
description; at times he is lost in ecstasy, almost sexual, and when
he strikes, the force of the blow is continued by his mind and the
look of concentration and satisfaction is devastating.

Two months later I was at a Hollywood party raving about Bruce
Lee and Chinese-boxing movies when I ran into Fred Weintraub, veteran
of the Bitter End in Grennwich Village, Neil Diamond and the Woodstock movie.

"Bruce? Why he's a good friend of mine. As a matter of fact I'm
just leaving for Hong Kong to negotiate a deal with him and Warner
Bros. We both knew the impact that a westernized version of this
type would have on the American audience.

The months pass. I see Freddie occasionally, delirious with
excitement as "Enter The Dragon!" is progressing. Then it is complete. I am eagerly awaiting the results when on July 20; while
singing in Toronto I pick up a paper and read to my shock and amazement " Bruce Lee Dead at 32 in Hong Kong of a Brain Hemmorage."
Impossible...it can't be;..tears of disbelief. But it is true. The
healthiest and most athletic man on the screen is snatched away by
the cruel joke of death.

It is my feeling now that Bruce Lee will become a James Dean
figure of the seventies. James Dean was a great actor finishing
three films before dying in a car crash at age 24. Bruce Lee was not
that kind of actor, but on a physical level he will survive in the
imagination as long as there are movies. They both found their way
into mythology by a brief but totally magical presence on the screen
followed by a sudden and meaningless death.

There is a great tradition of screen adventure first popularized
by Douglas Fairbanks Sr:then Jr, followed by Errol Flynn and continued by Burt Lancaster & Toshiro Mifune.

To be a star on this order requires not only a great face, an
extraordinary athletic body, a strong and graceful movement, but also
a certain charm and elan that you see in the eyes of Fairbanks in
"The Thief of Bagdad," or of Flynn in Captain Blood."

One of The last moments of pure adventure I saw on the screen was in
1952 when Lancaster slashed the rope of the high mast in "The Crimson Pirate" and flew to the top, his golden hair blowing against the
blue sky, shouting something like "Follow me mateys!"

Coincidentally I saw "The Crimson Pirate" in Bangkok, two weeks
before the Bruce Lee experience. By the expansion of body discipline;

-3-

Lee will change the course of adventure films of all countries.
The following information is based on information provided by
Bill Stern at WB publicity, Fred Weintraub, a magawine called
"Fighting Stars" whose opening editorial reads, "We all feel the
lack of the right words to say, expecially those that would give comfort to his stricken family and friends. For all of us the world
is a much smaller place."
Bruce Lee was born in San Francisco in 1940 and from age three
to 18 was raised in Hong Kong. His father was a star in the Chinese
opera. He studied martial arts from his early teens and was a master
at age 18. He entered the University of Washington in Seattle where
he got a degree in philosophy. There he met and married an American
girl named Linda. They have two children, Brandon and Shannon, age
eight and four. He also was a child actor in Chinese films.
He used to go to Long Beach for the karate tournament where he
would put on exhibitions of his own particular style, jeet kune do.
There he was noticed by a television producer who at first
wanted to cast him as the number one son in a Charlie Chan series.
But he changed his mind and Lee first emerged into the western
consciousness as Kato in the "Green Dragon" series.
International distribution made him a hero in Hong Kong. He
had trouble getting movie roles in the US and appeared occasionally,
once as a villain in "Marlowe" and a strong segment of "Longstreet "
with James Franciscus called "Way of the Fist."
Finally Raymond Chow of Golden Harvest Studios in Hong Kong offe
red him his first feature, "The Big Boss" to be filmed in Thailand
in July 71. The location was so remote that Lee lost ten pounds from
lack of meat in his diet.
Its opening in Hong Kong turned out to be a cinematic revolution.
It became the first film to outgross the champ, "The Sound of Music"
2.8 million for 'Music' and 3.2 million for 'Boss'.
Then everyone went crazy. He quickly finished "The Chinese Connection; like the first it was directed by Lo Wei.
This was followed by the only picture he directed "The Way of
the Dragon" (as yet unreleased in the US) by reputation the best of
his four. It was also the first Chinese film to do location shooting
in Europe. The dragon name is used twice since Lee's name in Chinese,
Lee Hsiao-lung means little dragon.
At this point arrives Weintraub, associate producer Paul Heller,
and Warner Brothers. Lee is heading for the throne of Eastwood and
Bronson and there is no question that, had he lived, he would have
been the highest paid actor in movies.
What follows is based on a conversation with Fred Weintraub at
WB.

-4-

"   "I met Bruce when Sy Weintraub brought him over to my house.
Sy studied with him along with James Garner, Steve McQueen; James
Coburn and Lee Marvin. He didn't like to teach and consequently
charged 100 dollars per hour.

Fred believes that part of the appeal of his pictures will lie
in the fact that most people have not been threatened by a gun, but
everyone has been hit; they will provide total identification.

"I think Bruce is a great exploitation actor, like Eastwood,
Wayne etc.They believe what th they do at the moment they are doing
it, no matter how outrageous; these actors are worth their weight-in
gold."

He said Bruce was totally absorbed with his body and his abiliti-
ies. " Often he would meet somebody and within a couple of minutes
he would say, 'Feel or punch my stomach. Sometimes he would take
his shirt off at screenings.

I remember standing in line at some restaurant and Bruce would
suddenly lash out a punch next to my face. I could feel the brush of
air, but I was never afraid; he had absolute control, he never
missed, he was like a sharshooter.

He was an expert in the use of his body. He went to all the best
teachers in each school and mastered their technique, every specialty.

He loved looking at his body.He lived in an eleven room mansion
in Hong Kong with a college size gym. He worked out for hours every
day including a three mile run; there were mirrors so he could watch
his own movements.

But it wasn't all physical. He would lock himself away for days
to read books on the philosophy of fighting, books on John L. Sullivan.
The art of kick-fighting.

I remember once we were having dinner with John Tunney and John
asked; " Do you think you could have beaten my father? "

Bruce said ;" 'To tell you the truth, I could beat anybody in
the world. Of course, if I sat still and your father hit me, or
Clay did, forget it. The question is could they ever get close to
me;"

He went on to describe a couple of books that Gene Tunney had
written that no one had heard about. He had the most unbelievable
library on the science of fighting. No one knew more about all kinds
of fighting than he did.

He liked to tell stories from Chiness legends. His favorite
was the one about the praying mantis. A cruel emperor was ravaging
China. Suddenly his army column stopped.Enraged, he rode to the
front and asked what was the matter.

The commander said there is a praying mantis in front of us.

So?

-5-

He is standing on his legs and is prepared to attack.

The emporer thought and agreed; the whole column rode around
the mantis. [*mantis*]

Fred describes an incident that occured when the picture was
2/3 complete. " Hong Kong is a pretty rough place. Where ever
Bruce went he was besieged for autographs and often people would
challenge him to fight on the streets; he tried to ignore them.

There was a young karate student who was an extra on the
picture walked up and said, 'I don't think you're so fast; I
think I can beat you."

I froze. I thought Oh my God, suppose he got hurt.

Bruce pulled away from me, raised his hands and stamped
his feet three times, the signal he was ready to fight. Suddenly
he swerved around and laid him on the floor with a kick in the
face, walked away without a word to him and said, 'Let's do
the next scene.'

Basically he was a loner. He didn't trust anybody. The only
people close to him were Raymond Chow and especially his wife
Linda. He adored and spent a lot of time with his kids."

Many Chinese-Americans have an incredible sense of insecurity
about themselves. Young well-to-do- Chinese often make self dep-
redating jokes about themselves doing laundry etc. Bill Stern tells
of driving Bruce through Coldwater Canyon, taking the curves
quickly and Bruce said, 'I can see by the way you drive this car,
you would like to have a car like mine, a Porsche 3" He has also ordered a $2,000 dollar Rolls Royce for Hong Kong.

This is often covered by an air of superiority.

Fred- "I wouldn't say this in public, but while making 'Dragon'
he personally fed stories to the local Chinese papers of how he
had fired the American writer on his picture. It's partially a
colonial mentality; or if you can picture a dead-end kid suddenly
becoming a millionaire.

If I could send a note to Bruce right now, it would be,
'Dragon' outgrossing 'The Getaway' in every engagement; Nothing
would make him more happy."   The biggest they ever had there,

Bruce Lee had two funerals. The first one in Hong Kong brought
out over 30,000 bereaved fans, and at his actual burial in Seattle
Steve McQueen and James Coburn were among his pall-bearers.

Fred- "His death affected many high-ego people I know; to think
that he of all people could die so suddenly..."

He blacked out six months before his death for no known reason. He had a complete physical check-up after that with the best
doctors in Los Angeles and they gave him a clean bill of health.

The offical cause of death is listed as an aneurism, a

—6—

congenital weakening of a vessel in the brain.
     Maybe he did die of an aneurism.
     There were rumors in Hollywood of Cocaine.
     Maybe he was killed by some crazy person or some rival
business faction.
     Maybe he wasn't meant to be cast as a James Bond figure, serving
the interests of Interpol.
     Maybe he lived more intensely than any human being can live.
     Or maybe he died for the same reason James Dean died. They
had taken too much of the fire, and the Gods were jealous.

                    Written by ~~Robert Sam Anson~~ in Addis Ababa ~~on the tour~~
                              Sept 1 1971

Mike

Please send copies to ~~weakly news~~ weakly news   Robin Love,   Bert. Barb   Ga Straight
and to Bill Stern & Fred wentush at WB.   univ. Review
                                                                 Grt. Speckled
                                                                 Bird

          arrival in Addis Sept 1   & will be in Nairobi Kenya
                                        on Sept 5,

                              God luck,

                                    P. Oh

               Let's spread this around eh ?
                    I like it

          any news?   send to Nairobi
                    trip starting slow — but a regional
                    my luggage — hard to melt people —
                    will see Lfodin in a cuple of days

P.S. WB will send photos to newspapers — please
                                        ask B. Stern

Brezhnev Makes A Deal

by Phil Ochs

My sources in Washington have informed me that there was much
discussion on the best possible way of presenting Premier Leonid
Brezhnev to the American public on television.

The more conservative elements wanted a straight face-the-camera
approach with a map of Russia in the background; in one corner would be
the Soviet flag; and in the other a hammer and sickle over the Chase
Manhatten Bank.

However some advisors suggested a more adventurous approach. They
argued that the most effective path to reach the American public was
through a game show format so the message could be absorbed in the exact
way the public is programmed.

Brezhnev's advisors were open to any suggestions, so for the sake of
argument a secret tape was made to see how it would work. A hush-hush
call was made to Monty Hall, and the noble experiment was on. The Russian
Premier would make a surprise appearance on Let's Make a Deal", disguised
ah what in a polar bear costume.

The details were worked out as Brezhnev was treated to a private
screening of "I Was a Communist For the FBI" and "Deep Throat."

Although the idea was finally rejected, my Hollywood contacts
arranged for me to see a bootleg tape of the failed experiment. The
following is a transcript of some of the highlights.

Monty Hall (MH)- Wow, what a great audience. I bet you're all ready for
fun and games and money, money, money. We're going to ask you to price
some items, and see if you'll sell out or go for the big one. Who's
gonna win the big prize today?", he chuckles, pinching a girl in a pink
bunny suit outfit clutching a giant carrot.

"I've got a five dollar bill. Would you like a five dollar bill?"

Hysteria fills the studio. Monty eludes the grasping hands and gives
the bill to a World War I veteran hopping on the floor dressed as a frog.

-2-

~~cr........ .... back pocket. They it's ....~~
~~there's money for everybody."~~

"Ladies and Gentlemen we are ~~especially~~ *deeply* honored to have with us
today a very special guest, a man who is bullish on America, someone
you housewives have never seen up close.

A bear lumbers up. "Yes behind this mask is the MC of the biggest
game show in the world, yes it's Lenny B̶reshnev host of the Union of
Soviet Socialist Republics."

Audience cheers and gasps.

(MH) Now Lenny, you've seen the demographics on our audience and you
know some of them are anti-communist due to previous conditioning. So
just to put people at their ease, will you explain to them that you're
really not a socialist, are you?

Brezhnev (LB) No, as a matter of fact its one of the most amazing misprints
in history. I have carefully re-read Lenin's writing, and his original
notes read the Union of Soviet Satiated Republics.

"Beautiful, here's ten dollars."

LB hesitates. "Well, uh I don't mean to be boorish, but could I
take it in German marks?

MH- You're beautiful. I can't tell you how proud we are that you have
chosen "Let's Make a Deal" to get across your true message to the
American public. Here's a fifty.

"You know last week we had Pat and Dick Nixon on. He came dressed
as a ~~burglar~~ *plumber* and she as ~~the wax figure of an Avis girl~~ *She first manne(un)* We had three
giant doors. Behind the first were homes in California, Florida, and
Washington with an extra two million dollars for improvements; behind
the second was a hard-bound edition of every monitored phone conversation
of the twentieth Century. Behind the third was Costa Rica.

LB- Whi̶hh one did he pick?

MH- Uh, unfortunately, he didN't have time. Just before the choice he
arrested himself.

-3-

LB- I hope he has a good lawyer.

MH- Lenny, you're a card. Here's 500 marks. Now forthe big deal of
the day. Here's one million rubles.Now you can keep this, spend it on
anything you want, or gamble it in-exchange-for and take whatever is
behind this iron curtain."

The audience bellows, "Do it, do it, go for broke!"

LB hesitates and says,"what the hell, the cold war is over."

The Iron Curtain Rises. Out comes Jill St. John and Liv Ullmann
with a   copy of "Maps to Stars Homes" [Henry Kissinger's Phone book]. Yes Mr. Brezhnev for
your first prize you get twoo weeks at the fabulous new Sinai Hilton
with these international beauties, plus hundreds of celebrities for
company.

LB- Small potatoes. Is that all I get?

MH- No there's much more. The second curtain rises.

Yes its a twenty year supply of Wheaties, Wonder Bread, and Hostess
Twinkies, plus 245 million Parker Paper-mate pens to hand out to each
Soviet citizen as a souvenir to commemorate the hundreds of treaties
you signed last week.

More cheers.

LB- What is this, a joke?

MH- Wait, here's the third. It rises againg.

The astounded audience views two eskimoes laboring under a heavy
pipe hoisted on their shoulders. Yes its the biggest freezer in the
world, Alaska, brought to you by Standard Oil with optional icebergs
on the side for the busy Premier who doesn't have the time to chill
his own champagne.

MH- [I've never seen a bear jump so high,] By the way did you and the President discuss Watergate?

LB- What's watergate?

MH- Oh you must have heard, the President and thirty of his closest
aides were caught breaking into the opposition party, and then spent

-4-

several months lying and covering it up.

LB- Well, I don't know if it will hurt him or help him, but he did say

in M˘scow that he was finally beginning to understand the advantages of

a one party system.

MH- Any final word to the American public?

LB- Better bread than red.

MH- Thanks Lenny, regards to little Tanya, and thanks for showing that

you too can make a deal. Now stay tuned for a double feature "The

Meaning of Stalingrad" brought to you by Pepsi Cola and ~~President Nixon~~ *Bebe Rebozo*

in his first appearance on "I've Got a Secret."

-30-

CODA

SOHO BAR ATTACKED
Unpublished

A drunken Phil Ochs smashed 5 windows of a bar called "Che."

He had bought 80% of the bar, but during negotiations had been thrown out repeatedly by his partner Robert Bonic.

Bonic signed a letter of intent until Sept. 15. If he receives $32,000 Phil Ochs is the official owner pending S.L.A. approval.

Ochs was so drunk earlier in the evening he threatened several lady customers when they complained that the juke box was too loud.

His own bouncer then decided to lock him out. It was a monumental battle. Before Ochs could climb thru the broken glass he was halted by 4 police cars.

They took him into custody, but after hearing the full story they released him without charges.

THE SALE OF ONE CITY
Unpublished, circa December 1975 (?)

I cannot find a cop
even tho I've just been stuck up
the garbage is all piled up

The car has lost a tire
the second floor's on fire
you'd know I'd be a liar
if I said we were happy

There's no water in the hose
the supermarket's closed

I picked up the telephone
it felt I was all alone
because the operator said hang up
and make it snappy

Chorus:
Oh what a sad tale
but a city is for sale

We left the house in style
I've reached the first half mile
soon we'll reach the top of the pile of the garbage

SAVE NEW YORK CITY
Unpublished, 1975

A Proposal
The Greatest Show on Earth
For
The Greatest City on Earth
Save New York City

Starring
Frank Sinatra   Barbra Streisand   Bob Dylan
Carole King   Neil Diamond   John Denver
Shea Stadium
M.C. Joe DiMaggio
Also . . . Stevie Wonder, Simon and Garfunkel, Ella Fitzgerald, John Lennon,
N.Y. Philharmonic Orch. with Leonard Bernstein, N.Y.C. Ballet, Woody Allen,
Ethel Merman, Bette Midler, Tito Puente, Liza Minnelli, Martin + Lewis,
Bob Hope, Bill Cosby, Arthur Rubenstein, Joe Namath, John + Bonnie Raitt,
Sammy Davis Jr., Beverly Sills, Zero Mostel, Herbie Hancock, Harry Chapin,
George Jessel, Al Green

Televised on CBS   National   Film of N.Y.C. History
Plus: Twenty minute slots from every ethnic group in city. Folklore and dance from
the Albanians, Poles, Chinese, etc.
Could be one to three days. Possible daytime fair at the stadium with all
neighborhoods from city participating.
Front row seats for $1,000 city bond. Also $500 and $100 available.
$5.00 general admission.

The idea is based on the fact that New York City is the cultural mecca of America. Almost everybody who made it had to make it here.

New York was the testing ground and New York gave the rewards. My feeling is, now that the city appears to be in deep and genuine trouble, all those who feel they might owe something to this town would have a chance to repay it.

The purpose is twofold. One is to raise a substantial amount of money and perhaps provide patterns of future revenue for the city.

The other, and more important in my opinion, is to focus national and worldwide attention on the idea of New York City. What has been its contribution to America, what are its problems, can they be overcome, and is it worth it?

I think so. Save New York City.

Could be July August September

OUT OF THE ARCHIVES (CODA)

CHORUS:

OH WHAT A SAD TALE
BUT A CITY IS FOR SALE
WE LEFT THE HOUSE IN STYLE
I'VE REACHED THE FIRST
HALF MILE

SOON WE'LL REACH THE
TOP OF THE PILE
OF THE GARBAGE

The Committee to Save New York presents

Save NYC !

Madison Square Garden

Starring (Jan. 76)

Frank Sinatra

Bob Dylan

Liza Minelli

(Three Nights)

MC's Joe DiMaggio   Robert Wagner
Danny Kaye
Bob Hope

with   Barbra Streisand
Neil Diamond   Carole King   Bill Cosby
Sammy Davis Jr.   Bruce Springsteen   Woody Allen

Dean Martin + Jerry Lewis
Elton John   John Lennon
   Bette Midler   Betty Davis
Myrna Loy   Tony Perkins

NY Philharmonic
   L. Bernstein

   Ballet   Opera

   Singing   Cop

John Denver   Joni Mitchell
Danny Kaye   George Jessel

A Proposal

THE GREATEST SHOW ON EARTH

FOR

THE GREATEST CITY ON EARTH

SAVE   NEW YORK CITY

STARRING

FRANK SINATRA   BARBRA STRIESAND   BOB DYLAN

CAROLE KING   NEIL DIAMOND   JOHN DENVER

SHEA   STADIUM

M.C. JOE DI MAGGIO

ALSO...STEVIE WONDER   SIMON AND GARFUNKLE ELLA FITZGERALD   John Lennon

N.Y. PHILHARMONIC ORCH. WITH LEONORD BERNSTEIN N.Y.C. BALLET   Woody Allen

ETHEL MERMAN   BETTE MIDLER TITO PUENTE   LIZA MINELLI   Martin a Lewis

BOB HOPE   BILL COSBY   ARTHUR RUBENSTEIN   JOE NAMATH   John o Bonnie Raitt

SAMMY DAVIS JR.   BEVERLY SILLS ZERO MOSTEL   HERBIE HANCOCK   Harry chapin

George Jessel   Al Green

TELEVISED ON CBS   NATIONAL   FILM OF N.Y.C. HISTORY

PLUS Twenty minute slots from every ethnic group in city. Folklore and

dance from the Albanians, Poles, Chinese, etc.

Could be one to three days. Possible day time fair at the stadium

with all neighborhoods from city participating.

Front row seats for $1,000 city bond. Also $500 and $100 available

$5.00 General admission.

The idea is based on the fact that New York City is the cultural mecca of America. Almost everybody who made it had to make it here.

New York was the testing ground and New York gave the rewards. My feeling is now that the city appears to be in deep and genuine trouble all those who feel they might owe something to this town whould have a chance to repay it.

The purpose is twofold. One is to raise a substantial amount of money and perhaps provide patterns of future revenue for the city.

The other and more important in my opinion is to focus national and worldwide attention on the idea of New York City. What has been its contribution to America, what are its problems, can they be overcome and is it worth it?

I think so. Save New York City.

Phil Ochs   56 Irving Place
                      NYC NY 10003
GR 3 2622

or c/o Michael Ochs 223   651 5530

Could be July   August   September

FOOTNOTES TO HISTORY

These notes are not intended to be a critical analysis of each piece included in this book. Indeed, the pieces speak for themselves. The notes are merely meant to provide additional information, historical context, or further Ochs-related branches, such as his songs, that could profitably be explored by those in search of additional Ochsiana.

THE FIGHT

The two stories from the *Scimitar*, "The Fight" and "White Milk to Red Wine," represent Phil's earliest attributable writings. However, Phil was also listed as a features writer for the Staunton Military Academy's newspaper, the *Kablegram*, beginning with an announcement of incoming newspaper staff in volume 41, number 2 (October 25, 1957) and continuing through number 6 (February 7, 1958). Issues number 7 and 8 were not able to be traced for verification, so the last issue to which Phil contributed cannot be definitely determined. By the publication of number 9 (April 18, 1958), Phil is no longer listed under features writers.

Unfortunately, in the surviving issues there are no bylines attributed to Phil (although he is given an entry in the paper's "Rogues Gallery" column of April 18, 1958—as "Ochsy," whose claim to fame is "last minute homework," whose racket is "Drum and Bugle Corps guide," whose jinx is "Schmandt," and who is sentenced, in a moderately remarkable geographical feat of prognostication (if nothing else), to "Columbia University." One uncredited piece, on page 4 of the November 15, 1957, issue, "With 'Mutnik' in 'Sputnik,'" is a possible Ochs contribution, with a tone similar to his later satirical pieces in Ohio State University's *Sundial*—and also includes a reference to one of Phil's favorite musicians of the era, Elvis Presley, by working "all shook up," a hit single for Elvis in March 1957, into the article text. However, with no direct evidence at hand, this must be regarded as an unconfirmed theory.

WHITE MILK TO RED WINE

The imagery of the highway used in this award-winning ($10!) story is something that Phil would return to throughout his career. Beginning with an early unreleased demo song (circa 1963), "Red was the Blood of the Man" (a.k.a. "Legend of the Highway"):

> Black was the tar on the highway
> White was the cold desert sand
> Yellow and gold was the cat it's been told
> Red was the blood of the man

all the way through to "My Kingdom for a Car" from his last studio album, *Greatest Hits*:

> How I love the highway
> Picks me up and takes me wherever I please
> I race through the trees
> Bring space to her knees
> I am master of all that's flying past me.

NARROW VIEW

This letter to the editor represents Ochs's first published thoughts on the Castro regime and was written in response to R. Christopher Powell's letter to the editor of April 25, 1961, entitled "No Assistance." Ochs's earliest surviving song, "Ballad of the Cuban Invasion," would likewise focus on this topic:

> They were told when they arrived
> They'd be helped by Castro's men
> But they found out, those who survived
> That the CIA was wrong again

By way of historical footnote, it is worth mentioning an even earlier song, "Three Dreams," a rock 'n' roll number. Referenced by Ochs in several interviews, "Three Dreams" was co-written in early 1960 with an African-American songwriter from New Orleans (whose name, thus far, is lost to history), while Ochs was in Florida taking a break from Ohio State. Alas, no fragment of this song is known to survive.

DISALLE, LAW STUDENTS DEBATE CAPITAL PUNISHMENT QUESTION

Capital punishment is another theme Phil would explore more than once in song—examining the question of deterrence and the dubious and racially biased justice of the electric chair in "The Iron Lady" (on *I Ain't Marching Anymore*):

> Stop the murder, deter the crimes away
> Only killing shows that killing doesn't pay
> Yes, that's the kind of law it takes
> Even though we make mistakes
> And sometimes send the wrong man to the chair

In another early song, "Paul Crump," collected on *A Toast to Those Who are Gone*, Phil extrapolates from the specific case of one person spared from execution through the avenue of rehabilitation:

> But Paul Crump is alive today
> He's a-sittin' in a cell, he's got somethin' to say
> Every man has got something to give
> And if a man can change, then a man should live.

SAMUEL FARBER

Attendance at the Circle Pines Center summer camp in Delton, Michigan is a recently uncovered chapter in Phil's early history. As assistant editor of the *Youth Manual*, Phil contributed several pieces that are included in the present volume, reprinted for the first time since their initial publication, to very limited circulation, in the summer of 1961. The pieces well display Ochs's preference for looking at all sides of an argument in order to better find the heart of the matter. It is this selfsame quality that Phil praises in Farber, when he describes him as, "a man who searches for facts, not propaganda to suit his personal biases," when he presents an overview of the speakers in "A Critique of the Sessions." One piece written for the *Youth Manual*, "Only in Cuba; or, Listen Circle Piners," was later "conserved" with minor amendments as "Only in Cuba; or Listen Ohio Staters" (the latter version included in this volume). In a similar vein, he would later find new life for his 1965 song "Here's to the State of Mississippi," with a re-vamped villain, as "Here's to the State of Richard Nixon." In certain ways a timeless core of a song, an update, even in the present day, could still be considered quite topical and apropos.

RODRIGO ALAMOS

Hearing Alamos speak may well have been Phil's first introduction to the political and cultural situation in Chile. He would gain firsthand knowledge a decade later with a trip to Chile in 1971, along with Jerry Rubin and Stew Albert, to see democratic socialism in action, in the guise of the elected government of Salvador Allende. While not covered in the left wing or musical press of the day, the trio's activities caught the eye of the American intelligence community, and details can still be found in Phil's 400-plus-page FBI file.

Through a stroke of good fortune, Phil met Victor Jara, a singer-songwriter who managed to blend the political (he had campaigned extensively for Allende) with the popular (he was revered by the populace at a level to which Ochs, seemingly banned from national television coverage in the U.S., could only dream). They would sing together to the miners at El Teniente and appear on Chilean national television.

After the Pinochet coup, the torture and murder of Jara in Estadio, Chile (the national sports stadium in Santiago, renamed Estadio Victor Jara in 2004), and the suicide of Allende at the Palacio de La Moneda on September 11, 1973, Phil would help organize a huge benefit concert, An Evening with Salvador Allende, on May 9, 1974, at the Felt Forum in New York City. In a tragic twist, Ochs's own memorial concert would be held in that self-same hall, scarcely two years later, on May 28, 1976.

ONE VERSION OF WHY AND HOW NEHRU DID WHAT HE DID TO SEIZE GOA

Once more, a letter to the editor from Phil comes in response to an earlier piece, in this case a December 26, 1961, Cleveland *Plain Dealer* editorial, "Look What Nehru Started," accusing Prime Minister Nehru of hypocrisy in using force to seize territory in India. Phil's letter provokes a response from S. Yanchar, "Imperialism Defined," which saw print on January 6, 1962. Yanchar takes Ochs to task for not fully understanding the meaning of imperialism and being inconsistent in response to different examples of cross-border intervention. Ochs would touch on this topic, the passing away of imperialism, in his song "Changing Hands," which appeared on the *Broadside Reunion* album:

> From the master to the servant, from the owner to the slave
> Colonial days are buried in a deep and dirty grave;
> It's so easy to see and well to understand
> That this old world is changing hands.

DISCUSSION OF CONSTITUTION SUBMITTED TO STEEB HALL

The origins of this piece cannot be definitively verified. The specificity and subject matter argue against it being written as reportage for *The Lantern* or as a class assignment (although the latter is a possibility). The typescript is held in the Phil Ochs Papers at the Woody Guthrie Center (Box 35, Scrapbook 1, page 3), with no identifying marginalia. It has long been supposed that nothing from Phil's political dorm paper, *The Word*, has survived. It cannot be ruled out that this politically aware piece was written for inclusion therein, although this is mere theory.

11 AFROTC INSTRUCTORS MAINTAIN FLIGHT STATUS

For the other side of the aviation coin, see Ochs's "Talking Airplane Disaster" on Vanguard's *New Folks Volume 2*:

> Pilot said we hit an air pocket
> Must've been a pocket with an awful big hole in it.

TOPICAL SONGS AND FOLKSINGING, 1965

Other participants in this symposium on the meeting point between the political and the commercial in folk music were Don West (Georgia poet and founder of the Highlander Folk School), Ewan MacColl (famed Scottish singer-songwriter, whose songs "The Ballad of the Carpenter" and "The Shoals of Herring" Ochs would cover), Chad Mitchell (of the Chad Mitchell Trio), John Cohen (of the New Lost City Ramblers), Moses Asch (Folkways Records) and Josh Dunson (author of *Freedom in the Air: Song Movements of the Sixties* and a frequent contributor to *Broadside*).

CHANGES (LINER NOTES)

Phil would become the second Ochs to supply liner notes to a Jim and Jean album, pipped to the post by his wife Alice, who had written the liners to their eponymous first album on Philips. Jim and Jean would cover a fair few Ochs songs, including "What's That I Hear," "The Bells," "There But for Fortune," "Changes," "Crucifixion," "Rhythms of Revolution," "Cross My Heart," and a unique take on Phil's "City Boy" as "City Girl" on the CBC broadcast *The New Generation*. Phil would send tapes of his new songs to Jim and Jean for their consideration, and the surviving "Glover Tapes" represent a trove of early Ochs songs, some unique to those tapes.

Jim was a college roommate of Phil's at Ohio State, introducing him to folk music and left-wing politics and supplying Phil's first guitar—won by Ochs in a wager with Glover over the Kennedy/Nixon election of 1960. Ochs and Glover would form a short-lived duo, the Sundowners (a.k.a. the Singing Socialists), performing at Columbus's Sacred Mushroom coffee house. A version of "Black Girl (In the Pines)" on the "Glover Tapes" features both Phil and Jim singing and may date from the Sundowner period; however, this cannot be verified and may, alternatively, be from Phil's early days in New York City (he crashed at Jim and Jean's apartment upon his arrival in 1962).

Jim would later reappear in Phil's life providing harmonies for "No More Songs" at the infamous gold suit concert at Carnegie Hall in March 1970, as well as appearing with Phil on the *Midnight Special* TV show (after Phil had broken his hand during a residency at New York City's famed Max's Kansas City). Jim and Jean would perform at Phil's memorial concert in 1976 and, after having been separated for many years, sang as a duo one final time on March 18, 2006, at the People's Voice Café, before Jean's death on August 19, 2007.

LOVE IS A RAINBOW

The Poems section commences, as it will end, with a song. In this case an unreleased song from approximately 1965 (a similarity in lyrical feel to "Changes" cannot be dismissed), which never appeared in any publication and for which there are no known recordings by Phil.

AND HERE COMES DAVID BLUE

Reiterating a point made in the introduction, the poems are presented here as per the author's final intent, as far as is discernable, incorporating any handwritten corrections. In cases where there is extensive emendation, or in some cases where only a fragment survives, a reproduction from the original manuscripts, as held in the Phil Ochs Papers at the Woody Guthrie Center, is presented in the Out of the Archives section, so readers can reach their own conclusions.

David Blue, born Stuart David Cohen, was a songwriter and an early friend of Phil's in the Village. Phil would transmit two of Blue's songs to *Broadside* ("Cruel Years" and "More Good Men Going Down"), singing them among the songs of his own that he recorded on Gordon Friesen and Sis Cunningham's reel-to-reel tape recorder. Many of the *Broadside* tapes, representing early work by Ochs, Dylan, Paxton,

Andersen, Spoelstra, and many others, are preserved in the Broadside Collection (1962–1991), held in the Southern Folklife Collection at the University of North Carolina, Chapel Hill. See Phil's article "Man Against Music" (included in this volume) for additional commentary on Blue and his music. Blue also died quite young of a heart attack, while jogging in New York in December 1982.

COBBWEBS

A close friend of Phil's, Ron Cobb is a cartoonist—and judging from his inspired pictures of Phil (some of which are included in this book), a skilled photographer. A frequent contributor to the *Los Angeles Free Press*, among many other venues, Cobb would join Phil on a tour of Australia in 1972, with Ochs singing and Cobb presenting his artwork. Cobb would later move to Australia and contribute design work on numerous films, including *Star Wars*, *Alien* and *Conan the Barbarian*.

LETTERS TO THE EDITOR

This is Phil's poetic response to a letter to the editor from one Bill Wargo of Harrison, New Jersey (*Village Voice*, November 30, 1967), in which Wargo answered Ochs's query "Have You Heard? The War is Over" (*Village Voice*, 23 November 1967) in the most definitive negative, deriding Ochs's position as deluded and puerile.

POOR ZALMAN, OR THE FAILURE OF THE JEW IN AMERICAN SOCIETY

It might do well, in the context of this poem, to consider the case of Zalman "Zal" Yanovsky, Canadian folk-rock musician and member of the Lovin' Spoonful. In 1966 Yanovsky was arrested on a drugs charge and, in return for not being deported, provided the police with information on his dealer.

TALKING CHICAGO JAIL BLUES

A great deal has been written about the Democratic National Convention in Chicago, 1968, and there is no need to recapitulate all of that in these notes. Suffice it to say, the Yippies (Youth International Party, a group cofounded by Abbie and Anita Hoffman, Jerry Rubin, Nancy Kurshan, Paul Krassner, and Phil, among others) brought their anarchic and absurdist "Festival of Life" protest to Chicago in 1968. Mayor Daley brought his police and their clubs. Phil would later refer to Chicago as the death of America (or at least his ideal of America), and it served as one turning point in his life. Seeing violence (and the inside of a jail) firsthand, Ochs returned home thinking he would compose thunderous protest songs. In the event, much of what was finally released on his next album, *Rehearsals for Retirement*, was quiet and introspective. This poem may well date from that first surge of rage in the aftermath of his experiences, but still deals with the subject matter with typical Ochsian humor.

WHO WAS THAT MAN IN THE GOLD LAMÉ SUIT

Readers are pointed back, by way of comparison, to the opening line of Phil's poem "The Torture Garden." The wearing of a gold lamé suit, as supplied by Nudie the tailor (Nudie Cohn, originally Nuta Kotlyarenko), was the sartorial signature of the 1970 concerts where Phil tried to meld Elvis Presley and Che Guevara, to mixed results. Judge for yourself by listening to the *Gunfight at Carnegie Hall* album—or, alternatively, bootlegs of full sets on this tour, from Carnegie (March 27, 1970) or, for a friendlier audience reception, at the Troubadour in Los Angeles (February 1, 1970).

I WILL NOT HURT YOU

We end the Poems section, as we began, with a song. Just as with "Love is a Rainbow," this song was never printed in any publication, nor are there any known recordings. It is listed in one of Phil's notebooks alongside "Tape from California," although to what end is unclear (perhaps in consideration of inclusion on the album of the same name?) It survives thanks to the conservation power of the U.S. Copyright Office.

PHIL OCHS DISCUSSES POLITICS OF SONGWRITING

Until quite recently (June 16, 2019, in fact) this piece was thought to be previously unpublished. Publication was uncovered in, of all places, Staunton Military Academy's student newspaper *Kablegram* (Volume 51 number 4, December 15, 1967, where Phil had been a features writer a decade before. An editor's note in the *Kablegram* indicates that it is a reprint of a recent article by Ochs, but any prior appearance in print has yet to be traced. The more complete text, adhering to the author's intent as per the typescript held in the Woody Guthrie Archives (where it is designated "Phil Ochs, October 24, 1967"), has been followed.

PLEASURES OF THE HARBOR (LINER NOTES)

Those interested in the reference to Cynara are pointed in the direction of the poem "Non sum qualis eram bonae sub regno Cynarae" by Ernest Dowson, as well as Horace's *Odes* (Book 4, 1), which Dowson references in his turn.

TAPE FROM CALIFORNIA (LINER NOTES)

Noted in passing: The original postcard used on the *Tape from California* back cover is held in the Michael Ochs Papers at the Woody Guthrie Center. On the reverse it reads, "Welcome to Chicago."

LEAVING DARWIN

This is a rarity in the realm of Phil's surviving papers, in terms of personal narrative detail. Most of the other extant journals contain a mix of very brief notes; lists of items of interest; reminders of things to do; articles cut out from newspapers or magazines; preliminary ideas for songs; and basic contact information, such as addresses and phone numbers. Journals that can be viewed as diaries, full of the details of everyday life, are (alas!) uncommon indeed in the Ochs Archives.

A few notes of clarification regarding some of the references Phil made in these entries:

Bob Garcia, the recipient of the air-expressed diary, was Director of Publicity and Public Relations at A&M Records.

Jan Wesley-Smith was an artist, cowinner of the Caltex Art Award in 1971, and art teacher, married to Rob Wesley-Smith. Both were activists who demonstrated against the Vietnam War and as a result were under surveillance by the Australian Security Intelligence Organisation for a number of years. It is not known if any surveillance was conducted at the time of their acquaintance with Ochs.

Mount Batur did indeed erupt in 1963.

Finally, these excerpts do not include all text from the journal entries, mainly excising brief, nonnarrative notes regarding geography, history, and culture. Those wishing to view the original are pointed to Box 25, Journal 4 in the Phil Ochs Collection at the Woody Guthrie Center.

REQUIEM FOR A DRAGON DEPARTED

The most widely published of Ochs's articles, appearing in *Take One* (Montreal) 4 no. 3 (January-February 1973); *Los Angeles Weekly News* (21–28 September 1973); *Zoo World* (8 November 1973); *Time Out* (London) 207 (15–21 February 1974); and *Strange Things Are Happening* (UK) 1 no. 3 (August 1988) with differing levels of abridgment. The text included in this volume follows the most complete published version, that in the *Los Angeles Weekly News* (with the reproduction of Phil's original typescript, by way of comparison, in the Out of the Archives section).

OPPOSES POT DECRIMINALIZATION, FREEP PRESS PASSES

Results from the April 3, 1973, Democratic primary for Mayor of Los Angeles, for the politically and historically curious: Tom Bradley (233,789), Sam Yorty (190,649), Jesse M. Unruh (114,693), and Thomas Reddin running as an Independent (83,930).

THE LAST WORD

The last word belongs, as it must, to Phil Ochs: "Ah, but in such an ugly time, the true protest is beauty."

INDEX